PETERSON'S

PANIC PLAN

FOR THE

SAT

Peterson's
Thomson Learning™

About Peterson's

Founded in 1966, Peterson's, a division of Thomson Learning, is the nation's largest and most respected provider of lifelong learning online resources, software, reference guides, and books. The Education Supersite[SM] at petersons.com—the Web's most heavily traveled education resource—has searchable databases and interactive tools for contacting U.S.-accredited institutions and programs. CollegeQuest[SM] (CollegeQuest.com) offers a complete solution for every step of the college decision-making process. GradAdvantage[TM] (GradAdvantage.org), developed with Educational Testing Service, is the only electronic admissions service capable of sending official graduate test score reports with a candidate's online application. Peterson's serves over 55 million education consumers annually.

Thomson Learning is among the world's largest providers of lifelong learning information. Headquartered in Stamford, CT, with multiple offices worldwide, Thomson Learning is a division of The Thomson Corporation (TTC), one of the world's leading information companies. TTC operates mainly in the U.S., Canada, and the UK and has annual revenues of over US$6 billion. The Corporation's common shares are traded on the Toronto, Montreal, and London stock exchanges. For more information, visit TTC's Internet address at www.thomcorp.com.

Visit Peterson's Education Center on the Internet (World Wide Web) at
www.petersons.com

Excerpts from *The Uncollected Wodehouse* copyright © 1976; *Germany: 2000 Years*, by Kurt F. Reinhardt, copyright © 1961; and *To Secure the Blessings of Liberty*, by William Shepherd, copyright © 1985, by permission of Continuum Publishing Company.

Excerpts from *It Began with a Stone*, by Henry Faul and Carol Faul, copyright © 1983, and from *Animal Behavior*, by C. J. Barnard, copyright © 1983, reprinted by permission of John Wiley and Sons, Inc.

Excerpt from *Celtic Mysteries*, by John Sharkey, copyright © 1975 by John Sharkey. Reprinted by permission of Thames and Hudson.

SAT questions selected from SATI®: Reasoning Test, College Entrance Examination Board and Educational Testing Service, the copyright owners of the test questions. Permission to reprint the above material does not constitute review or endorsement by Educational Testing Service or the College Board of the publication as a whole or of any other questions or testing information it may contain.

Library of Congress Cataloging-in-Publication Data

Carris, Joan.
    Panic plan for the SAT / Joan Carris with Michael Crystal.
        p.   cm.
    ISBN 0-7689-0503-6
    1. Scholastic Assessment Test—Study guides.   I. Crystal, Michael R., 1964-   .
    II. Title.
    LB2353.57.C36   1998
    378.1'662—dc21
                                                                98-8129
                                                                CIP

Printed in Canada

10 9 8 7 6 5 4 3 2

CONTENTS

Answer Section

Exercises

ACKNOWLEDGMENTS

In our attempt to gather the most helpful material for students preparing for the SAT I and PSAT, we are indebted to the two parent books, *SAT Success, Success with Words,* and the first edition of *Panic Plan for the SAT* for much of this material. For math problems contained in *SAT Success,* we say thanks to William R. McQuade of the Hun School in Princeton—a master teacher and problem designer.

A textbook covers many areas—such as definition and etymology—which often spark differences of scholarly opinion. When confronted with a problem, we used the following authorities: *Webster's Ninth New Collegiate Dictionary,* Robert W. L. Smith's *Dictionary of English Word-Roots,* Warriner's *English Grammar and Composition,* and Brewer's *Dictionary of Phrase and Fable.*

For permission to reprint passages similar to those on SATs, we thank Continuum Publishing Company for excerpts from *The Uncollected Wodehouse,* by P. G. Wodehouse; *Germany: 2000 Years,* by Kurt F. Reinhardt; and *To Secure the Blessings of Liberty,* by William C. Shepherd.

We are grateful to John Wiley and Sons for excerpts from *It Began with a Stone,* by Henry Faul and Carol Faul, and from *Animal Behavior,* by C. J. Barnard. We also thank Thames and Hudson for permission to reprint from *Celtic Mysteries,* by John Sharkey. Peterson's supplied material from *Jobs for English majors and Other Smart People,* by John L. Munschauer.

Additional reading passages were supplied by folks long gone and definitely not forgotten: Benjamin Franklin, who left us his inimitable *Autobiography,* and Guy de Manpassant, who wrote "The Hole," from which we excerpted a small segment. We thank Herman Melville for an excerpt from *Moby Dick* and Theodore Dreiser for a portion of *Sister Carrie.* Owen Fellham and Thomas Henry Huxley provide essays on education, and reading passages about the Maoris came from *The Journals of Captain Cook* and from *The Encyclopedia Britannica,* 11th edition.

The loudest thanks are reserved for last, for the staff at Peterson's who worked so hard to design, copyedit, and proofread this book in a determined effort to make it the most accessible, clear, and concise text in the field.

Joan Carris and Michael Crystal

PLAN OF ATTACK:

WEEK ONE

DAY		☑ ASSIGNMENT	PAGES

A TWO-WEEK STUDY PLAN

WEEK TWO

DAY		☑ ASSIGNMENT	PAGES
DAY 8	VERBAL	☐ Review How to Answer Critical Reading Questions	46–71
		☐ Do Practice Critical Reading 3 and 4	83–88
		☐ Depressing Adjectives & Roots	105–107
	MATH	☐ Coordinate Geometry	168–173
DAY 9	VERBAL	☐ Practice Critical Reading 5 and 6	89–93
		☐ Words from Science & Roots	107–108
		☐ Review all new vocabulary to date	
	MATH	☐ Basic Algebra (Important! Spend extra time.)	174–182
DAY 10	VERBAL	☐ Actual SAT questions	222–228
		☐ Evaluate your study needs	
		☐ Pleasant Verbs & Roots	108–110
	MATH	☐ More Algebra	182–194
		☐ Actual SAT questions	214–221
DAY 11	VERBAL	☐ Review Analogy and Sentence Completion strategies	
		☐ Potluck (A great assortment.) & Roots	110–111
	MATH	☐ Comon Algebraic Applications	194–202
DAY 12		☐ Take Practice SAT under *timed* conditions. Set aside 2½ hours	229–271
DAY 13	VERBAL	☐ Evaluate practice SAT results and review whatever you need most.	
		☐ Word Groups Worth Knowing & Roots	112–113
	MATH	☐ Evaluate Practice SAT results and review rough spots	
		☐ Less Common Algebraic Applications	202–209
		☐ For the brave: Practice with the Final Few	210–212
DAY 14	REST DAY	☐ Stop preparing for the test. Play like crazy all day. Run around your bed twenty times, and then fall into it.	

LIST OF ABBREVIATIONS

AS (Anglo-Saxon)
Gr (Greek)
L (latin)
Rom (Roman)

lit. (literally)
opp. (opposite)
pl. (plural)
ref. (referring/refers)
usu. (usually)

adj. (adjective)
n. (noun)
v. (verb)

UNIT 1

FIRST . . . SOME VITAL INFORMATION

Are you on schedule?
Check the prep plan on pages vi and vii.

Repeat after me: **It's not too late to study for the SAT I or PSAT.**

That's right, it is not too late to learn many things that will make an all-important difference in your test score. For example:

- How to find the correct answers

- Why, when, and how to guess at answers

- Fast, smart approaches to all verbal questions

- Logic and reasoning techniques for all problems

- Directions to all question types so you won't waste a minute on test day

Also, with review, much of what you thought you'd forgotten will come back to you. Make flashcards of anything you just can't seem to remember. **Flashcards work!**

Put these flashcards all over the place—in your jeans pocket, in your purse, next to your bed, in the bathroom, on the kitchen table. Review wherever you are. As new words and math formulas become known items, your confidence will zoom upwards.

Study with a friend whenever possible. It's more fun.

Give your preparation an honest effort: 40+ minutes a day for verbal study, another 40 for math. If you want to concentrate on only the verbal or the math part of the test, be sure to spend at least an hour a day in review.

With careful preparation, you can make a wonderful difference in your test score. Others have; why not *you?*

1

Big Truths and Helpful Hints

The SAT and PSAT have gotten somewhat tougher in the last couple of years, but perhaps tougher in ways you will like.

1. Antonym questions are gone altogether.

2. Reading passages are longer, but more interesting. They're less likely to be peppered with chemical symbols or flooded with facts.

3. Critical reading questions that test how well you understand written material are just over half of the verbal questions.

4. Math problems may test several concepts in one problem, making them harder to solve . . . but now you can use a calculator if you want.

5. Ten of the math questions require you to compute the answers and record them on a numbered grid.

Remember: SAT and PSAT closely reflect the kind of work you will be doing in college. So . . . you're learning material and skills that you will use in college, *not* just for a test.

Last-minute reviews obviously have limits. You can't fix ten years of near-zero recreational reading with a few hours of vocabulary review. If you've always hated math, you won't turn into Einstein in two weeks. But you *can learn* hundreds of useful, interesting words, and math formulas do come back with review.

• Ask your favorite teacher for help if some area of study really worries you.

• How about reviewing old math or English tests?

• What about creating a Power-Study Group? (Law and medical students say they couldn't survive without their study groups.)

Know this: You have millions of unused brain cells. We all do. You'll be amazed at how many of your brain cells you can stuff with new information in a short time.

Also, if your math or verbal PSAT score was low, real study now will pay big dividends. People with low scores have a much better chance of raising them than those whose scores were quite high to begin with.

Remember: Your SAT or PSAT score is only one test score on one day of your life. It does not say who you are. You decide that for yourself.

How SAT Scores are Used

The SAT came about because colleges needed one standard measure for all applicants, no matter where they attended high school. The College Board asked Educational Testing Service (ETS) to design this test for college-bound seniors, and it is still widely used, along with the ACT from American College Testing—a similar test taken by almost half of our college-bound students. In general, admissions personnel use these criteria for accepting or rejecting you:

1. Your high school transcript, including activities

2. SAT I (or ACT) scores; SAT II: Subject Test (formerly Achievement Test) scores (at some schools)

3. The application itself, including essays and recommendation letters, if required

4. A personal interview (at some schools)

You can see that the SAT score (or the ACT score if you're a typical Midwesterner) is *only one part* of the admissions decision. For nearly all colleges, your high school record is the most important document.

At schools requiring a personal interview, such as William and Mary in Virginia, admissions folks tend to rely almost equally on the four criteria listed above. At those schools, your interview carries equal weight with your SAT score. (How are your interviewing skills, by the way?)

Schools with very demanding course work (Caltech, MIT, Berkeley, Princeton, etc.) look for high test scores. These schools attract powerhouse students, remember? As President Harry Truman said, "If you can't stand the heat, get out of the kitchen." To be happy at college you must be able to compete fairly in the classroom.

At most schools there is a cutoff point in test scores—one that says to admissions officials: "This is too low. A student with scores below X just can't make it here, will be in hot water the first semester, and will go home hating college." To be sure, students are not rejected casually, but on the basis of long experience with the demands of each university or college.

Admissions officials say that SAT scores predict freshman academic success with about 50 percent accuracy. The high school transcript predicts with equal accuracy, and, obviously, two predictors are better than one.

Your Job as a College Applicant

To smooth the path of your senior year, you need to know as much as possible about applying to college. Collect all the information you can from seniors who went before you, from guidance counselors, and from colleges you're interested in.

For instance, at the college you're considering, what is the average SAT score of the freshman class? If your own score is more than 10 percent below that average, your chance of acceptance there dwindles.

If you know you could succeed at a particular school, even though your scores are iffy, it's your job to make that point with the admissions people. How? Here are only a few of many ways:

- A portfolio of special work, or a film you made as a senior project

- Letters from summertime employers

- Tapes of your last trumpet solo

- A video of your routine in a gymnastics competition

- A sample of a game you designed

- Several school newspapers featuring your articles

- Original artwork of any kind

Give your applications to college a great deal of care and thought, but for goodness' sake, *do them yourself.* If you cannot complete the application without lots of help, how can you possibly survive at that school?

PSAT Facts Length: 2 hours and 10 minutes

- **Verbal questions:** 91 total
  Two 25-minute test segments, and one 30-minute segment
  - 13 sentence completions
  - 13 analogies
  - 26 critical reading questions
  - 39 questions testing English effectiveness and correctness

- **Math questions:** 40 total
  Two 25-minute test segments
  - 20 multiple-choice questions on arithmetic, algebra, geometry
  - 12 quantitative comparison questions
  - 8 student-answer, grid-in questions on arithmetic, algebra, geometry

The acronym PSAT/NMSQT stands for Preliminary Scholastic Assessment Test/National Merit Scholarship Qualifying Test. The NMSQT part means that this is the qualifying test for students who want to take part in the nationwide competition run by the National Merit Scholarship Corporation.

Being a National Merit Finalist or Semifinalist or receiving a Letter of Commendation is solid gold at college application time. Doing well on the PSAT is worth all the effort you can muster.

SAT I Facts Length: 3 hours

- **Verbal questions:** 78 total
  Two 30-minute test segments and one 15-minute segment
  - 19 sentence completions
  - 19 analogies
  - 40 critical reading questions

- **Math questions:** 60 total
  Two 30-minute test segments and one 15-minute segment
  - 35 multiple-choice questions in arithmetic, algebra, geometry
  - 15 quantitative comparison questions
  - 10 student-answer, grid-in questions

- **Experimental Questions:** One 30-minute segment, either math or verbal questions

---

The SAT and PSAT Test

- Acquired knowledge in math and language
- Logic and reasoning skills
- Math computation skills
- Vocabulary and reading comprehension
- Your attention to absolute accuracy

These are life skills—not fancy extras—not just for the college-bound.

Current Scores

PSAT and SAT scores were "recentered"—recalibrated to a new norm or average—during the 1994-1995 school year. The average SAT I verbal score nationwide is now 500 and the average math score is 500, for a combined average of 1000. Before the recentering, average verbal scores were running in the low 420s and math scores in the high 470s, with a combined average of just over 900. It's not that students are doing any better on the test—SAT scores have been either falling or holding steady for years now—but that the College Board decided to do some statistical tinkering to make the scores easier for colleges to work with.

The Night Before the Test

Reviewing the night before an SAT or PSAT is usually upsetting. You're bound to find something you don't know, so let's forget the whole idea.

Instead, go to a party or a movie or a friend's house. But don't toddle home at 3 A.M. Get a good night's sleep—enough sleep to make you feel rested—and eat a sensible breakfast.

What to Take to the Test

- **Absolute musts:** Your #2 pencils and ID card

- **Your calculator,** if you want one. Don't get a special new "killer calculator" either; take an old buddy calculator that makes you feel comfortable.

- **Your snack**—fruit juice or tea and a sandwich for the break. No candy. Too much sugar gives you a high, then a sleepy low—something to avoid at all costs.

- **Your time**—enough time on each question to record a thoughtful answer. It's not a crime to run out of time before the last few questions in a test segment. They're the toughest ones anyway. No one is expected to score a perfect 800 on either the math or verbal half of this test, although it happens occasionally for a rare few.

UNIT 2

HOW TO ANSWER VERBAL QUESTIONS

Are you on schedule?
Check the prep plan on pages vi and vii.

As you probably already know, verbal SAT and PSAT questions come in three varieties: analogies, sentence completion questions, and critical reading questions. They all test your developed ability in language. Assuming you can develop verbal abilities, let's get busy and develop some more!

Basic How-To

1. **Never grab the first appealing answer.** Always eliminate answer choices one at a time. Cross them out in your test booklet.

2. **Always make an educated guess** whenever you can eliminate one or two wrong answers. If you've never seen any portion of the question before—if it's totally from outer space and you can eliminate not one answer—better leave it blank.

    Example: On a group of ten PSAT multiple-choice verbal questions, you get six right without guessing, for a score of roughly 60 points. You guess carefully on two more and get them right, for 20 more points. You miss two questions by guessing wrong. Since one fourth of the points you can earn is deducted for each wrong answer, we'll subtract half a question's worth (¼ + ¼) for those two wrong answers.

    Your score looks like this: 60 + 20 = 80 − 5 = 75.

    If you had left four questions blank, your score would have been about 60. For sure, the score of 75 is better.

    Note: On the SAT I: Reasoning Test, each verbal question is worth about 7.7 points. On the PSAT, a verbal question is worth about 6.5 points.

3. **Don't dither around on any question,** for any reason. If it's too hard or too weird, move on to the next question. You can revisit the weirdos later if there's time.

4. **The "killer questions" are all those questions you can't answer.** Usually, tougher questions come near the end of any set; however, critical reading questions are *not* arranged in order of difficulty. A nasty question can occur anywhere.

5. **Answer your best kinds of questions first!** Save the ones you don't do as well for last. Your job is to record as many right answers as possible before time runs out, not to prove you can do questions in the order they're presented.

   Each right answer is worth the same number of points, no matter how easy or hard or how long it took you to get it.

6. **Be meticulous.** Watch where you record each answer to be sure the question number matches the number on your answer sheet. Some folks like to record answers in their test booklet first, then transfer them to the answer sheet in a batch. Others keep one finger on the question number while they locate its mate on the answer sheet.

7. **Keep track of the time.** Get a feeling for a 25- or 30-minute test segment by practicing at home. Managing time is a major testing skill.

8. **The unknown is sometimes the right answer.** If you've eliminated all but one answer, and that answer is unknown to you, pick it anyway. The others were wrong, remember, so this one has to be right.

9. **Choose direct, simple answers.** Often the longer answers are designed to sound impressive so you'll pick them.

10. **Study the questions and the answers for clues to the correct answer.** Practice with various question types will help you to get better and better with this critical skill.

Tips on Time Management

You are in charge of your time on any timed test. Don't let the test push you around, okay?

First, quickly scan the timed segment. Decide what you do the best and do it first. Then do your next-best kind of questions, and so on.

Are you a slow-but-thorough reader? If so, save plenty of time, at least half of every verbal segment, for reading the passages and answering the critical reading questions.

For paired reading passages, be efficient. You'll have 15 minutes to read two passages and answer twelve or thirteen questions. Read the first passage and answer the questions that pertain to it immediately; then read the second passage and answer the remaining questions. Only the last few questions will expect you to compare and contrast the two passages.

Above all, don't bog down on a tough analogy question or a wordy sentence completion question. No answer is worth 3 minutes of your time unless you have tons of time left over.

How to Answer Analogy Questions

An analogy is a relationship of one thing to another. When you say that your friend Brad is as crazy about skiing as you are about ice hockey, you are making an analogous comparison. In briefer language, it looks like this:

Brad : skiing :: I : ice hockey

In other words, *Brad feels about skiing just as I feel about ice hockey.* Each of us is related to the sport named in the same way—we're just crazy about it.

Here are directions for completing analogy questions. They're pretty simple—simpler than the questions themselves. The directions on the SAT never change, so reading them is a waste of precious seconds. Learn what the directions say now, and you'll never have to read the directions again.

The following questions are based on analogous relationships. Choose the lettered pair that most accurately reflects the relationship expressed by the pair in capital letters.

Always express the relationship of the first pair in a clause. The answer you seek must complete the sentence with another pair that expresses exactly the same relationship.

Note: The order of terms in analogies must be the same on both sides of the double colon. *Brad* and *I* must appear in the first slot and the sports we're mad about must appear in the second slot on each side. Positioning is critical. Move any item to another position and the analogy falls apart.

Common Distinctions to Keep in Mind

- *Negative vs. positive:* If one or both sides of an analogy require a negative word, for instance, you can discard any answers that show positive words in that particular slot.
- *Human vs. animal vs. plant vs. mineral:* Comparing a human worker to another human worker is a better analogy than comparing human to animal.
- *Live vs. inanimate (nonlive):* A comparison between a human and an animal is more accurate than one between a live thing and an inanimate thing. *A man uses a hammer just as an otter uses a rock,* for example, is a fair analogy that compares how one living thing uses a tool to the way another living thing uses a tool.

Use your knowledge of *prefixes* and *roots* to help decode a strange word. Negative or positive prefixes can be especially helpful. Also, if a word *sounds* very negative, it probably is. Words are funny that way; they often sound nice or nasty, and that may point toward their meanings. Your ear is a valuable language tool.

Common Analogous Relationships

Analogies fall into patterns or types that tend to repeat on tests. Being comfortable with some of the basic ones should prove helpful. (The PSAT and SAT rarely use type 1 or type 2 below, but these types illustrate correct analogous relationships.)

1. **Antonyms**

   celestial : mundane :: pinnacle : nadir

   Your sentence reads: *Celestial* is the direct opposite of *mundane,* just as *pinnacle* is the direct opposite of *nadir.* Total opposites on both sides.

2. **Synonyms**

   stingy : miserly :: indigenous : native

   Stingy means *miserly,* just as *indigenous* means *native.* Both sides of the analogy balance because both show synonyms.

3. **Degree**

   warm : boiling :: cool : gelid

   Warm is much less hot than *boiling,* just as *cool* is much less cold than *gelid* (frigid, frozen). Analogies of degree are favorite toys of people who make up tests. You'll get quite good at these with a bit of practice.

4. **Person Related to Tool, Major Trait, or Skill/Interest**

   surgeon : scalpel :: bricklayer : trowel

   A *surgeon* uses a *scalpel* as one major tool in his work, just as a *bricklayer* uses a *trowel* as one of his main tools.

   orator : words :: artist : design

   An *orator* is dependent upon *words* or uses *words,* just as an *artist* is dependent upon or uses a *design.* What is on the right side of each pair is that person's "stock in trade." These are popular analogous relationships on tests.

accountant : accurate :: judge : incorruptible

An *accountant* is expected to be *accurate,* just as a *judge* is expected to be *incorruptible.*

Note that a *noun* representing a person is in the first slot of each pair and the *adjective* we expect as the major describing trait is in the second slot of each.

Remember: Make a sentence that states the relationship of the first pair, and make it as precise as possible.

5. **Person Related to Least Desirable Characteristic or to Something Lacking**

accountant : inaccurate :: judge : corrupt

The *last thing* an *accountant* should be is *inaccurate,* and the *last thing* a *judge* should be is *corrupt.* Again, the noun (person) is in the first slot, and the adjective naming the least desirable characteristic is in the second slot of each pair.

liar : truthful :: lunatic : rational

A *liar* is not *truthful,* just as a *lunatic* is not *rational.*

bigot : tolerance :: dilettante : expertise

A *bigot* (prejudiced, opinionated person) lacks *tolerance,* just as a *dilettante* (dabbler) lacks *expertise.*

6. **One of a Kind**

petunia : flower :: maple : tree

A *petunia* is one kind of *flower,* just as a *maple* is one kind of *tree.*

7. **Part of a Whole**

verse : poem :: stanza : song

A *verse* is one part of a *poem,* just as a *stanza* is one part of a *song.*

8. **End Product Related to Substance**

car : metal :: furniture : wood

A *car* is typically constructed of *metal*, just as *furniture* is often constructed of *wood*.

9. **Cause and Effect (or Typical Result)**

aggression : war :: discord : altercation

Aggression can lead to (or result in) a *war*, just as *discord* (disagreement) can lead to (or result in) an *altercation* (heated, angry argument).

10. **Noun Related to Logical Action/Purpose**

centrifuge : spin :: scissors : cut

A *centrifuge spins,* just as *scissors cut.*

stable : shelter :: warehouse : storage

The purpose of a *stable* is to provide *shelter,* just as the purpose of a *warehouse* is to provide *storage.*

11. **Relationships of Location/Description**

camel : desert :: alligator : swamp

A *camel* is an animal of the *desert,* just as an *alligator* is an animal of the *swamp.* (This does not mean we only see camels in the desert or alligators in a swamp, merely that each is a natural denizen of the named area.)

egg : oval :: brick : rectangular

An *egg* is often *oval,* just as a *brick* is usually *rectangular* in shape. (Again, not all eggs must be oval nor all bricks rectangular.)

12. Implied Relationships

clouds : sun :: hypocrisy : truth

Clouds hide (or block out) the *sun,* just as *hypocrisy* hides (or blocks out) *truth.*

chauffeur : livery :: soldier : uniform

A *chauffeur* typically wears *livery* (as a uniform), just as a *soldier* wears a *uniform.*

Note: These implied relationships are the analogies most common on current PSATs and SATs.

QUICK TIPS

Express the relationship of the given pair in a clause or sentence.

Choose your own idea of a good answer—your own pair of words—before looking at the answer choices.

Eliminate bad answer choices one by one.

Cross out the answers you've eliminated in your test booklet.

Be aware of common distinctions used in analogies.

Common distinctions include *negative vs. positive, human vs. animal vs. plant vs. mineral,* and *live vs. inanimate.*

Select an answer and mark it on your answer sheet.

Or circle it in your test booklet if you plan to record all of your answers to analogy questions at once. Guess if you need to, but *try not to leave any answer slots blank.*

PRACTICE ANALOGIES 1

Choose and circle the lettered pair that best expresses a relationship like that of the first pair. Remember to express the relationship in a sentence, and cross out the wrong answers as you eliminate them. Answers appear at the end the book on pages 274-276.

1. VERSE : SONG ::

    (A) play : drama
    (B) rug : carpet
    (C) paper : typewriter
    (D) bicuspid : teeth
    (E) barn : door

2. FISH : SCHOOL ::

    (A) chick : hen
    (B) herd : tribe
    (C) geese : gaggle
    (D) rooster : coop
    (E) mammal : pack

3. FORTITUDE : HEROINE ::

    (A) talent : artist
    (B) blend : musician
    (C) fabric : model
    (D) ocean : diver
    (E) sedan : chauffeur

4. FOOD : HUNGER ::

    (A) acumen : bankruptcy
    (B) hope : fear
    (C) desire : greed
    (D) transportation : car
    (E) water : thirst

5. STUDIO : ART ::

    (A) conservatory : music
    (B) school : business
    (C) office : contracts
    (D) laboratory : experiments
    (E) museum : crafts

6. SCALPEL : INCISION ::

    (A) knife : blade
    (B) needle : insertion
    (C) awl : repair
    (D) trowel : plaster
    (E) plow : furrow

7. MEDIA : NEWS ::

    (A) home : rule
    (B) government : laws
    (C) legislature : bureaus
    (D) library : words
    (E) market : vegetables

8. ENERVATE : EXHAUSTION ::

    (A) rescind : solution
    (B) penalize : misdemeanor
    (C) certify : profession
    (D) negate : testimony
    (E) assimilate : uniformity

9. ACCORD : DISSENSION ::

   (A) chicanery : guile
   (B) obloquy : reproach
   (C) refinement : denigration
   (D) gentility : coarseness
   (E) wariness : desiccation

10. TORTUOUS : PATH ::

   (A) wretched : miscreant
   (B) worthless : solution
   (C) convoluted : prose
   (D) heinous : crime
   (E) ignominious : defeat

Note: A few tough words here, right? The vocabulary used in PSAT/SAT I questions has become more demanding in recent years. Please learn the words in the foregoing ten questions. Most have appeared on past tests, and many will return to haunt you.

PRACTICE ANALOGIES 2

Complete each analogy with the best pair possible. Are you remembering to cross out answers as you eliminate them?

1. ORCHESTRA : PIT ::

   (A) skaters : rink
   (B) acting company : screen
   (C) troupe : podium
   (D) choir : rostrum
   (E) band : quartet

2. MONARCHY : GOVERN-MENT ::

   (A) anarchy : chorus
   (B) building : school
   (C) fruit : vegetable
   (D) sonata : music
   (E) despotism : economics

3. ARTICLE : NEWSPAPER ::

   (A) journal : ledger
   (B) account : diary
   (C) potato : field
   (D) egg : cake
   (E) scene : play

4. GRANDEUR : SCALE ::

   (A) design : geometric
   (B) monument : statue
   (C) harmony : balance
   (D) edifice : marble
   (E) aesthetics : rules

5. STARS : CONSTELLATION ::

(A) ships : ocean
(B) mountains : continent
(C) electricity : transformer
(D) theories : philosophers
(E) particles : solution

6. EAGER : ZEALOUS ::

(A) ecstatic : rapturous
(B) inane : insipid
(C) artless : ingenuous
(D) bovine : perspicuous
(E) generous : prodigal

7. CLUMSY : MOVEMENT ::

(A) hastiness : retort
(B) emulation : art
(C) inarticulate : speech
(D) rashness : dancing
(E) propriety : behavior

8. MALIGN : VILIFICATION ::

(A) appraise : confusion
(B) deride : accreditation
(C) castigate : reduction
(D) satirize : mockery
(E) embellish : austerity

9. CONNOISSEUR : DISCRIMI-NATION ::

(A) monk : asceticism
(B) gourmand : diet
(C) bibliophile : stamina
(D) novice : dedication
(E) diplomat : style

10. EDIFY : ENLIGHTENMENT ::

(A) isolate : amendment
(B) codify : dissolution
(C) announce : assembly
(D) persuade : accord
(E) pulsate : electron

Check your answers against the key at the end of this unit. Did you guess on some? How many of your guesses were correct? Remember to make a serious attempt at an educated guess for each question. This is a technique you can perfect with practice.

PRACTICE ANALOGIES 3

1. TIGER : FEROCIOUS ::

    (A) deer : timorous
    (B) cow : grumpy
    (C) proud : lion
    (D) dog : stealthy
    (E) mule : tractable

2. HONEY : HIVE ::

    (A) water : tub
    (B) liquid : bowl
    (C) wine : cask
    (D) batter : pan
    (E) thermos : soup

3. RADIANCE : GLIMMER ::

    (A) glow : shine
    (B) sparkle : glitter
    (C) dark : bright
    (D) heat waves : shimmer
    (E) midday : dawn

4. PIONEER : APATHY ::

    (A) designer : taste
    (B) envoy : diplomacy
    (C) disciple : rebellion
    (D) advocate : documentation
    (E) caterer : innovation

5. LAW : REGULATION ::

    (A) arrival : timetable
    (B) glory : retreat
    (C) outline : structure
    (D) tension : harmony
    (E) mystery : detective

6. DIFFICULT : ARCANE ::

    (A) assiduous : clear
    (B) engaging : abrupt
    (C) tenuous : impalpable
    (D) willful : venerable
    (E) acerbic : low-spirited

7. CHILD : MATURE ::

    (A) bud : burgeon
    (B) spine : flex
    (C) shrub : wither
    (D) stalk : support
    (E) youth : imitate

8. CARICATURE : CHARACTER ::

    (A) clown : person
    (B) child : infant
    (C) boxer : athlete
    (D) actress : lady
    (E) ghost : corpse

9. INCISE : HACK ::

    (A) crash : collapse
    (B) edit : revise
    (C) pour : leak
    (D) embrace : seize
    (E) recite : narrate

10. SLOTH : TORPID ::

    (A) gazelle : willful
    (B) amphibian : gelid
    (C) mammal : carnivorous
    (D) ant : assiduous
    (E) bluejay : ascetic

Check your answers at the end of each practice set. Are you becoming a better guesser? *Note when you guess* so that you can watch your progress.

PRACTICE ANALOGIES 4

1. BEE : SWARM ::

(A) wrestler : opponent
(B) editor : staff
(C) spectator : throng
(D) athlete : horde
(E) actor : bevy

2. DRENCH : SPRINKLE ::

(A) suppose : speculate
(B) drive : impel
(C) refute : confirm
(D) abide : rest
(E) squander : spend

3. SLEEP : FITFUL ::

(A) dream : wakeful
(B) idea : ludicrous
(C) design : original
(D) thought : chaotic
(E) manuscript : trite

4. PERSEVERANCE : SUCCESS ::

(A) curiosity : knowledge
(B) scrutiny : results
(C) hope : confirmation
(D) endeavor : trials
(E) consternation : answer

5. HEED : ADVICE ::

(A) rejoice : good fortune
(B) enjoin : rumor
(C) prevent : acclaim
(D) vanish : thin air
(E) synchronize : thoughts

6. RUMINATE : PLAN ::

(A) scheme : conspire
(B) defy : succumb
(C) violate : disturb
(D) guess : think
(E) write : outline

7. OBLIGATORY : OPTIONAL ::

(A) remarkable : peculiar
(B) incredible : genuine
(C) incessant : sporadic
(D) judicious : legal
(E) mordant : impressive

8. NARCOTIC : DULL ::

(A) notice : admit
(B) inhalant : irritate
(C) bandage : wound
(D) license : prohibit
(E) unguent : soothe

9. CONSTITUTION : AMEND-MENT ::

(A) index : appendix
(B) will : codicil
(C) newspaper : headline
(D) adjunct : corollary
(E) church : nave

10. EMULSION : DISINTEGRATE ::

(A) sanction : improve
(B) congregation : individual-ize
(C) contentment : emulate
(D) probability : enumerate
(E) encumbrance : mortify

More Practice with Analogies

By now, you're probably more comfortable with analogy questions than you were when you carted this book home from the store. Practice makes a tremendous difference.

So, if you have a copy of *Real SATs,* get it out and do all of the analogy questions for two complete tests. Forget the other kinds of questions for now. *You are determined to conquer analogies.* On those two tests you will answer 38 analogy questions, and I'll bet your results will surprise you.

If you answer 15 (out of 19 total) analogies correctly on one test, you can earn roughly 115 points. Added to the base score of 200, you have 315 for openers—and you have worked with only *one* question type. That's a great start!

Dealing with Unknown Words

Sometimes you don't know one of the two key words in the first part of a given analogy. Once in a while, you don't know *both* words. And fairly often, one or more of the answer choices in either analogies or sentence completions contain unknown words. There are steps you can follow when you think you have never seen a word before.

QUICK TIPS

Examine the unknown word.

Look for a prefix. Prefixes can tell you whether the word is positive, negative, or neutral. (*Trans = across* is an example of a neutral prefix.) If possible, decide whether the unknown word is negative or positive.

Look for a word root. The root—the guts of the word—can give you an approximate meaning. Jot this meaning in the margin next to the question in the exam booklet.

Determine the part of speech being tested. Suppose your mystery word, the second half of an analogy, is *censor*. If the second half of the answer choices are verbs, *censor* is being tested as a verb, not a noun.

Try to remember a context for the word. Maybe you don't know the exact meaning of the word, but you think it sounds vaguely familiar. Try to remember a sentence using the word, if possible, or who used it. If you can recall the context, you may get a glimmer of meaning.

Prefixes to Remember

Prefixes That Are Usually Negative

a, an *(not, without, lacking)*	atypical
ab, abs *(from, away)*	abdicate
anti *(against, opposing)*	antisocial
contra *(against, opposing)*	contradict
counter *(against, opposing)*	counteract
de *(away, from, off, down)*	destruct
di, dif, dis *(off, opposing, away, down)*	diverge, dissent
for *(against, away)*	forbid
il, im, in, ir *(into, within, not, opposing)*	illegal, irregular
mal *(bad, badly)*	maladjusted
mis *(amiss, wrongly, bad)*	misfortune
non *(not)*	nonsense
ob, oc, of, op *(over, against, toward)*	obstacle, offense
un *(not, opposing)*	unwilling

Prefixes That Are Usually Positive

bene, bon *(good, well)*	beneficial
co, col, com, con, cor *(with, together)*	cooperate, correlate
eu *(good, well)*	euphemism
pro *(for, in favor of)*	promote

Prefixes of Time, Location, Size, or Amount

ana *(up, back, again)*	anachronism
ante, anti *(before, previous)*	antecedent, anticipate
cata *(down, away)*	catacombs
circum *(around)*	circumnavigate
e, ef, ex *(from, out, away)*	emit, exit
em, en *(in, among, within)*	embrace, enfold
epi *(outside, over, outer)*	epidermis
exter, extra, extro *(outside, beyond)*	external, extrovert
fore *(before)*	foretold
hyp, hypo *(under, beneath)*	hypodermic
inter *(among, between)*	interact
intro, intra *(inwardly, within)*	intramural
magn, meg, mega *(great, large)*	magnify, megaphone
mini *(tiny, miniature)*	miniskirt
neo *(new, latest of a period)*	neophyte
omni *(all)*	omnivorous
pan *(all, every)*	panorama
per *(through)*	permeate
peri *(around, near)*	perimeter
post *(after, following)*	postpone
pre *(before, in time)*	predict
re *(back, backward, again)*	retract
sub, suc, suf, sug, sum, sup, sus *(under, beneath)*	submerge, support
tele *(far, distant)*	telegram
trans *(over, across)*	transpose, transcend

Words to Remember

Certain words crop up repeatedly in literature, newspapers, speeches
. . . *and* on the SAT I and PSAT. These words appear in the analogy
and sentence completion exercises; more are listed in the vocabulary
section of this book (pp. 95–113). A few appear in the following
exercises. These same words parade by, test after test—and you must
know them. *Memorize the ones you don't know well.*

Try out these practice exercises. Choose the best antonym (word opposite in meaning) for each numbered word from the selections that follow word number 5, and write it on the correct line. Answers appear on pages 276–277.

Antonyms A

Antonym   *Word and Meaning*

_____ **1.** apathy (lack of interest, emotion, or caring)

_____ **2.** decrepit (broken down, aged, no longer useful)

_____ **3.** atrophy (waste away, degenerate, wither)

_____ **4.** plethora (vast amount, excess amount)

_____ **5.** capitulate (to yield, give in, give up)

Choices: burgeon, paucity, resist, vigorous, zeal

Antonyms B

Antonym   *Word and Meaning*

_____ **1.** ingenuous (innocent, trusting, naive)

_____ **2.** staid (serious, sober, sedate, restrained)

_____ **3.** indifferent (neutral, without prejudice)

_____ **4.** discerning (astute, perceptive, able to distinguish between one thing and another)

_____ **5.** revere (to honor or esteem highly, worship)

Choices: exuberant, disdain, sophisticated, obtuse, biased

If these words are becoming all mixed up—like a recipe for goulash—here's an idea. Ask your English teacher to offer 5 minutes of vocabulary review a day. That's 25 minutes a week for the two weeks preceding your exam. You'll be amazed at what you can learn in that amount of regular, concentrated time.

Antonyms C

Antonym	Word and Meaning
_____	1. rant (to denounce angrily, rave noisily)
_____	2. ignominy (utter shame and disgrace)
_____	3. elucidate (to make perfectly clear, explain)
_____	4. extricate (to disentangle, work one's way out of a predicament)
_____	5. hypocrisy (lack of honesty, sincerity, or truth)

Choices: esteem, embroil, sincerity, talk pleasantly, confound

Antonyms D

Antonym	Word and Meaning
_____	1. expendable (unnecessary, extra)
_____	2. defunct (useless, dead, finished)
_____	3. copious (superabundant, plentiful)
_____	4. provincial (of narrow, restricted outlook; lacking polish or sophistication)
_____	5. ambiguous (lacking clarity, vague)

Choices: sparse, broad-minded, extant (existing), definite, irreplaceable, and vital

Antonyms E

Antonym	Word and Meaning
_____	1. impartial (not biased, fair, neutral)
_____	2. meager (scanty, skimpy, sparse, lacking in quality or quantity)
_____	3. denounce (to condemn, criticize, talk against)
_____	4. repudiate (to reject, repulse, decline)
_____	5. candor (honesty, frankness, openness)

Choices: adopt, laud, prejudiced, guile, opulent

QUICK TIP

Words often function as many different parts of speech.

For example: Think of the word *rank*.

As verb—I *rank* high in my class.

As noun—What *rank* has she attained in her class?

As adjective

—The *rank* growth of weeds clogs our pond. (lush or excessive)

—Jim is a *rank* amateur at tennis. (as an intensifier)

—The *rank* odor of sewage hurts my nose. (offensive)

—Their *rank* disobedience needs correcting. (flagrant)

If the answer choices don't seem to go with the given words in an analogy, you might be looking for the wrong meaning of a word. Ask yourself, what other meaning can this word have?

How to Answer Sentence Completion Questions

Sentence completion questions ask you to select the word or words that best complete the meaning of a sentence. Students who read a great deal do well on this question type. The reluctant reader has more trouble, but practice makes a big difference, so let's get on with it.

First, the directions. They will read something like the box shown here. Learn the directions now, and you will never have to refer to them again.

Blanks appear in one or two places in each of the following sentences to indicate a missing word or phrase. Choose the word(s) or phrase(s) that best complete the meaning of each sentence.

"Test Smarts" You Can Use

Key words point to the answer you want in every sentence.

Note the italicized words in the following examples. They are your clues to the needed words and sentence type.

Example A

Although Janie was *normally* _____, *she became* extremely _____ when it was time to get out of the pool, *insisting* that she needed more practice with the kickboard.

1. Is Janie behaving normally?

2. How is she behaving? Is she being insistent?

3. Is she normally the insistent type?

4. Is Janie's normal behavior the opposite of how she's acting now? Yes.

5. *This is a sentence of contrast:* one behavior contrasted with (opposed to) another.

6. The answer will be opposing words, such as *docile. .stubborn.* Try reading the sentence with those words inserted. It makes complete sense, doesn't it?

Example B

The critic labeled the film _____, saying that *it was poorly cast and lacked substance.*

1. Why so many key words in a row?

2. Do the italicized words after the blank act as a definition of the unknown word? Yes.

3. *This is a definition sentence:* the key words explain, amplify, or define the missing word.

4. Try plugging in a word that fits the definition, such as *shallow* or *tasteless.* Now the sentence makes complete sense.

Example C

The *aggressive* _____ *and commitment* required to open the American West are *reflected* today in the _____ of modern business entrepreneurs.

1. Is that little word *and* really significant? You bet it is.

2. *And* links *similar* words, certainly not opposites.

3. The missing word and *commitment* must be closely linked and well described by *aggressive* to make logical sense.

4. These two nouns, _____ and *commitment,* are *reflected* (they show up again) in modern business entrepreneurs—today's pioneers in the business field.

5. *This is a sentence of comparison or coordination of similar ideas:* the key words told you so.

6. Try reading the sentence again, with words inserted: The aggressive *drive* and commitment required to open the American West are reflected today in the *actions* (or *thrust*) of modern business entrepreneurs.

Example D

Due to the _____ of qualified instructors, the obvious *concern* of modern education *is not the curriculum but* the _____ required to give it life.

1. *Due to* means *because of,* right?

2. *Because of* some problem with qualified instructors, the *concern* (worry) in education is *not* curriculum (what is being taught) *but* that problem with teachers.

3. *This is a cause and effect sentence* or *cause and result:* the key words tell you that one thing/situation is resulting in another.

4. Go ahead now and plug in your own words. Write your complete sentence here:

_____

_____

_____

_____

5. Did you come up with something like this? Due to the *lack* of qualified instructors, the obvious concern of modern education is not the curriculum but the *personnel* required to give it life.

Key Word Alert!

Certain words in sentence completion questions should grab you. Words indicating a **contrast** include *but, although, nevertheless, on the other hand, atypically, uncharacteristically, abnormally, illogically, yet, however, curiously, even though, except, strangely, oddly, ironically,* etc.

Words that hint at **similar or like ideas being compared or coordinated** include *and, moreover, like, always, ever, faithfully, reflected, echoed,* etc.

Words that suggest a **cause and effect** sentence include *so, because, as a result, since, unless, except, but,* etc.

These are the so-called "little words," but they are the *big words* when it comes to determining the feeling of any sentence. You must take the pulse of your sentence by noting these key words right away. Many will be conjunctions or adverbs. Others will be verbs such as *echoed* or *reflected.*

Certain Sentence Types Repeat

Learn these sentence types.

1. Contrast of one thing/situation with another. (Read Example A on page 27.)

2. Definition or explanation. (Read Example B on page 27.)

3. Comparison/coordination of similar ideas. (Read Example C on page 28.)

4. Cause and effect/result. (Read Example D on page 28.)

Knowing what sentence type you are working with will tell you what sort of words must be used to complete the meaning. Although not all sentences on standardized tests fit into these categories, you'll be surprised at how many do.

Negative vs. Positive Concepts Abound

Remember this example? *The critic labeled the film _____, saying that it was poorly cast and lacked substance.* Did the critic like the film? No. The word for this blank must be a *negative* word. Any positive or even neutral word offered as an answer choice will be wrong and can be crossed out immediately.

How about this example? *The aggressive _____ and commitment required to open the American West are reflected today in the _____ of modern business entrepreneurs.* Is this a negative sentence as a whole? No, it appears to be fairly positive. Any negative answer choices can be eliminated immediately. *Commitment* is a fairly positive word, and the word linked to it by *and* must also be positive. For the second blank, a positive word or one with no negative connotations is a must. Why? Because the two nouns (_____ and *commitment*) are *reflected* today. They show up again in modern business pioneers, and they are still positive qualities.

Be alert for negative and positive word requirements. Ask yourself whether you want good words or bad ones. Is the general idea nice or nasty?

The Last Sentence Completion Questions Are Often Harder

In any set of sentence completion questions, the first few are apt to be relatively simple. One-word completions are the easiest and will take you only a few seconds. As you work through the problem set, however, the going may get rougher, and the answer choices may be words you've rarely seen. Eliminate all the answers you *know* to be wrong. Then choose the best one of those remaining.

Reasoning Your Way Through to the Answer

Let's work through a question of medium difficulty to demonstrate the reasoning process. This always looks long in print, but your mind is the best computer ever made, and it will do all this work in seconds.

Example
Choose the word or words that best complete the meaning of the entire sentence.

Q: The bygone belief that education was the province of the _____, and not required by the masses, has been supplanted by our conviction that education is absolutely _____ for everyone if our nation is to progress.

    (A) monarchy. .logical
    (B) church. .impossible
    (C) populace. .desirable
    (D) elite. .mandatory
    (E) educators. .required

1. Read the sentence carefully. Read it again.

2. Note key words pointing to the required answer: *not required by the masses* sets up a contrast with the first clause; *supplanted by* (replaced) further emphasizes the contrast with *bygone belief. Conviction* and *absolutely* are strong words, pointing to a strong word for the second blank.

3. Sentence type? An obvious contrast—old with modern. Education long ago compared with education today.

4. Whomp up the answer. Let's try: *The bygone belief that education was the province of the wealthy or upper class, and not required by the masses, has been supplanted by our conviction that education is absolutely necessary for everyone if our nation is to progress.* Does the "guess" answer make total sense?

5. Eliminate answers.

(A) **monarchy. .logical**

No. Factually wrong, as the wealthy were also educated. And *logical* makes little sense in the second slot. This sentence poses the problem of *who* must have an education, not whether it is logical or illogical.

(B) **church. .impossible**

True, the church once did most of the education, but *church* is not an opposite of *the masses,* which is required in this sentence. *Impossible* makes no sense in the second blank. No. Cross out.

(C) **populace. .desirable**

Populace is a good synonym of *the masses,* not the contrasting word we need. *Desirable* works, but is very weak when you remember the strong words *conviction* and *absolutely.* No. Cross out.

(D) **elite. .mandatory**

Elite would include the monarchy and the wealthy, who were educated in bygone days, and *mandatory* (essential, vital) completes the idea of contrast between then and now. Circle this one to KEEP.

(E) **educators. .required**

Educators is not an opposite of *the masses* and makes little sense, although it's vaguely possible. *Required* works well in the second blank. KEEP, for now.

You are left with answer **(D)** and answer **(E)**. Which one is *more specific?* Which one is closer to your idea of a good answer? Because *elite* fits so much better in the first blank, and because *mandatory* is a stronger word than *required,* you should choose **(D)**. Answer **(D)** is correct for this sentence.

QUICK TIPS

Read and reread the given sentence.

Examine it like a bug under a microscope. Circle key words if it helps you.

Note the key words as clues.

Pay special attention to the "little words": *so, because, and, yet, since, most, least, although, enough, moreover, typically, normally, curiously, however, uncharacteristically, unless, even though, nevertheless,* etc. Note all *adverbs.*

Decide on sentence type—is it one of these?

(1) *Contrast* of one thing with another?
(2) *Definition,* with the word you're looking for defined or explained in the sentence?
(3) *Comparison* or *coordination* of similar ideas?
(4) *Cause and effect* or *result?*

Whomp up your own answer for the blank(s) before looking at the answer choices.

Do you want a positive or negative word? Positive word in the first blank and negative word in the second blank? What does the sentence need to make absolute logical sense?

Eliminate answer choices systematically.

Cross out the wrong ones in your test booklet, and circle the answers to keep for final decision time.

Timing for Sentence Completion Questions

Look ahead to see how many sentence completion sentences are on a given portion of your timed test. Normally you will see sentence completion questions in sets of nine or ten on an SAT.

Students often spend longer on these questions than they should.

Allow yourself 30 seconds to 1 minute per question. Practice with sentence completion questions should help make you a speedy, accurate worker. Plan to spend roughly 6–8 minutes on a set.

As you practice, note how long it takes you to do a ten-question series of sentence completion problems.

PRACTICE SENTENCE COMPLETIONS 1

Directions for all practice exercises: Circle the word or words that best complete the meaning of the entire sentence. Answers begin at the end of the book on pages 277–279.

1. Americans seem committed to the exploration of space, aware that the variety of information gained in the attempt is of _____ value—beyond precise calculation.

(A) dubious
(B) medical
(C) inconclusive
(D) inestimable
(E) calculable

2. James was _____ about joining a fraternity; yes, he wanted the society of compatible, like-minded friends, but he also craved _____.

(A) confused. .education
(B) ambivalent. .diversity
(C) delighted. .companion-ship
(D) determined. .solitude
(E) uninformed. .knowledge

3. The principle behind media-
tion is _____, wherein
people with _____ goals
or philosophies reach agreement on common ground,
with each side conceding a
point now and then.

   (A) arbitration. .identical
   (B) historic. .similar
   (C) compromise. .disparate
   (D) modern. .current
   (E) dissension. .divergent

4. Despite warnings from
financial experts, some
_____ investors still
_____ dubious get-rich-
quick schemes.

   (A) innocent. .adhere to
   (B) credulous. .succumb to
   (C) timorous. .retreat from
   (D) skeptical. .wait for
   (E) arbitrary. .care for

5. Patience, who possessed
_____ temperament at
odds with her name, learned
that office work was too
repetitive and predictable for
one of her nature.

   (A) a placid
   (B) a volatile
   (C) a remote
   (D) a benevolent
   (E) an amicable

6. A dedicated sculptor,
Wharton found himself
_____ with his new
acquaintances because they
valued him more for his
ability to regale them with
_____ at endless parties
than for his hard-won artistic
achievement.

   (A) conversant. .grisly
       details
   (B) incompatible. .witty
       repartee
   (C) blessed. .professional
       skills
   (D) disgusted. .information
   (E) malcontent. .frivolity

7. It is an unfortunate _____ that the countries most in need of restructuring their economic systems are the ones whose history, customs, or rulers have _____ the acquisition of modern education and technology.

   (A) situation. .encouraged
   (B) error. .frustrated
   (C) paradox. .inhibited
   (D) concern. .realized
   (E) contretemps. .promoted

8. More scientific progress was made during the twelve _____ years of war than during the preceding fifty years of _____ and peaceful commerce.

   (A) disordered. .frugality
   (B) subversive. .intrigue
   (C) chaotic. .tranquillity
   (D) glorious. .depression
   (E) uneventful. .sterility

9. Miracles are not _____ to scientific proof; their _____ rests entirely on faith.

   (A) immune. .power
   (B) opposed. .evidence
   (C) amenable. .inevitability
   (D) convertible. .vitality
   (E) susceptible. .efficacy

10. Literary styles change, and Dickens or Hawthorne would be as astonished by the deliberate _____ of Hemingway, as Hemingway was appalled by their _____ of words.

   (A) terseness. .profusion
   (B) prose. .paucity
   (C) approach. .variety
   (D) morass. .style
   (E) passages. .mastery

PRACTICE SENTENCE COMPLETIONS 2

1. Clara Peeters, a distinguished Flemish painter, is among the best of many talented women who have _____ the history of still life and flower painting.

   (A) created
   (B) enriched
   (C) rescued
   (D) validated
   (E) extended

2. Frontier settlements had only makeshift jails in empty storerooms and livery stables; in addition, security was _____ and guards were easily _____, so that escapes were not uncommon.

   (A) formal. .angered
   (B) established. .induced
   (C) feeble. .converted
   (D) intermittent. .investi-gated
   (E) lax. .bribed

3. Rhonda's belief that people's lives are predestined, determined by God or perhaps fate, makes her championship of free will and independence especially _____.

   (A) understandable
   (B) incongruous
   (C) specious
   (D) suspect
   (E) reprehensible

4. Ralph's young, ingenuous appearance belied his _____ bargaining skill in awkward negotiations, so that opponents were often surprised by his _____.

   (A) honest. .approach
   (B) clever. .failures
   (C) canny. .acumen
   (D) innovative. .retreat
   (E) plausible. .illogic

5. As anyone who watches TV can _____, the determination of advertisers to feed us their messages along with our entertainment continues _____.

(A) attest. .unabated
(B) reveal. .to diminish
(C) state. .to be mystifying
(D) deny. .as before
(E) verify. .to wane

6. Emily found that her pet monkey had not only a _____ tail but a mind to match it; his inventive exploits displayed a _____ intelligence far beyond what she had expected in so young an animal.

(A) talented. .kind of
(B) simian. .destructive
(C) sedulous. .brief
(D) prehensile. .precocious
(E) clever. .malicious

7. In times past, society suffered from a _____ of information about diet and exercise, but recently we have been _____ reams of information on both topics.

(A) deluge. .deprived of
(B) dearth. .inundated with
(C) paucity. .denied the
(D) plethora. .showered with
(E) misdirection. .given

8. Known for her _____ and generosity, Mavis astonished her community by withdrawing her customary support from a charity and establishing a rival one in her own name, a gesture labeled as pure _____ by disgruntled former associates.

(A) keenness. .philanthropy
(B) aggressiveness. .conceit
(C) geniality. .insensibility
(D) idealism. .rudeness
(E) altruism. .narcissism

9. Because of our cherished conception of the friar as an honest _____ who has no need of worldly goods, Chaucer's portrayal of the _____ and mendacious cleric comes as a shock.

(A) priest. .perspicacious
(B) cleric. .efficacious
(C) ascetic. .avaricious
(D) fanatic. .grasping
(E) lunatic. .craven

10. When informed that their ideas are _____, many people both old and wise have refrained from sharing their patiently garnered knowledge with the young and smug whom they deem too _____ to appreciate it.

(A) perceptive. .conceited
(B) ludicrous. .grateful
(C) revolutionary. .hide-bound
(D) vicarious. .insular
(E) obsolescent. .myopic

Stop!

Are there, by any remote chance, some words given as answer choices in these exercises that you *didn't know??* If so, you'd better check on their meanings. These words were taken from PSATs and SATs of recent years, and many are repeat offenders.

PRACTICE SENTENCE COMPLETIONS 3

1. Can we restructure education so that it teaches logic and _____, rather than the collection and recitation of facts divorced from useful application?

   (A) cohesiveness
   (B) reasoning
   (C) problem-solving skills
   (D) proven data
   (E) historical precedent

2. Popular in the seventies, the young adult problem novel, as it was known in the publishing trade, was essentially _____ in nature, bent on conveying a moral lesson in modern slang.

   (A) frivolous
   (B) boring
   (C) modern
   (D) equivocal
   (E) didactic

3. Her school performance was consistently _____; in conferences, her parents debated with the instructors whether she was _____ or just plain bored.

   (A) lackluster. .incapable
   (B) insipid. .gifted
   (C) meteoric. .attentive
   (D) slow. .bright
   (E) erratic. .deficient

4. Apparently greatly _____, the secretary of the corporation accepted the generous apology of her board chairman.

   (A) perplexed
   (B) mollified
   (C) exaggerated
   (D) maligned
   (E) stimulated

5. An optimist by nature, Harold faced a difficult adjustment when his investments turned sour, and he was slow to regain his customary _____ after the _____ .

(A) cheer. .process
(B) hardiness. .event
(C) wariness. .disaster
(D) sanguinity. .debacle
(E) outlook. .result

6. Because the front-runner in a state election focused on _____ interests rather than the parochial ones of his constituency, he lost to a _____ who told the citizens what they wanted to hear about their own narrow concerns.

(A) private. .campaigner
(B) catholic. .demagogue
(C) wide-ranging. .pioneer
(D) specific. .candidate
(E) centralized. .politician

7. For authors, composers, and painters who must work alone, an occasional, stimulating meeting with others in the solitary arts serves to _____ their self-imposed _____ .

(A) combat. .isolation
(B) expand. .endeavors
(C) mitigate. .agony
(D) destroy. .talent
(E) allay. .fears

8. Although E. B. White enjoyed the success of his children's novel *Charlotte's Web*, he was _____ to have it translated into a movie, which he feared might _____ the book.

(A) resigned. .reproduce
(B) delighted. .magnify
(C) reluctant. .inaccurately reflect
(D) hesitant. .skillfully depict
(E) ecstatic. .lampoon

9. Many of the antique "finds" she holds most dear have been strictly _____, the result of happenstance or what is often termed serendipity.

   (A) characteristic
   (B) preposterous
   (C) brilliant
   (D) immaculate
   (E) fortuitous

10. For too many faculty members and researchers, computers are still _____ challenge; for growing numbers of students, however, these remarkable machines are _____ the way they learn.

    (A) an interesting. .inhibiting
    (B) a formidable. .revolutionizing
    (C) an absorbing. .subverting
    (D) a disabling. .codifying
    (E) a euphoric. .solidifying

PRACTICE SENTENCE COMPLETIONS 4

Remember to put the trickier sentences into your own words. Know what sort of word you need for each blank before you eliminate answers.

1. While critics praised the play highly, viewers did not flock to the theater, and the playwright reaped only _____ reward from its brief run.

   (A) a just
   (B) a modest
   (C) an embarrassed
   (D) a monetary
   (E) a precise

2. My economics textbook is _____ to read, yet when I read attentively, I understand the theories presented.

   (A) exciting
   (B) annoying
   (C) objectionable
   (D) demanding
   (E) idealistic

3. The scientist decided to risk failure rather than _____ the data just so that he could be published in the leading scientific journal.

   (A) augment
   (B) implement
   (C) rationalize
   (D) distort
   (E) gauge

4. Although children need shelter and protection, their need for _____ is just as great if they are to evaluate themselves and their world honestly.

   (A) homes
   (B) affection
   (C) truth
   (D) adjustment
   (E) instruction

5. The considerate personality of Dr. Jekyll underwent a total _____ as he became Mr. Hyde, _____ character bent on evil.

    (A) alteration. .a dubious
    (B) refurbishing. .a masterful
    (C) indoctrination. .an original
    (D) advancement. .a different
    (E) metamorphosis. .a ruthless

6. If, as Shelley wrote, "The great instrument of moral good is the imagination," then we must not allow _____ to exclude totally our _____.

    (A) harsh reality. .idealistic goals
    (B) creativity. .fantasies
    (C) unpleasant facts. .daily lives
    (D) religion. .perception of life
    (E) practicality. .constructive ideas

7. In the nineteenth century, women on the American frontier were people of _____ determination whose _____ helped them conquer loneliness and privation.

    (A) questionable. .character
    (B) fortunate. .morality
    (C) average. .modesty
    (D) relentless. .tenacity
    (E) aristocratic. .attitude

8. Even though certain forms of cancer now respond well to treatment, others have remained _____ continuing to puzzle physicians.

    (A) a pestilence
    (B) an allusion
    (C) an eccentricity
    (D) an enigma
    (E) a provocation

9. A number of psychologists appear to believe that human intelligence is largely _____ and that to provide large sums of money to _____ intelligence in a structured environment is wasteful.

(A) proven. .portray
(B) spiritual. .define
(C) theoretical. .calculate
(D) innate. .cultivate
(E) accessible. .test

10. Believing himself supported by more than a _____ of evidence, the professor endeavored to prove that Beowulf was not the _____ his colleagues claimed, but an actual man whose existence was the basis for the Old English epic.

(A) shred. .persona
(B) modicum. .chimera
(C) fabrication. .demon
(D) particle. .heresy
(E) aggregation. .protagonist

More Practice with Sentence Completion Questions

After you have recovered from the foregoing exercises, if you feel the need for further practice and you have a copy of *Real SATs,* do as many of its sentence completion questions as you can stand. You will find that you are *much* better than you were. In fact, you will rarely miss any but the very nastiest—and maybe not even those. Still, out of 19 total sentence completion questions, you can miss three or four without serious damage to your overall verbal score.

How to Answer Critical Reading Questions

On each SAT, 40 of the 78 questions are based on critical reading skills. One verbal segment usually has two passages, one of about 450 words with six questions and one of about 600 words with nine questions or so. Another section has one longer passage. A shorter, 15-minute verbal section consists entirely of two related passages and twelve to fourteen questions about them.

Most of these readings are fairly interesting. They seem to have improved recently, maybe as a result of a law requiring ETS to publish used test forms, or maybe because SAT tutors have criticized the reading passages as the worst-written material imaginable. Still, many are convoluted in sentence structure and suspiciously packed with "SAT words." Few of your college textbooks will be as dull as some SAT passages.

The reading passages include material from the physical and social sciences and from the humanities. One selection is usually fiction, and another focuses on an ethnic group or minority and/or on women. A passage about either women or minorities will normally be positive in tone.

Why Are Reading Passages Such a Big Part of a Verbal Test?

College entrance exams are developed at the request of colleges themselves. As nearly as possible, these tests are designed to discover how well a student will do with college-level reading material. Your college work will *directly depend* on your ability to read and understand written material. **Some authorities have stated that as much as 90 percent of your work in college is reading based.**

So . . . you are learning to read in an *involved* way, *not just for a test* but because you will need to read the same way as a college student.

How Should You Read?

We all do at least two distinct varieties of reading:

1. Pleasure Reading: Garfield and his lasagna and/or "The Wildest Girl/Boy in Town."

2. Information/Study Reading: the biology book, American history, and how-to manuals, like this one.

As you know, these two kinds of reading are done for very different purposes. The way that they are performed must be just as different.

The kind of reading you want to perfect is demanding reading because it asks for *all* of you, not just your funny bone. It expects you to be totally involved with the passage. And if you are, the answers are there, waiting for you to spot them and answer the questions with no strain.

Key Words . . . One More Time

Remember the key (or clue) words from page 29 in the section on sentence completion questions? Words such as *but, yet, since, although, except, moreover, unless,* and *nonetheless* will be just as helpful to you in critical reading territory. *Key words in sentences signal a shift, a qualification, an anomaly—SOMETHING you should note.* More than half of the questions will come from sentences containing key words. The answers will be either stated or implied in the passages, just as the test directions say.

The answers are there. And you will learn how to spot them by doing this section.

What Kinds of Questions Are Asked?

If you think for a minute, you'll know what kinds of questions can be asked about a relatively short passage. Someone out there will want to know whether or not you grasped:

1. The **main point** or central theme of the passage

2. The author's **intent, attitude, or tone**—how the writer *feels* about what he or she is saying, as well as the techniques used to convey those feelings

3. The **basic facts** contained in the material

4. The **implications** of the material, including the drawing of logical conclusions

5. How the author uses particular words—**vocabulary in context**

Improving Your Critical Reading

You probably know your strengths and weaknesses as a reader. And if you're normal, you want to get better, not only for a PSAT or SAT, but for college reading.

Good readers, like good writers, get that way through practice. No one can prescribe rules, because you are unique. What works for you may not work for someone else.

But . . . *you can learn to be a good reader by practicing the skill of involved reading.* What follows is a class-tested, time-proven way to do it. Try it. It can make your life a great deal easier.

How to Read for the Main Point or Central Theme

Everything written or said has a point to make. Why write or speak if you don't have a point?

Typical SAT Questions on the Main Point

1. The author's main purpose in the passage is . . .

2. The passage is primarily concerned with . . .

3. The passage suggests that . . .

4. Which of the following best expresses the main point of the passage as a whole?

In order to find the answers, follow these steps:

1. *Skim all questions* rapidly *before* you read the passage. Now you know what to read for. (Some detest this method. Don't follow any suggestion you hate. Read the passage first if it's the only way you're comfortable.)

2. *Look for the main idea* in the first paragraph. Not there? Then maybe it is summarized near the end of the passage.

3. *Read the passage quickly* when looking for the central theme or main point. Asterisk (***) or underline all meaty sentences that sound as if they're expressing a main idea, major conclusion, or focal point. You'll need to find these sentences later on.

4. If, after one quick reading, you're unsure of the main idea, begin answering other questions. As you work, the major focus of the piece will become clearer and you'll be able to answer the question on the main idea.

What Will the Answers Be Like?

Typically, for *many* questions on an SAT or PSAT, *not just those on the main point,* you will find that:

1. *One answer covers too much ground.* It is too broad—too "big" in some way.

2. *One or more answers are too narrow*, too restricted in outlook—too "small" in some way.

3. *One answer is apt to parrot the passage,* repeating exact phraseology. It may be tempting but is typically too narrow/ limited in scope.

4. *One answer may be off the wall*—wacko—illogical.

5. *One will be right.* It will be specific and will stand up to any tests you apply for accuracy.

QUICK TIPS
for Reading Passages

Answer sentence completion and analogy questions before you tackle critical reading.
Spending too long on reading passages can cost you points. Answer the quicker kinds of questions first.

Skim the questions first.
Reading rapidly over the questions will give you an idea of what the passage is about and what will be asked.

Skim through questions to find the easy ones.
Reading questions are *not* arranged in order of difficulty as they tend to be on the rest of an SAT. The last question about a passage may be the easiest.

Read quickly.
The only time you will be tested on this material is in the next 10 minutes. You don't have to memorize it.

Focus on main ideas.
Use the first paragraph as an indicator of the main idea of the passage as a whole. The first and last sentence of each subsequent paragraph will usually tell you what that paragraph is about.

Circle key words as you read the passage.
See the key word alert on page 29. A majority of answers will come from sentences containing key words.

Eliminate answers one by one.
The answer that jumps out at you from the page was put there to do just that. Make sure it's better than all the other answers if you decide to choose it.

Avoid answers that express strong emotion.
Except for the fictional passages, strong feelings just don't appear on the SAT. Likewise, avoid strongly negative answer choices when determining the author's attitude, style, or mood.

And now to put all these techniques into practice . . .

Reading for the Main Idea

Passage A

Line Interviewers are not going to pull information from a reluctant
interviewee. They will simply ask a question that will give you a
lead. They feel that one way to assess your abilities is to judge
how well you present yourself. Put yourself in a recruiter's shoes
5   and judge for yourself how well you come across. The recruiter's
mission is to screen applicants and refer them to managers who
will do the actual hiring. If, in a sales training program interview,
you say you are unsure of your interest in sales but wonder about
something in administration, the recruiter is going to be annoyed.
10   He is exhausted from traveling around the country looking for
people interested in sales, and you focus on an entirely different
job area. What is he supposed to do? Report back to his manager
and say, "I have a candidate, a very nice person, but I am not
sure he wants to sell"?
15   If you were in the recruiter's shoes, you would not recommend such a candidate. Nor would you recommend one who says
"you know" at the end of each thought, nor one who laces
sentences with unnecessary "filler" words. Help the recruiters.
They look long and hard for candidates who will be a credit to
20   their judgment. What they want an interview to be is just what
you want it to be—an exchange between two people sincerely
trying to establish whether they have a mutual interest, with
neither party trying to intimidate or manipulate the other. The
recruiters, however, are the questioners; if you are not prepared
25   with answers, you are going to feel as if you were on trial.

Question

Which of the following best summarizes the main point of the passage?

(A) The process of interviewing for employment can be difficult.

(B) Interviewers should try to put themselves in the place of their interviewees.

(C) Interviewers sometimes try to trip up their interviewees with difficult questions.

(D) Interviewees can be more successful if they understand what interviewers want from them.

(E) Interviewees should be careful to let their interviewers ask most of the questions.

Answer

Eliminate answer choices one by one.

(A) Too broad.

(B) Appealing at first, but note that this choice reverses the emphasis of the passage. The passage gives advice to *interviewees,* not *interviewers.*

(C) Off the wall. This idea might be one that many people hold, but it isn't expressed in the passage.

(D) Yes! This one summarizes an idea that appears more than once in the passage, in lines 4–5, 10–12, 15–16, and 18–20.

(E) This choice might have appealed to you if you hadn't already seen a better one, but it's really too narrow.

Some passages state their main ideas in the first or last paragraph; increasingly, many do not. *Especially* when the main idea is implied rather than stated, process of elimination is *indispensable.* All the answers are there to appeal to you, and they are apt to express ideas that *do* appear in the passage. Your task, though, is to focus on *the passage as a whole.*

Reading to Decode Attitude, Style, or Mood

Frequently, one of the questions based on passages of reading material asks you to determine the authors' attitudes toward their material. How do they *feel* about what they are saying? *Why* are they bothering to write all this down for posterity? And what is the *result* of this attitude? The *mood* of the passage.

Authors *reveal attitude by their word choice.* If they say that homeless people are "pitiable creatures," then you know their feeling is one of *pity* for those people. Certain words are very revealing of author attitude, and you must note these words or ideas as you read through a passage for later reference about author attitude.

Passages written mainly to inform do just that, usually without intruding mood or feeling. The tone, therefore, is unimportant, as long as the *authors' feelings* about what they're writing are not part of the message. Educational materials typically are written to inform, and that is their sole purpose. (The words *tone* and *mood* are often inter- changeable and since they rarely apply to informative passages shouldn't cause you any problems.)

When to Beware

When reading for authors' attitudes toward their material or the mood or tone of the passage, *avoid answers that are strongly negative.* Violently critical material—highly disputatious stuff—just isn't going to appear. Authors' attitudes may be *admiring, appreciative, approving, respectful,* or *deferential,* but authors never *loathe* the person or group they are writing about—not for the SAT anyway.

If the passage you're reading is fiction—not fact—the author's tone or style may be *satirical,* as in the following passage, but it will *never* be *dogmatic, pedantic, explanatory,* or *informative,* because *those tones (moods) are not appropriate for fiction.* On one SAT, the author's atti- tude toward a fictional subject was one of *detached sympathy,* and the answer choices *cold objectivity, clear distaste,* and *veiled disdain* were decidedly wrong.

Some words have *never* been correct answers to describe the author's attitude or the style or mood of an SAT passage. Avoid like the plague: *ambivalent, condescending, vitriolic, pompous, apathetic, skeptical* (or *suspicious*), and *apologetic.* When you see other words like these, be extremely careful. These words are altogether too negative.

In the following brief passages, read for author's attitude and mood. After each passage, write in the margin a few words that describe the passage in terms of mood or tone. Answer the questions, and see how closely you pegged the tone of each piece. *Circle* words that guide you to the answers.

Passage B

Line   "Sylvia!"

        "Yes, papa."

        "That infernal dog of yours—"

        "Oh, papa!"

5   "Yes, that infernal dog of yours has been at my carnations again!"

        Colonel Reynolds, V.C., glared sternly across the table at Miss Sylvia Reynolds, and Miss Sylvia Reynolds looked in a deprecatory manner back at Colonel Reynolds, V.C.; while the dog in ques-

10   tion—a foppish pug—happening to meet the colonel's eye in transit, crawled unostentatiously under the sideboard, and began to wrestle with a bad conscience.

        "Oh, naughty Tommy!" said Miss Reynolds mildly, in the direction of the sideboard.

15   "Yes, my dear," assented the colonel; "and if you could convey to him the information that if he does it once more—yes, just once more!—I shall shoot him on the spot you would be doing him a kindness." And the colonel bit a large crescent out of his toast, with all the energy and conviction of a man who has

20   thoroughly made up his mind. "At six o'clock this morning," continued he, in a voice of gentle melancholy, "I happened to look out of my bedroom window, and saw him. He had then destroyed two of my best plants, and was commencing on a third, with every appearance of self-satisfaction. I threw two large

25   brushes and a boot at him."

        "Oh, papa! They didn't hit him?"

"No, my dear, they did not. The brushes missed him by
several yards, and the boot smashed a fourth carnation. However,
I was so fortunate as to attract his attention, and he left off."
30   "I can't think what makes him do it. I suppose it's bones.
He's got bones buried all over the garden."

"Well, if he does it again, you'll find that there will be a few
more bones buried in the garden!" said the colonel grimly; and he
subsided into his paper.

Question

The tone of this selection could best be described as

(A) serious
(B) literary
(C) irritable
(D) humorous
(E) familial

Answer

The answer to this piece lies in the words chosen by its author, P. G.
Wodehouse, one of the most famous English humorists of all time. If
you did as suggested and circled words that point to tone or mood,
you might have circled lines 9–12, which show the pug wrestling
"with a bad conscience." That in itself is a laughable approach, as is
the picture of Sylvia's father, whose voice is one of "gentle melancholy," line 21. Last, the colonel's threat to add a few more bones to
the garden isn't treated very seriously by the author, and probably not
by Sylvia.

All in all, you can eliminate any serious answers, as this is *not* a
serious piece; that gets rid of (A), (B), and (C) in short order. And
while it pictures a family at table, the talk is not family centered,
which eliminates (E), *familial.* Therefore, by elimination, you choose
(D), *humorous,* which does fit the mood of this piece. Its tone is light,
and we know that Sylvia is not really frightened by her father, although he'd probably wish her to be at least awed.

Passage C

Line When I disengaged myself, as above mentioned, from private
business, I flattered myself that, by the sufficient though moderate
fortune I had acquired, I had secured leisure during the rest of my
life for philosophical studies and amusements. I purchased all Dr.
5   Spence's apparatus, who had come from England to lecture in
Philadelphia, and I proceeded in my electrical experiments with
great alacrity; but the public, now considering me as a man of
leisure, laid hold of me for their purposes, every part of our civil
government, and almost at the same time, imposing some duty
10   upon me. The governor put me into the commission of the
peace; the corporation of the city chose me one of the common
council and soon after an alderman; and the citizens at large
elected me a burgess to represent them in Assembly. This latter
station was the more agreeable to me, as I was at length tired
15   with sitting there to hear debates, in which, as clerk I could take
no part, and which were often so uninteresting that I was
induced to amuse myself with making magic squares or circles or
anything to avoid weariness; and I conceived my becoming a
member would enlarge my power of doing good. I would not,
20   however, insinuate that my ambition was not flattered by all these
promotions; it certainly was; for considering my low beginning,
they were great things to me; and they were still more pleasing,
as being so many spontaneous testimonies of the public's good
opinion, and by me entirely unsolicited.

Question

The primary purpose of the passage is to

(A) recount a historical event
(B) explain the author's feelings about certain events in his life
(C) counter charges made against the author by his detractors
(D) amuse by pointing out the foibles of persons of the author's
     acquaintance
(E) inspire awe in the author's many talents

Answer

This passage clearly seems to be about someone's life. In fact, it is a portion of Benjamin Franklin's well-known *Autobiography,* the 1848 version as published by Harper & Brothers. While it does recount historical events, as suggested by answer (A), the autobiographical intent—to tell the facts, but *as they affected the author*—is better expressed in answer (B). Answers (C), (D), and (E) express emotional nuances that are too strong for this relatively even-tempered piece of writing.

Often, two or even three answers to a mood or author-attitude question seem very tempting. Whenever you can choose the more *specific* answer, you should do so.

The combined effect of the author's attitude and purpose *leads* to mood or tone. This total effect is often called "the author's point of view."

Remember that you can accomplish a great deal in a quick reading by *circling or underlining words* that give you an indication of mood, tone, and author's attitude.

If you feel that circling or underlining is tiresome, time-consuming, or unnecessary, don't do it. Nonetheless, this technique does help many to stay involved with the material and concentrate only on it, not on a growling stomach or the promise of a wonderful evening to come.

Pollyanna or Dr. Pangloss?

To do well on SAT factual passages, keep in mind two characters from literature named Pollyanna and Dr. Pangloss. They were unfailingly positive and even-tempered—no matter what. When you and I would shout and stamp around, *they* might admit to "mild distress." The test makers at ETS must be related to them because they *never print emotionally charged material.* They especially avoid writings of skeptical or censorious authors when they select factual, serious reading passages.

When you see answers expressing strong feelings, be suspicious. Here's a sample of what I mean, using answers from recent SATs. The choices in the first list were always wrong; the ones in the second list were correct. Remember that this guideline—*avoid answers too strongly worded or too emotional*—applies to serious passages, e.g., history, science, and biography.

Too Emotional = Wrong	**Nicely Restrained = Right**
argumentative *(too controversial)*	impersonal
apologetic *(too wimpy)*	objective
passionately	analytical
harsh	informative or explanatory
hazy	lucid
defensive	pragmatic or practical
wildly excited	dissatisfaction
opinionated *(too negative)*	
capricious *(as bad as hazy)*	
vengeful	

Reread Passage A on page 51, and then answer this question.

Question

The author's style and tone in this passage combine to give an overall impression of

(A) formality
(B) corporate bias
(C) encouraging friendliness
(D) professional detachment
(E) unabashed enthusiasm

Answer

A basically informative, how-to passage will avoid any *bias,* answer (B), as well as strong emotion, answer (E). Answers (A) and (D) are too cold and detached if you consider paragraph 2. That leaves only (C), *encouraging friendliness,* as the correct answer. (Whenever an author speaks to "you"—the reader—directly, as in paragraph 2, the tone warms up considerably.)

> ## QUICK TIP
>
> ### For factual passages, choose neutral or positive answers.
>
> Factual passages, material about ethnic groups, and "serious" subjects (law, government, medicine, science, education) are indeed serious business to the folks who design your test. They will print material restrained in tone, style, and author attitude—and you must choose answers in this same vein.

Reading to Isolate Key Facts and Examples

A third type of critical reading question on an SAT is based on facts in the passage. The point authors wish to make is often buttressed by facts and examples that help to make the meaning clear and to support their thesis.

Reading Technique

As you read a sample of written material, make a *check mark in the margin* next to sentences containing examples or facts. A typical question on an SAT is "All of the following examples are mentioned in the passage EXCEPT . . ." And then you must determine which example was *not* mentioned. You cannot do that unless you know what examples *were given* and how to find them *quickly*. If check marks pinpoint the location of each example, your job becomes easier.

These questions should be like gifts, and I think you'll feel that way as soon as you make a habit of marking the passage wherever you see examples or key facts that have been included.

Try your hand at the following question based on Passage A on page 51.

Question

The advice given to an interviewee can best be summarized by

   I. It is important to present yourself well.

   II. Be honest about your lack of interest in sales.

   III. Express an open interest in administration.

   IV. Give direct, clear answers that are well-phrased.

   V. Prepare penetrating questions beforehand.

    (A) I and IV
    (B) II and IV
    (C) I and III
    (D) III and IV
    (E) IV and V

Answer

This type of roundup question is not one that students are used to seeing. If you haven't involved yourself sufficiently in the reading passage, it comes as a rather rude shock. Not only do you have to have *all* the facts in mind, but you have to sum them up and let one or two (or possibly three) of the chosen Roman numeral answers represent your fact roundup. Oh boy!

Look back at the passage, and see if you have checked lines 3–4, 6–9, and 15–18, plus 23–25 as a summation sentence. If you have, you can see that Roman numeral I sums up the advice shown by examples in the first paragraph, and Roman numeral IV sums up what the second paragraph is saying. Thus, both can act as themes of the key points to be gleaned from these two paragraphs.

Answer (A), then, *I and IV,* is the correct choice.

Note also that this type of question is a mixture of the main-point question and the factual or example variety.

QUICK TIP

Note the central idea of each paragraph as you read.

Each paragraph has one major point to make. That is its contribution to the piece as a whole. Questions often center on the main point of a paragraph.

Reading for What Is Suggested or Implied But Not Stated

A very important word in the directions for questions based on reading material is the word *implied.* It tells you to read with extreme care, as questions may be asked about what was *not explicitly* set forth in the passage.

Usually answering an inference question requires you to put together information from two different spots in the passage. The trick is to go *only* as far as the information in the passage will let you but *not* to make any wild imaginative leaps.

Practice 1

Reread Passage B on pages 54–55 that was written by P. G. Wodehouse in a humorous style. Then do the following exercise.

Question

It can be inferred from the passage that the pug dog named Tommy

    (A) rarely was in the flower garden

    (B) disliked carnations

    (C) was in the colonel's favor most of the time

    (D) was a joy to Sylvia, his mistress

    (E) had repeatedly destroyed the colonel's carnations

Answer

Your first clue to the answer was in lines 5 and 6, in the colonel's comment that the dog had been "at my carnations *again*," which says that he's done damage in the garden at *other* times. Later, in lines 30–31, Sylvia wonders why her dog digs in the garden and says that he has bones buried "all over the garden." Therefore, answer (E), *had repeatedly destroyed the colonel's carnations,* is the best answer.

We might guess that the pug disliked carnations, answer (B), but there is no supporting evidence for that guess, just as there is no evidence to support answer (D), that he was a joy to his mistress. We might find that to be true later, but in this specific example, only answer (E) is corroborated.

Practice 2

Reread Passage C on page 56 from Benjamin Franklin's *Autobiography.* Then, do the next exercise.

Question

It can be inferred from the passage that the public considered the author "a man of leisure" (lines 7–8) because he

(A) had amassed a considerable fortune
(B) was no longer involved in private business
(C) had temporarily laid aside his experiments with electricity
(D) often engaged in making or solving puzzles in his spare time
(E) found that government work left him with a great deal of spare time

Answer

Your answer lies in the first sentence. Right at the beginning, Franklin states that he has retired from business. He has a "moderate" fortune, not a large one, so (A) is out. Answers (D) and (E) describe things that happened *after* the public got the idea that Franklin, as a man of leisure, ought to be put to public use. And answer (C) is contradicted in the passage—Franklin was pursuing his electrical experiments "with great alacrity" or speed (lines 6–7). Answer (B) is correct.

Reading Vocabulary in Context

Often one or two of the questions about a passage ask you the meaning of a word or phrase *as it is used in the passage.* These are *not* simply vocabulary questions, and answering them doesn't depend on your knowing the meaning of the word. In fact, usually *all* of the answer choices are possible definitions of the word or phrase. Your job is to decide which of those five definitions makes the most sense in the context of the passage.

You'll be given a word or phrase to be defined and the line number(s) in which it appears. Go to that spot, and read the sentence the word or phrase is in (and sometimes the sentences before and after). Substitute each of the answer choices in turn for the target word or phrase, eliminating the ones that make no sense in the sentence. Usually you'll have just one choice left; otherwise, choose the leftover choice that makes the *most* sense in the passage.

Remember, this question is testing a reading skill, not your vocabulary. Don't panic if you've never heard the word before, though usually you have. (You could answer this question using the answer choices and the sentence from the passage without even looking at the target word.) Likewise, don't eliminate an answer choice because you've never heard the word used in that sense. Chances are the word *is* sometimes used *in that sense.* The question is which answer choice makes the *most* sense *in the context of the passage.*

Practice 1

Turn back to Passage C on page 56 to answer these two questions:

Question
In line 9, the word "imposing" most nearly means

(A) placing
(B) taking advantage of
(C) establishing by authority
(D) bringing about by force
(E) passing off as if to deceive

Answer

It may take you a while to figure out what's happening in this sentence, but what it comes down to is that "the public . . . laid hold of me . . . *imposing* some duty upon me." Try answer (A), "placing": "*placing* some duty upon me." Hey, that works! Keep (A) for now.

Try the others: "*taking advantage of* some duty upon me," "*establishing by authority* some duty upon me." Nope—though if you'd tried to answer the question without looking at the passage, you might have chosen one of those two because you've heard *imposing* used in those ways: "He's always *imposing* on our good will" or "The government *imposed* a tax."

When you try (D) and (E), you see that they don't fit any better than (B) and (C) do—so you're left with (A) as your answer. Note that (A) is the simplest of the answer choices. If you've gotten the impression that a hard test always has hard answers, get rid of that impression now, okay?

Question

In line 21, the word "low" most nearly means

(A) not high
(B) not loud
(C) humble
(D) depressed
(E) unfavorable

Answer

The actual words tested will not necessarily be hard ones. You've been able to read the word *low* since second grade . . . but here it is on a standardized test.

Just plug in the answer choices: "my *not high* beginning"? Hardly. "My *not loud* beginning"? No. "My *humble* beginning"? Sounds good; keep for now. "My *depressed* beginning"? Maybe, though it doesn't sound as good as (C). Trying (E) gives you the same reaction.

You could, at this point, just go with your gut and choose (C). You'd be right. If you wanted to make sure, you'd look at the fuller context. You'd see that the author writes about being "flattered by all these promotions" and about how "they were great things to me"—all of which he contrasts with his *low* beginning. Sure enough, *humble* is the only choice that makes sense in context.

The Good News About Vocabulary Questions

Vocabulary-in-context questions are great when you're short on time or confidence because you can answer them quickly. Skim for a vocabulary-in-context question—"In line _____, the word _____ most nearly means"—locate the line in the passage, read the sentence, and choose the answer choice that best fits the sentence. (To be safe, read the whole paragraph.) You've just completed a critical reading question and collected one more right answer.

Reading Paired Passages

One short section of the SAT I consists of two related critical reading passages and twelve to fourteen questions, which you have 15 minutes to answer. Usually the passages discuss the same subject from two different viewpoints. Sometimes they will cover two different but related subjects, and then your job will be to find the similarities.

The Good News and the Not-So-Bad News

The good news is that both the passages and the questions come in the same types as in the other critical reading passage sets. Passages will be about the humanities, science, or the social sciences. Questions will test your understanding of main ideas, specific details, tone and attitude, logical inference, techniques, or vocabulary in context.

The bad news isn't that bad, really. This section differs from the other critical reading sections only in asking you to *compare* or *contrast* both passages. You should concentrate and use all of your critical reading skills in order to do well on this section.

How to Tackle Paired Passages

Most of the questions in a paired reading set refer to one or the other of the passages. Only a few questions at the end of the set ask you to consider both passages. You should treat the first reading passage of the pair and its questions *exactly as you treat any other reading passage*. First, read any explanatory material in italics that begins the two passages. Next, skim the questions, quitting when you get to the first question that asks about Passage 2. Now read Passage 1, and then answer those four to six questions about Passage 1. If you can't answer a question, leave it blank, but mark it in your question booklet— something in Passage 2 or the following questions might spark an idea.

Skim all the rest of the questions, the ones about Passage 2 and those about both passages. (Don't do this if skimming questions goes against the grain; in that case, go directly to Passage 2.) Read Passage 2 carefully, *keeping Passage 1 always in mind.* Make a mark—maybe a circled number 1—next to anything that seems similar or in marked contrast to something you read in Passage 1. And now you can answer the questions. Do the ones on Passage 2 first, unless an answer to one of the questions about both passages is right there in the front of your mind. And then do the ones on both passages, referring back to both as necessary.

The questions that follow these two brief passages will give you an idea of the ways in which you will be asked to compare two passages.

Passage 1

Line *One Hundred Years of Solitude,* Gabriel Garcia Marquez's most
famous novel, is often cited as the seminal work in the movement
in Latin American fiction known as magic realism. Some critics have
argued that magic realism was a departure from the tradition of so-
5 cial realism in Latin American fiction that so often concerned itself
with the struggles and oppression of poor or indigenous people.
However, the presence of magical events in the novels of the magic
realists does not mean that those authors have abandoned social
commentary. Rather, they have immersed themselves so fully in the
10 belief systems of their characters—usually poor people with strong
ties to native or African roots—that the appearance of supernatural
beings or the occurrence of strange events occasions no surprise or
disbelief. Indeed, what is "real" in magic realism is the magic itself;
it is fully accepted by both author-narrator and characters as simply
15 part of normal life. The presence of the supernatural distinguishes
magic realism from other types of realism; the fact that the supernatural is mingled with the real world distinguishes it from science
fiction or fantasy, and this acceptance of the supernatural as normal
and real distinguishes magic realism from ghost stories and other
20 tales of the supernatural.

Passage 2

While carefully chronicling the struggles of African American
people at various points in U.S. history, Toni Morrison's novels
often include elements of the magical or supernatural, so much so
that many critics have mentioned Morrison's works in the same
25   breath with those of the magic realists of Latin America. *Song of
Solomon,* for instance, ends with Milkman, the protagonist,
apparently having learned to fly; the title character of *Beloved* is a
ghost, killed in infancy and now come to life as a young woman
the age the baby would have been had it lived. When asked about
30   the presence of the supernatural in her novels, Morrison says, "I
want my work to capture the vast imagination of black people.
That is, I want my books to reflect the imaginative combination of
the real world, the very practical, shrewd, day to day functioning
that black people must do, while at the same time they encom-
35   pass some great supernatural element. We know that it does not
bother them one bit to do something practical and have visions at
the same time."

Question

According to information provided by the passages, which of the
following is a similarity between *One Hundred Years of Solitude* and
Beloved?

(A) Both feature ghosts as main characters.

(B) Both emphasize the magical over the realistic.

(C) Both combine realistic events with supernatural events.

(D) Both are considered to be seminal works of magic realism in
their respective countries.

(E) Both draw on African folk traditions for their depiction of
magical events.

Answer

This question asks you to pull together information from both passages. Neither author actually says very much about the novels in question; you have to take what the author of Passage 1 says about magic realism in general and what the author of Passage 2 says about Morrison's novels in general and apply those comments to the novels mentioned in the question to come up with the right answer, which is (C).

Look at the wrong answer choices. In questions that compare two passages, at least some of the wrong answer choices are likely to apply to one passage but not the other.

Answers (A) and (E) apply only to *Beloved* in Passage 2. Passage 1 does mention "African roots" in line 11, but we don't know whether any African folklore appears in *One Hundred Years of Solitude.*

Answer (D), meanwhile, applies only to Passage 1. The author of Passage 2 does say that some critics have linked Morrison's works to magic realism, but that doesn't make them *seminal,* which means *seedlike, having the power to originate or create.*

Answer (B) is just plain wrong, using the language of both passages to say the *opposite* of what both passages say.

Question

Which of the following techniques is NOT used in EITHER passage?

  (A) defining a term
  (B) refuting an assertion
  (C) providing an example
  (D) quoting an authority
  (E) analyzing a literary text

Answer

These "NOT questions" can be tricky. You have to be careful in eliminating answer choices. In this case, check each answer choice to see whether *either* author uses that technique. If the technique appears in Passage 1 *or* Passage 2, you can eliminate it.

Does either author *define a term?* Yes, in fact, Passage 1 "is primarily concerned with" (to use SAT language) defining magic realism.

Does either author *refute an assertion?* Yes, Passage 1 refutes the assertion that magic realism is a departure from social realism.

Does either author *provide an example?* Both do—Passage 1 opens with an example and Passage 2 cites two novels by Morrison.

Does either author *quote an authority?* Well, what is Toni Morrison if not an authority on her own novels?

Luckily, choice (E) is right; neither passage *analyzes* a literary text. Although both passages are about literature, they do not analyze the work itself. Neither author breaks a literary text down into its parts in order to understand it better.

Question

Would the author of Passage 1 be likely to agree with the characterization of Toni Morrison's novels as examples of magic realism?

(A) Yes, because Morrison immerses herself in the struggles of African American people.

(B) Yes, because Morrison's characters accept magical events as real within a realistic setting.

(C) Yes, because the examples cited in Passage 2 show that Morrison includes supernatural events in her fiction.

(D) No, because magic realism is indigenous to Latin America.

(E) No, because Morrison's emphasis on practicality and shrewdness is incompatible with magic realism.

Answer

The *because* clauses are more important here than whether you think the answer is *yes* or *no.* In order for the author of Passage 1 to agree that Morrison's novels are magic realist, the novels would have to meet author 1's criteria for magic realism. Passage 1 says that magic realist novels combine the supernatural and the realistic and, perhaps most importantly, *the supernatural is accepted by narrator and characters as normal and real* (lines 13–15). Morrison makes a similar point about her own novels at the end of Passage 2: "It does not bother them one bit to do something practical and have visions at the same time." (As you were reading Passage 2, this would have been a good place to mark a circled 1 or somehow indicate that this comment corresponds closely to something said in the first passage.) The answer, then, is (B).

Answers (A) and (C) would have Morrison meeting only part of author 1's criteria. Answers (D) and (E) give as reasons things that the author of Passage 1 does not cite as criteria for magic realism.

Summary: Know-How for Critical Reading Questions

Remember to use the steps that lead to correct answers:

Step 1. *Skim the questions before reading the passage.* (If this task drives you bats, don't do it. Begin by reading the passage quickly to determine the main idea.)

Step 2. *Read the passage as quickly as you can,* concentrating first on the main points that the author is making. Be sure to underline or asterisk meaty, summation-type sentences. If you are ready at the end of the first reading, answer any questions on main point or central theme.

Step 3. *Mark the reading passage* with check marks in the margin for fact-filled areas or specific examples on your second reading.

Step 4. *Mark all words* (a quick slash before the word works well) *that indicate a shift in viewpoint* or *something different coming up*, e.g., *but, however, although, nevertheless, ironically, atypically, nonetheless,* and *unless.* If a *date* is given, it's there for a reason. Also, note words that indicate tone or mood.

Step 5. *Answer the questions with the elimination method* so that you select your answer because none of the *other* answers can be correct.

Timing for Critical Reading Questions

On sections that contain both reading passages and the quicker analogies and sentence completions, make sure you do the quick ones first, but don't spend too much time on them. Reading questions seem to take forever, but they are tremendously important, and you want to have plenty of time for them. On a short passage of 500 words or less and its five to six questions, plan to spend less than 10 minutes. The medium-size passages, with seven to nine questions, should take maybe 10–12 minutes. Those really long passages—the 800-word ones with up to fourteen questions—can take as long as 15–20 minutes.

As you practice, see how quickly you can grasp the main point of the passage. Use the marking system described above so you can find answers to questions quickly if you need them. Use the line numbers, when they are given in the question, to help you find the spot quickly—but don't assume that the answer to the question will be right there.

Always look through the questions to find the easiest ones. Don't waste time on a stumper when the very next question could be easy for you. Skip any questions you find difficult—be careful to skip on your answer sheet too!—and go back to them later. As you search for the answer to another question, you might happen across an answer to that earlier tough question.

But *be sure to record an answer to each question for a given passage before leaving that passage.* If you go on and finish a section and *then* try to come back to an earlier reading passage, you will have forgotten it and will have to start over.

For paired passages, you have 15 minutes in which to read both passages and answer the questions. Dividing that time equally between the passages might be a mistake. You'll need *more time for Passage 2* because that's when you respond to questions about both passages as well.

Instead, try working about 4-6 minutes with Passage 1 and its questions at the beginning of the question set. That should leave enough time to read Passage 2, and answer all remaining questions.

Practice Reading Passages

For the following reading passages, practice reading and answering questions as rapidly as you can. Learn the directions now, so that you won't waste time with them on test day.

Answer the questions based on what is stated or implied in the passage as well as any introductory material that might be supplied.

The passages are as close to actual test passages as possible. As on standardized tests, they come from a variety of reading materials. Answers appear on pages 280-282.

PRACTICE CRITICAL READING 1

The following passage is from a nineteenth-century American novel about the whaling industry. The setting is on board the ship Pequod. *Here, the chief mate of the ship, Starbuck, is presented and his character described. The historical time is about 1850.*

Line
    The chief mate of the *Pequod* was Starbuck, a native of Nantucket. He was a long, earnest man, and though born on an icy coast, seemed well adapted to endure hot latitudes, his flesh being hard as twice-baked biscuit. Transported to the Indies, his
5 live blood would not spoil like bottled ale. He must have been born in some time of general drought and famine. Only some thirty arid summers had he seen; those summers had dried up all his physical superfluousness. But this, his thinness, so to speak, seemed no more the token of wasted anxieties and cares, than it
10 seemed the indication of any bodily blight. It was merely the condensation of the man. He was by no means ill-looking; quite the contrary. His pure tight skin was an excellent fit; and closely wrapped up in it, and embalmed with inner health and strength, like a revivified Egyptian, this Starbuck seemed prepared to
15 endure for long ages to come. For be it Polar snow or torrid sun, like a patent chronometer, his interior vitality was warranted to do well in all climates. Looking into his eyes, you seemed to see there the lingering images of those thousand-fold perils he had calmly confronted through life.
20   Yet, for all his hardy sobriety and fortitude, there were certain qualities in him which at times seemed well nigh to over-balance all the rest. Uncommonly conscientious for a seaman, and endued with a deep natural reverence, the wild watery loneliness of his life did therefore strongly incline him to
25 superstition, which in some organization seems rather to spring, somehow, from intelligence than from ignorance. Outward portents and inward presentiments were his. And if at times these things bent the iron of his soul, much more did his far-away domestic memories of his young Cape wife and child, tend to

30   bend him still more from the original ruggedness of his nature,
      and open him still further to those latent influences which, in
      some honest-hearted men, restrain the gush of dare-devil daring,
      so often evinced by others in the more perilous vicissitudes of the
      fishery. "I will have no man in my boat," said Starbuck, "who is
35   not afraid of a whale." By this, he seemed to mean, not only that
      the most reliable and useful courage was that which arises from
      the fair estimation of the encountered peril, but that an utterly
      fearless man is a far more dangerous comrade than a coward.
          Starbuck was no crusader after perils; in him courage was
40   not a sentiment; but a thing simply useful to him, and always at
      hand upon all mortally practical occasions. Besides, he thought,
      perhaps, that in this business of whaling, courage was one of the
      staple outfits of the ship, like her beef and her bread, and not to
      be wasted. Wherefore he had no fancy for lowering for whales
45   after sun-down; nor for persisting in fighting a fish that too much
      persisted in fighting him. That hundreds of men had been so
      killed Starbuck well knew. What doom was his own father's?
      Where, in the bottomless deeps, could he find the torn limbs of
      his brother?
50   With memories like these in him, and, moreover, given to a
      certain superstitiousness, as has been said; the courage of this
      Starbuck, which could, nevertheless, still flourish, must indeed
      have been extreme. But it was not in reasonable nature that a
      man so organized, and with such terrible experiences and
55   remembrances as he had; it was not in nature that these things
      should fail in latently engendering an element in him, which,
      under suitable circumstances, would break from its confinement,
      and burn all his courage up. And brave as he might be, it was that
      sort of bravery chiefly visible in some intrepid men, which, while
60   abiding firm in the conflict with seas, or winds, or whales, or any
      of the ordinary irrational horrors of the world, yet cannot
      withstand those more terrific, because more spiritual terrors,
      which sometimes menace you from the concentrating brow of an
      enraged and mighty man.
65   Men may seem detestable as joint stock-companies and
      nations; knaves, fools, and murderers there may be; men may
      have mean and meager faces; but, man, in the ideal, is so noble

and so sparkling, that over an ignominious blemish in him all his
fellows should run to throw their costliest robes. That immaculate
70 manliness we feel within ourselves, so far within us, that it
remains intact though all the outer character seem gone; bleeds
with keenest anguish at the undraped spectacle of a valor-ruined
man. But this august dignity I treat of, is not the dignity of kings
and robes, but that abounding dignity which has no robed
75 investiture. Thou shalt see it shining in the arm that wields a pick
or drives a spike; that democratic dignity which, on all hands,
radiates without end from God; Himself! The great God absolute!
The center and circumference of all democracy! His omnipres-
ence, our divine equality!

1. The word "transported"
   (line 4) describes which of
   the following?

   (A) "flesh" (line 3)
   (B) "biscuit" (line 4)
   (C) "blood" (line 5)
   (D) "ale" (line 5)
   (E) "He" (line 5)

2. Starbuck was thin chiefly
   because he

   (A) was burdened with
       worry and anxiety
   (B) had an inherited
       digestive illness
   (C) was still a very young
       man
   (D) had a compact, efficient
       constitution
   (E) had a rare sort of blood
       disorder

3. In line 7, the word "arid"
   most nearly means

   (A) long and fretful
   (B) dull and uneventful
   (C) dry and parched
   (D) unhappy and painful
   (E) disturbing and frighten-
       ing

4. Starbuck is compared to an
   Egyptian mummy (lines
   12–15) in order to emphasize
   his

   (A) strong belief in a
       preordained fate
   (B) extraordinary durability
   (C) intellectual strength and
       interests
   (D) antecedents in historical
       time
   (E) rigid moral convictions

5. In line 23, "endued with" most nearly means

(A) possessed of
(B) in need of
(C) weakened by
(D) wishing for
(E) sanctified by

6. Which of the following best describes the author's attitude toward Starbuck?

(A) He understands and respects Starbuck.
(B) He feels Starbuck is weak and fearful.
(C) He envies and fears Starbuck.
(D) He feels Starbuck is cruel and mean.
(E) He thinks Starbuck is good and faultless.

7. By describing Starbuck as "uncommonly conscientious" (line 22), the author implies that most seamen are

(A) unskilled and lazy
(B) violent and aggressive
(C) self-indulgent and weak
(D) reserved and individualistic
(E) careless and indifferent

8. Starbuck's natural predisposition toward bold, courageous action was tempered chiefly by

(A) the authority of the ship's captain
(B) the unpredictability of his crew mates
(C) his innate fear of dying
(D) thoughts of his family back home
(E) a humble spirit and fear of God

9. The "thousand-fold perils" that Starbuck "calmly confronted" in his life (lines 18–19) accounted for which of the following traits as primary in his character?

(A) A profound, sometimes disabling superstition
(B) Prudence and a capacity for judicious caution
(C) An occasional failure of nerve caused by memories of his father and brother
(D) A heroic yet reckless disdain for danger and imminent calamity
(E) A matchless self-confidence in his own talents and experience

10. The deaths of Starbuck's father and brother (lines 46–49) were most likely the result of

   (A) a vengeful fate
   (B) a violent storm
   (C) hapless accidents
   (D) reckless judgment
   (E) faulty equipment

11. The author implies that Starbuck's nobility of character can be compromised only by

   (A) the dangers and fury of a stormy sea
   (B) a cowardly and weak boat crew
   (C) the sinister power of whales
   (D) an angry and vengeful God
   (E) anyone possessed of a cosmic anger

12. The author would most strongly agree with which of the following ideas?

   (A) Life at sea for long periods provides people with unusual chances to purify the spirit.
   (B) A life of action is most often preferable to a life of contemplation.
   (C) Life on land nurtures domestic values; life at sea is destructive of human values.

   (D) Violence and egotism in human nature are common elements that will ultimately prevail.
   (E) Anger and hatred are always present in the human heart and when yielded to may destroy a person's soul.

13. The author's style or voice is best described as

   (A) informal and conversational
   (B) witty and sophisticated
   (C) formal and orotund
   (D) elegant and decorative
   (E) fearful and prophetic

14. In the final paragraph, the author's purpose is to

   (A) celebrate the glories of God
   (B) shift the focus from Starbuck to kings, God, and social leaders
   (C) end the narrative on a level of logical inquiry
   (D) transmute the particular person to the universal ideal human being
   (E) contrast Starbuck's virtues with his potential for failure

PRACTICE CRITICAL READING 2

> *The passages below are adapted from two different essays. The first*
> *was written in the seventeenth century, and the second was written*
> *about 1870. Both authors are English.*

Passage 1

Line   It is a capital misery for a man to be at once both old and
ignorant. If he were only old, and had some knowledge, he might
lessen the tediousness of decrepit age by divine raptures of
contemplation. If he were young, though he knew nothing, his
5   later years would serve him to labor and learn; whereby in the
winter of his time he might beguile the weariness of his pillow
and chair. But now his body being withered by the stealing length
of his days, and his limbs wholly disabled for either motion or
exercise, these, together with a mind unfurnished of those
10   contenting speculations of admired science, cannot but delineate
the portraiture of a man wretched.

A gray head with a wise mind is a treasury of grave precepts,
experience, and judgment. But foolish old age is a barren vine in
autumn, or a university to study folly in: every action is a pattern
15   of infirmity: while his body sits still he knows not how to find his
mind's action: and tell me if there be any life more irksome than
idleness. I have numbered yet but a few days,[1] and those, I know,
I have neglected; I am not sure they shall be more, nor can I
promise my head it shall have a snowy hair.
20   What then? Knowledge is not hurtful, but helps a good
mind; anything that is laudable I desire to learn. If I die tomor-
row, my life today shall be somewhat the sweeter for knowledge:
and if my day prove a summer one, it shall not be amiss to have
my mind my companion. Notable was the answer that Antis-
25   thenes[2] gave when he was asked what fruit he had reaped of all
his studies. "By them," saith he, "I have learned both to live and
to talk with myself."

---

[1] The author wrote this short essay before he was 20 years old.

[2] An Athenian philosopher who lived about 444–365 B.C.

Passage 2

Suppose it were perfectly certain that the life and fortune of
every one of us would depend upon our winning or losing a
30 game of chess. Don't you think that we should all consider it a
primary duty to learn at least the names and the moves of the
pieces? Do you not think that we should look with a disapproba-
tion amounting to scorn, upon the father who allowed his son, or
the state which allowed its members, to grow up without
35 knowing a pawn from a knight?

Yet it is a very plain and elementary truth, that the life, the
fortune, and the happiness of every one of us do depend upon
our knowing something of the rules of a game infinitely more
difficult and complicated than chess. It is a game which has been
40 played for untold ages, every man and woman of us being one of
the two players in a game of his or her own. The chessboard is
the world, the pieces are the phenomena of the universe, the
rules of the game are what we call the laws of Nature. The player
on the other side is hidden from us. We know that his play is
45 always fair, just, and patient. But also we know, to our cost, that
he never overlooks a mistake, or makes the smallest allowance for
ignorance. To the man who plays well, the highest stakes are
paid, with that sort of overflowing generosity with which the
strong shows delight in strength. And one who plays ill is
50 checkmated—without haste, but without remorse.

Well, what I mean by Education is learning the rules of this
mighty game. In other words, education is the instruction of the
intellect in the laws of Nature, under which name I include not
merely things and their forces, but men and their ways; and the
55 fashioning of the affections and the will into an earnest and loving
desire to move in harmony with those laws. For me, education
means neither more nor less than this. Anything which professes
to call itself education must be tried by this standard, and if it fails
to stand the test, I will not call it education, whatever may be the
60 force of authority, or of the numbers, upon the other side.

That man has had a liberal education who has been so
trained in youth that his body is the ready servant of his will, and
does with ease and pleasure all the work that, as a mechanism, it

is capable of; whose intellect is a clear, cold, logic engine, with
65 all its parts of equal strength, and in smooth working order; ready
like a steam engine, to be turned to any kind of work, and spin
the gossamers as well as forge the anchors of the mind; whose
mind is stored with a knowledge of the great and fundamental
truths of Nature and of the laws of her operations; one who, no
70 stunted ascetic, is full of life and fire, but whose passions are
trained to come to heel by a vigorous will, the servant of a tender
conscience; who has learned to love all beauty, whether of
Nature or of art, to hate all vileness, and to respect others as
himself.

1. In line 1, the word "capital" most nearly means

(A) centrally fixed
(B) critically important
(C) lesser quality
(D) little understood
(E) much discussed

2. According to the author in Passage 1, the pains of old age can be made more bearable if one

(A) is sufficiently wealthy
(B) has inherited good genes
(C) is well educated
(D) is naturally courageous
(E) has sympathetic friends

3. According to the author in Passage 1, the chief advantage in being young is that one has

(A) strength and good health

(B) opportunities to travel and meet new people
(C) prospects of good employment
(D) future years in which to study and acquire knowledge
(E) time to enjoy life without spending it all on tiresome work

4. In line 6, the "winter" of one's time most nearly means

(A) years of illness and bad health
(B) youth and its normal ignorance
(C) years of unrewarding hard labor
(D) times of misfortune and bad luck
(E) old age and its infirmities

5. Which of the following is the most striking characteristic of the language in Passage 1?

  (A) Rich use of figures of speech
  (B) Simple and direct sentences
  (C) Rhetorical questions and logical answers
  (D) Unusually complex verbal structures
  (E) Abstract diction and argument

6. In lines 26–27, the phrase "to talk with myself" is a metaphorical way of saying

  (A) loneliness is unavoidable
  (B) old age is a second childhood
  (C) being selfish loses friends
  (D) thinking is excellent conversation
  (E) a love of ideas will invite many admirers

7. The author of Passage 1 most disdains which of the following?

  (A) Old age and infirmity
  (B) Scandal and bad repute
  (C) Poverty and homelessness
  (D) Pain and death
  (E) Indolence and sloth

8. The fundamental assumption the author of Passage 2 makes about life is that

  (A) it is dominated by a cruel and malign force
  (B) behind the material world is a more or less benign power that challenges mankind
  (C) what happens to human beings is largely determined by chance
  (D) there is no force or power in the universe superior to mankind's intelligence
  (E) human beings can lay claim to having a part of the divine being within themselves

9. Which of the following best states the definition of the educated person as described by the author of Passage 2?

(A) A person is educated who through self-discipline has learned the ways of self, nature, and society and lives in harmony with those ways.

(B) An educated person is a gamester and a good sport, taking victory humbly and defeat with grace.

(C) An educated person has trained himself diligently in a profession or business and succeeds through a combination of struggle and good luck.

(D) An educated person is one who knows that fate is neutral and even careless in dealing with people but who still believes in victory.

(E) A person who has acquired an education is versed in the sciences and arts and is able to outwit fate and Nature in the game of life.

10. "The player on the other side" (lines 43–44) in its challenge to human players is best described as

(A) sinister and unknowable
(B) absolute and dictatorial
(C) generous and loving
(D) exacting and unforgiving
(E) dishonest and secretive

11. The phrase "to spin the gossamers" (lines 66–67) is a metaphor for

(A) developing architectural plans
(B) dreaming and imagining
(C) learning the mind's psychology
(D) getting rid of lazy thinking
(E) solving problems mathematically

12. According to the passage, a "stunted ascetic" is one who

(A) is born with a physical disability
(B) values natural law over artistic beauty
(C) has a kind and saintly manner
(D) needs much respect and affection
(E) is too strict and pinched in spirit

13. The authors of both passages value which of the following most highly?

   (A) Sociability and good spirits
   (B) Honesty and frankness
   (C) Knowledge and learning
   (D) Wealth and influence
   (E) Good health and longevity

14. The authors of both passages believe that acquiring an education is possible only

   (A) for those who are born to privilege and opportunity and take advantage of them
   (B) when society provides appropriate educational institutions and opportunities for its citizens to use them
   (C) when one strives to learn and makes being a diligent student a lifelong habit
   (D) for those born with above-average intelligence and a strong drive to succeed
   (E) for those who can play the game of life like a gambler and beat Nature and fate at their own game

15. The authors of the two passages are alike in that they both

   (A) are young men in their early twenties
   (B) speak with conviction
   (C) reveal their own weaknesses
   (D) are whimsical and only half serious
   (E) have served as professional educators

PRACTICE CRITICAL READING 3

Line   Although a complex nervous system is not essential for behav-
       iour—protozoans get by quite nicely with only rudimentary sense
       cells—the scope and sophistication of behaviour within the
       animal kingdom is quite clearly linked with the evolution of
5   neural complexity. The behavioural capacities of protozoans and
       earthworms are extremely limited compared with those of birds
       and mammals. What, then, are the properties of a nervous system
       which make complex behaviour possible?
              . . . True nervous systems are only found in multicellular
10   animals. Here they form a tissue of discrete, self-contained nerve
       cells or *neurons.* Like any other type of animal cell, neurons
       comprise an intricate system of cell organelles surrounded by a
       cell membrane. . . . Unlike other animal cells, however, they are
       specialised for transmitting electrical messages from one part of
15   the body to another. This specialisation is reflected both in their
       structure and their physiology.
              A neuron has three obvious structural components. The main
       body of the cell, the *soma,* is a broad, expanded structure
       housing the nucleus. Extending from the soma are two types of
20   cytoplasm-filled processes called *axons* and *dendrites.* Axons
       carry electrical impulses away from the soma and pass them on to
       other neurons or to muscle fibers. Dendrites receive impulses
       from other neurons and transport them to the soma. All three
       components are usually surrounded by *glial cells.* Although glial
25   cells are not derived from nerve tissue, they come to form a more
       or less complex sheath around the axon. In invertebrates, the glial
       cell membranes may form a loose, multilayered sheath in which
       there is still room for cytoplasm between the layers. In this case
       the arrangement is known as a *tunicated axon.* In vertebrates the
30   sheath is bound more tightly so that no gaps are left. The glial
       cells are known as Schwann cells and are arranged along the axon
       in a characteristic way. Each Schwann cell covers about 2 mm of
       axon. Between neighbouring cells there is a small gap where the
       membrane of the axon is exposed to the extracellular medium.

35 These gaps are known as the nodes of Ranvier. Axons with this interrupted Schwann cell sheath are called *myelinated* or *medullated* axons. The formation of the myelin sheath enhances enormously the speed and quality of impulse conduction.

1. The question in lines 7–8 serves primarily to
   (A) introduce the description of neural specialization that follows
   (B) signal a shift in topic from animal behavior to the capacities of nervous systems
   (C) cast doubt on the previous discussion of simple animal behavior
   (D) highlight one of the enduring mysteries of biology
   (E) emphasize the differences between simple and complex neural systems

2. According to the passage, the components of nerve cells that perform jobs opposite to one another are
   (A) the cell organelles and the cell membrane
   (B) the soma and the muscle fibers
   (C) the glial cells and the cytoplasm
   (D) the axons and dendrites
   (E) a tunicated axon and glial cells

3. It can be inferred from the passage that the neural systems of vertebrates receive
   (A) fewer messages than do the neural systems of invertebrates
   (B) interrupted messages due to the gaps known as the nodes of Ranvier
   (C) electrical messages at too great a speed for assimilation
   (D) electrical messages more quickly and accurately than do the neural systems of invertebrates
   (E) specialized electrical messages only

4. The word "medium" in line 34 most nearly means

   (A) an average or mean

   (B) a surrounding environment

   (C) a position between two extremes

   (D) a material used for a specific function

   (E) an agent through which something is transmitted

5. One major difference between invertebrate and vertebrate neurons is

   (A) their structural components

   (B) the tightness of the glial cell sheath

   (C) their neural complexity

   (D) the number of cytoplasm-filled processes known as axons and dendrites

   (E) the presence of a glial cell sheath

PRACTICE CRITICAL READING 4

Line While Austria had come out of the first phase of the Napoleonic
Wars weakened but not broken, Prussia had lost more than half
her territory, having been reduced to but four provinces: Branden-
burg, Pomerania, Prussia, and Silesia. Her economic life was
5   completely paralyzed by the immense war indemnities and by
Napoleon's "Continental Blockade" of England (decree of 1806),
which made it impossible for Prussia to continue the lucrative
export of agricultural products to the British Isles. The catastrophes of Jena and Auerstedt made the political leaders of Prussia
10   realize the mistakes and omissions of the past decades and made
room at last for those unselfish and patriotic men who had long
voiced their prophetic warnings in vain.

One such man was Baron Karl vom Stein, who said, "I have
but one fatherland which is called Germany. With my whole heart
15   I am devoted to it, and not to any of its parts." In 1804 Stein
received an appointment as Prussian Minister of State and was
given charge of the departments of finance and economics. He
immediately seized the opportunity to carry out some of the
much-needed reforms. An edict of 1805 decreed the suspension
20   of the inland duties in Prussia which had proven one of the major
stumbling blocks to the development of a unified national
economy. The substitution of private ownership of industrial
enterprises for State ownership served to break down the
economic system of the mercantile State and the elimination of
25   the corporate restrictions of the guilds was to prepare the way for
the introduction of the principle of freedom of trade.

In 1806, Stein's demand for reorganization of the whole
governmental system for the sake of greater efficiency and
responsible leadership went unheeded, and he was dismissed by
30   royal cabinet order. Within six months he was recalled and
shortly thereafter published his first great Reform Edict, having as
its main objectives the abolition of serfdom, the free exchange
and disposal of landed property, and the free choice of occupa-
tion. Up to this time, two thirds of the population of Prussia had

35 been bound to the soil, unable to leave their homes of their own
    free will and obliged to render personal service to the manorial
    lord. In the rural districts the medieval feudal system had survived
    essentially untouched.
        Stein recognized in the sudden and unparalleled breakdown
40 of Prussia the result of a political and social system of bureau-
    cratic and feudalistic tutelage. A partly paternalistic, partly
    absolutistic form of administration had gradually loosened the
    mutual bonds of loyalty and unselfish devotion between the
    people and their government and had bred an attitude of irre-
45 sponsibility and indifference among all classes of the population.
    Stein's program of national regeneration received its directives
    from his clear-sighted diagnosis of the national disease.

1. According to the passage, all
    of the following characterize
    Karl vom Stein EXCEPT

    (A) absorption with
         Germany's economic
         status in the world
    (B) understanding of the
         nature of the Germanic
         people
    (C) approval of the Prussian
         governmental leadership
         in the early 1800s
    (D) willingness to act in a
         decisive, revolutionary
         manner
    (E) perception to judge
         Prussian history and
         prophesy trouble ahead

2. When Baron vom Stein said
    of Germany, "I am devoted
    to it, and not to any of its
    parts" (line 15), he most
    probably meant that he

    (A) was not concerned with
         the separate Prussian
         states
    (B) was interested mainly in
         Germany's international
         role
    (C) was involved with
         leadership, not with
         warring factions
    (D) viewed his country as a
         single, united entity
    (E) was interested in
         Prussia, not Germany

3. The reason given for Prussia's lack of exportation to Britain was

   (A) Napoleon's blockade of the British Isles
   (B) the early phase of the Napoleonic Wars
   (C) lack of agricultural commodities to export
   (D) reduction in commodities produced for export
   (E) Prussian governmental policy on exportation to the British Isles

4. According to the author, Germany was hindered in its establishment of a unified national economy by

   (A) the massive war effort itself
   (B) its policy of imposing inland duties
   (C) the substitution of private ownership in place of State ownership
   (D) guilds that had historically operated without restrictions
   (E) the catastrophes of Jena and Auerstedt

5. Stein felt that Prussia had broken down as a country primarily because

   (A) the Napoleonic Wars had paralyzed its economy
   (B) Prussia's political leaders paid scant attention to their international role
   (C) the mercantile State had not kept pace with that of other countries
   (D) two thirds of her population was bound to the soil
   (E) her people no longer felt morally or emotionally bound to their homeland

PRACTICE CRITICAL READING 5

Line   Securing the rights of newly emancipated blacks in a practical way
was a cardinal objective of the Reconstruction Congresses. For this
reason, the thirteenth, fourteenth and fifteenth amendments were
drafted and offered to the states; they were ratified in 1865, 1868
5   and 1870, respectively. Theoretically, of course, the rights enumerated in the Bill of Rights would have sufficed to do the job of
implementing full citizenship for former slaves. But the circumstances were special, and obviously Jefferson's moral universalism
had never been put to this particular test. The thirteenth amend-
10   ment abolishing slavery, the fourteenth amendment guaranteeing
privileges and immunities, due process, and equal protection of the
laws, and the fifteenth amendment prohibiting denial or abridge-
ment of the right to vote took long further steps toward realization
of equal treatment for all Americans. More than a century later, that
15   ideal has not been fully reached. Yet the Republic has come a
considerable distance from the colonial period, in which rights
were accorded primarily to land- and slave-owners.
        Legal scholars dispute the original intention of the framers of
the fourteenth amendment. Indeed, "theories of legislation" in
20   general are disputed in American jurisprudence. If a statute enacted
by Congress unambiguously specifies rights and duties and if it
embodies a reasonable political goal, then few problems of
interpretation arise because there is substantial agreement about
new obligations to be enforced by the courts. Several factors must
25   combine if a statute is to achieve unambiguous clarity. In older
days, a preamble set forth the intent of the legislation, and the
language became an official part of the new law itself. Sometimes
now a committee report serves the same function, as do floor
speeches of legislators who are acknowledged sponsors of a given
30   bill. These factors, along with other more amorphous ingredients,
such as dicta and opinion among debators of a bill, comprise the
"legislative history" of a statute, what is often called by lawyers the
"original understanding." Clarity and binding force of interpretation

are further enhanced if good political arguments are available
35   justifying policies or principles advanced by the new law.

Unfortunately, with some legislation no agreed-upon original intention stands out, no general collective understanding of a bill's aim finds consensus, and possible justifications collide. Cases involving the fourteenth amendment and the 1871 Civil Rights
40   Act designed to enforce it tend to fall into this latter category, and no important decisions have escaped argument based on differing readings of legislative history and on projections of various conceivable principles and policies.

1. One purpose of the amendment passed in 1868 was to

   (A) abolish slavery
   (B) guarantee the right to vote
   (C) guarantee equal protection of the laws
   (D) set a precedent later followed by Jefferson
   (E) abolish due process

2. The author believes that the failure of the Bill of Rights to secure proper freedoms for the slaves was due in part to

   (A) Thomas Jefferson and his philosophy
   (B) moral universalism
   (C) the Congresses at the time of Abolition
   (D) special circumstances at the time
   (E) errors in the Bill of Rights itself

3. The real difficulty with the fourteenth amendment, as the author of the passage sees it, is that

   (A) it is fundamentally flawed
   (B) it imposes unrealistic expectations on the courts
   (C) it has generally been misunderstood by the public
   (D) the intent of its original framers is not clear
   (E) legislators have read it in too many different ways

4. In order that a statute achieve unambiguous clarity, which of these factors should exist, according to the passage?

I.   specification of rights and duties

II. clear outline of the courts' obligations

III. avoidance of any political goal

IV. an original understanding or legislative intent

V.   acceptance within our Constitutional framework

(A) II, III, and V

(B) I, III, and IV

(C) I, II, and IV

(D) II, III, and IV

(E) I and IV

5. The word "drafted" in line 4 most nearly means

(A) written down

(B) planned for

(C) sketched out

(D) compelled to serve

(E) selected from among a group

PRACTICE CRITICAL READING 6

Line   "The tears were in my eyes, and I knew that Madame Renard was
boiling with rage, for she kept on nagging at me: 'Oh, how
horrid! Don't you see that he is robbing you of your fish? Do you
think that you will catch anything? Not even a frog, nothing
5   whatever. Why, my hands are burning just to think of it.'

"But I said to myself: 'Let us wait until twelve o'clock. Then
this poaching fellow will go to lunch, and I shall get my place
again.' As for me, Monsieur le Judge, I lunch on the spot every
Sunday; we bring our provisions in the boat. But there! At twelve
10   o'clock the wretch produced a fowl out of a newspaper, and
while he was eating, actually he caught another chub!

"Melie and I had a morsel also, just a mouthful, a mere
nothing, for our heart was not in it.

"Then I took up my newspaper, to aid my digestion. Every
15   Sunday I read in the shade like that, by the side of the water.

"Well, then I began to tease my wife, but she got angry
immediately and very angry, so I held my tongue. At that moment
our two witnesses, who are present here, Monsieur Ladureau and
Monsieur Durdent, appeared on the other side of the river. We
20   knew each other by sight. The little man began to fish again, and
he caught so many that I trembled with vexation, and his wife said:
'It is an uncommonly good spot, and we will come here always.'

"As for me, a cold shiver ran down my back, and Melie kept
repeating: 'You are not a man; you have the blood of a chicken in
25   your veins'; and suddenly I said to her: 'Look here, I would rather
go away, or I shall only do something foolish.'

"And she whispered to me as if she had put a red-hot iron
under my nose: 'You are not a man. Now you are going to run
away and surrender your place!'

30   "Well, I felt that, but yet I did not move while the little man
pulled out a bream. Oh! I never saw such a large fish before, never!
And then my wife began to talk aloud, as if she were thinking, and
you can see her trickery. She said: 'That is what one might call
stolen fish, seeing that we baited the place ourselves. At any rate
35   they ought to give us back the money we have spent on bait.'"

1. Monsieur Renard is most probably relating his story in a
   - **(A)** town square
   - **(B)** town council meeting
   - **(C)** friend's sitting room
   - **(D)** courtroom
   - **(E)** local restaurant

2. The passage suggests that Monsieur Renard
   - **(A)** is intimidated by his wife
   - **(B)** respects his wife's feelings
   - **(C)** rarely pays attention to his wife
   - **(D)** abhors his wife
   - **(E)** enjoys his wife's company on fishing trips

3. Monsieur and Madame Renard's attitude toward the "little man" is best described as one of
   - **(A)** wounded indignation
   - **(B)** seething hatred
   - **(C)** abject depression
   - **(D)** magnanimity in defeat
   - **(E)** respectful admiration

4. Madame Renard's speeches are intended to
   - **(A)** taunt her spouse about his lack of masculinity
   - **(B)** goad her husband into action against the usurper
   - **(C)** drive Monsieur Renard to commit a crime
   - **(D)** tease her spouse to relieve the tedium of fishing
   - **(E)** inflict misery on her inactive husband

5. Monsieur Renard's narrative style can best be described as
   - **(A)** light-hearted, but somewhat dull and wordy
   - **(B)** terse and angry, but interesting
   - **(C)** rambling and disoriented, but entertaining
   - **(D)** amusingly loquacious, but eloquent
   - **(E)** intense and wordy, but penetrating

More Practice with Critical Reading Questions

If you have a copy of *Real SATs,* put your new knowledge to work on the real thing. Read and answer questions on *all* passages given as test material in two complete SATs.

Practice reading as swiftly as you can, reading for the main point of each selection and the central point of each paragraph. Pay attention to *time.* Allow yourself no more than 13–15 minutes for the longer passages and about half of that for each short one.

Do you see that some of the passages are really quite easy? The fiction passage and the one on minorities/ethnic cultures may even be enjoyable—certainly not "killer" reading.

Are you beginning to think like the test makers? To anticipate what kinds of questions will be asked on the reading material? *When that day comes,* and it will come with practice, you will know that *you're in charge of this test.*

UNIT 3

VOCABULARY REVIEW: WONDERFUL WORDS AND NECESSARY ROOTS

Are you on schedule?
Check the prep plan on pages vi and vii.

Certain words repeat—in magazines, in newspapers, in popular books, and college textbooks. And on tests. You need to know these words *for life,* not because you are taking an SAT or PSAT exam. But certainly, you will use many of the following words on Test Day.

Likewise, certain Latin and Greek roots are basic to our language. If you learn two or three roots a day, those thirty-odd roots will unlock the meanings of thousands of words for you.

Thirty words and three roots a day might seem like a lot, but it's not as if all these words are total strangers. Some you know, some you sort of know and need to be reminded of, and a few may be completely new.

Make flashcards of the unknowns. In only a couple of weeks before the test, you can learn dozens of new words or recapture once-familiar words and fix them in mind.

In all lists, *words shown in italics and given as definitions are important words to learn.* Also, definitions given here are those most often tested on SATs and PSATs.

Learning units (roughly thirty words and three roots) are divided by broken lines as an aid in helping you to plan your review.

Words of Number, Size, Quantity, and Amount

bountiful—in great supply; abundant

dearth—scarcity or lack; *paucity*

diminutive—tiny; *lilliputian*

disparity—difference, inequality

minuscule or **minute**—tiny (measurement of size or amount)

paucity—scarcity or lack; *dearth*

plethora—a vast amount; great excess

prevalent—widespread, *pervasive;* common to an area

prodigious—arousing awe; extremely large or impressive

profuse—flowing freely; *lavish,* extravagant (profuse praise)

scant, scanty—barely enough, *meager,* insufficient

voluminous—spacious; extremely wide or large (doesn't refer to volume of sound)

Nice (or at Least Neutral) Nouns

acumen—keen perception, *shrewdness, discernment*

altruism—unselfish giving of time, money, support to others

amity—friendship, *accord,* agreement

clemency—mercy (*clement* weather is *mild* weather)

coherence—the quality of logical consistency of parts of a whole, often applied to speech and writing but not limited to them

deference—honor and respect due an older or more experienced person; esteem (v., *to defer*)

diligence—faithful, careful attention to a task (opp. of *sloth, laziness*)

euphony—pleasing, agreeable sound (opp. of *cacophony*)

finesse—skillful, adroit handling or management

levity—lightness of mood, humor

nostalgia—recollection of "the old days" with fondness

penchant—natural tendency; fondness for; *affinity* (for)

philanthropy—lit., love of humankind; refers to charitable giving (person is a *philanthropist)*

propriety—what is proper or customary; *decorum,* politeness

resolution—determination, decision (v., *to resolve*)

respite—a pause, lull, or break; rest from activity

rigor—thoroughness; unyielding or inflexible strictness

sagacity—wisdom, *perception, keenness,* shrewdness (adj., *sage*)

Roots

CAP, CAPT, CEPT, CIP (L)   TAKE or SEIZE

had a ball playing *capture* the flag (take, seize)

a *captious* reviewer (critical, faultfinding)

receptive to ideas (willing to take in, receive)

DUC, DUCT (L)   LEAD, DIRECT

induce her cooperation (urge, encourage strongly)

the most *ductile* metal (easily shaped or molded)

abduct him at night (take away by force)

FAC, FACT, FICT, FECT, -FY (L)   DO, CREATE, MAKE

a *factitious* demand (not real, created artificially)

his affected air of unconcern (put on for *effect*)

work of *fiction* (an imagined, created story)

to *falsify* the evidence (misrepresent, to make false)

— —

Our Human Nature

acute—quick to comprehend, sharply intelligent (n., *acuity*)

aesthetic—referring to the sense of beauty

aloof—distant, unsociable, withdrawn, cool

ambivalence—lack of certainty or definiteness; a feeling of simultaneous, opposing attitudes toward a subject

apathy—lack of interest or feeling

audacity—extreme boldness; *chutzpah, nerve* (adj., *audacious*)

capitulate—to yield to pressure, give in, *concede*

civil—polite, well-mannered

conspicuous—noticeable, obvious

desultory—random, haphazard, casual (opp. of *purposeful*)

discriminate—to see clear distinctions or differences

eccentric—significantly odd or unusual; *idiosyncratic*

ephemeral—fleeting, short-lived (opp. of *eternal*)

fallible—capable of error (adj., *fallacious*)

fervor—deep feeling, passion, zeal

grave—extremely serious, solemn (n., *gravity*)

indifferent—neutral, unbiased, *impartial,* even apathetic

laconic—sparing of speech; concise almost to the point of rudeness

neophyte—beginner, *tyro, novice*
orthodox—according to traditional teaching; accepted, customary
pious—extremely, devoutly religious (n., *piety*)
premonition—a forewarning, omen
provincial—lit., from the provinces; *unsophisticated*
resignation—reluctant acceptance of conditions
reticent—untalkative; restrained in behavior; *reserved*
simulate—to approximate; to *assume, feign* (*simulated* = opp. of *genuine*)
solemn—serious and sober, *grave*
stoic—brave in the face of pain or sorrow; *impassive*
tentative—not final; hesitant, unsure
vehement—profoundly intense, passionate (opp. of *tepid*)
willful—strong-minded, stubborn, determined, headstrong

Roots

FER (L)   CARRY, BEAR, YIELD

transference of ideas (carrying across to a receiver)
a correct *inference* (a conclusion or assumption)
defer to her judgment (yield or give way in respect)

GRAPH, GRAM (Gr)   WRITE, WRITING

a *graphic* picture (delineated well, described exactly)
his witty *epigram* (brief, meaningful statement)
a skilled *graphologist* (handwriting expert)

LOG (Gr); LOQU, LOCUT (L)   SPEECH, STUDY, WORD, TALK

remnants of early *theology* (study of religion)
adding a memorable *epilogue* (words at a book's or play's end)
my *loquacious* cousin (extremely talkative, gabby)
lessons in *elocution* (effective speaking)

— —

Normally Negative Nouns

anarchy—absence of government, often resulting in disorder and lawlessness

animosity—a feeling of ill will; strong dislike

antagonist—enemy; opposing force (opp. of *protagonist* = *hero*)

apprehension—fear of evil, a foreboding (v., *to apprehend* = *to take hold of, physically or mentally*)

arrogance—a feeling of superiority shown by an overbearing manner; excess pride

clamor—loud outcry; continuous, insistent noise

complacence—smugness, self-satisfaction

contempt—feeling of hatred or loathing; *disdain*, disrespect

decadence—a state of decline or deterioration

depravity—a state of moral corruption and decay

detriment—harm; injury or damage

discord—lack of harmony or agreement; disagreement (opp. of *concord* and *accord*)

disdain—*contempt*, a feeling of superiority and disrespect

dissent—disagreement (opp. of *assent* and *consent*)

duplicity—deliberate double-dealing, deception

hypocrisy—saying or doing one thing while believing another; dissembling (adj., *hypocritical*)

indigence—poverty, *destitution* (adj., destitute) (Don't confuse with *indigenous* = *native.*)

indolence—laziness, idleness, *sloth*

languor—relaxed sleepiness, unwillingness to move (adj., *languid*)

negligence—lack of proper care and attention

parsimony—extreme thrift, often stinginess; *niggardliness*

trepidation—fear, worry, or *apprehension*

Medical/Psychological Terms

atrophy—to wither or waste away (opp. of *burgeon*)

debility—physical weakness; *infirmity* (v., *to debilitate*)

fester—to *rankle,* irritate, or worry

phobia—extreme, specific fear (usually illogical)

resuscitate—to revive, bring back to life; revitalize

salutary—promoting good health, curative, remedial

therapeutic—beneficial to recovery from illness or a problem

virulent—fast, powerful, often fatal in its progression; poisonous, *malignant,* evil in intent

Roots

MIT, MISS (L)   SEND

a guided *missile* (anything thrown or sent into space)

emitting a delicious odor (giving off, sending out)

remiss in sending thanks (negligent, careless, lax)

PLEX, PLIC, PLY (L)   FOLD or WEAVE

a ruddy *complexion* (color or appearance of the face, once thought to reveal character)

implicated in a crime (pulled or woven in by circumstances)

are you *implying?* (suggesting indirectly)

PON, POS (L)   PLACE or PUT

postpone a decision (put off until a later time)

an *expository* paper (informative, factual)

to *depose* a tyrant (lit., to put down; to remove forcibly)

— — — — — — — — — — — — — — — — — — — —

Nice (or at Least Neutral) Adjectives

arcane—known to a select few; secret, *esoteric,* mysterious

astute—wise, shrewd, *perceptive, perspicacious*

austere—reserved, somber, grave in manner; *unadorned*

benevolent—good-hearted, generous (n., *benevolence*)

blithe—merry, lighthearted; also, casual or heedless

candid—open, honest, frank

convivial—sociable, *gregarious, congenial*

demure—well-behaved, *sedate,* shy, and modest

dispassionate—unbiased, objective, lacking passion, neutral

docile—easy to direct or discipline; *complaisant,* amiable

eloquent—phrased in a moving, forceful manner; verbally skilled (n., *eloquence*)

elusive—hard to pin down or to understand; tending to escape description or capture (v., *to elude*)

fastidious—extremely particular or neat; picky

feasible—possible to do ("doable")

frugal—careful about the use of money or goods; economical

impartial—not biased or prejudiced; fair, just

incessant—continuous, unstopping, ceaseless, *unremitting*

lucid—clear and distinct; logical, intelligible

magnanimous—bighearted, generous and forgiving

novel—fresh, new, original, creative (v., *to innovate*)

objective—not biased or prejudiced (opp. of *subjective*)

palatable—acceptable, even pleasurable (to the mind or the taste buds)

potent—having strength or power; effective

pragmatic—sensible, practical

profound—deep, with serious meaning; showing perception

prudent—wise, sensible, *judicious* (showing good judgment)

subtle—not obvious; *elusive;* also, refined

succinct—brief and to the point; *concise, pithy*

urbane—polished and sophisticated (said of men, manners, prose, and other arts, but not used for women)

vigilant—watchful, on guard, *wary* (n., *vigil*)

Roots

SPEC, SPIC, SPECT (L)   SEE or LOOK

a *specimen* of his art (visible sample)

thoughtful, *perspicacious* fellow (observant, wise, shrewd)

speculate on the many clues (reflect, wonder, consider)

TEN, TIN, TAIN, TENT (L)   HOLD or CONTAIN

his long-held *tenet* (belief)

the *tenacity* of a bulldog (determination to hold on, *retention,* courage)

a monk's *abstinence* (refraining from worldly pleasures)

detain the culprit (hold back, restrain)

TEND, TENS, TENT (L)   STRETCH

a *tendency* toward lengthy speeches (a proneness toward, a natural learning)

on the *pretense* of being tired (false show, sham)

a *pretentious* display (showy, falsely grand)

— — — — — — — — — — — — — — — — — — —

Depressing Verbs

admonish—to warn strongly or show disapproval; *reprove*

blaspheme—to curse (adj., *blasphemous*)

censor—to edit for questionable material; to examine, with the goal of deleting material

censure—to criticize harshly, *chastise, castigate*

coerce—to force or compel (someone or something)

condescend—to come down in level; to unbend; to stoop, as, *she condescended to reply to my letter*

denounce—to accuse; to inform against; to criticize

deride—to make fun of, to ridicule or scorn (n., *derision*)

desecrate—to profane (foul) anything sacred (opp. of *consecrate*)

disparage—to belittle or downgrade another's accomplishments

dissipate—to use up in a worthless, foolish way; to waste

enervate—to sap, exhaust, weary

exacerbate—to irritate or worsen a situation or condition; to *aggravate,* intensify

hamper—to get in the way of, to *hinder* or obstruct

instigate—to egg on; to *foment* (something bad)

inundate—to overwhelm, as a flood

lampoon—to ridicule, make fun of; to satirize

malign—to slander, *defame,* speak ill of

mar—to damage the appearance or substance of (but not disastrously)

proscribe—to outlaw, *forbid,* prohibit

recant—to renounce (an opinion or belief); to confess error or wrongdoing

refute—to prove wrong by giving evidence to the contrary; to disprove, rebut, deny

reproach—to reprove or show displeasure (with someone)

repudiate—to reject, refuse to accept; to decline

rue—to regret with sorrow; to feel remorse (adj., *rueful*)

squander—to use in silly, extravagant ways; to waste or *dissipate*

sully—to soil or *defile*

thwart—to foil, baffle, or frustrate (someone's attempts)

usurp—to take (a position of authority) by force, often without the right to do so

vilify—to slander, *malign,* defame

Roots

DIC, DICT (L)   SPEAK, SAY, WORDS

an error in *diction* (word choice or usage)

the emperor's stern *edict* (order, forceful command)

a necessary *interdiction* (ruling that prohibits action or stops or impedes an enemy)

FLU, FLUCT (L)   FLOW

impressive *fluency* of our speaker (polished flow of words)

superfluous addition of lace (extra, extravagant, wasteful)

a *fluctuating* temperature (moving, not stable)

GEN (Gr and L)   CAUSE, KIND, BIRTH, RACE

regenerate your enthusiasm (give new life to)

a noble *progenitor* in our family (forefather, ancestor)

talk that *engenders* arguments (gives rise to, causes)

an *indigenous* species (native to the area, local)

Words from Mythology, Literature, and People's Names

chauvinist—an extreme patriot, loyal beyond reason (from Nicholas Chauvin)

chimera—wild dream or fanciful imaginative creature (Gr. myth)

cupidity—greed, avarice (Rom. myth)

halcyon—peaceful, tranquil (Gr. myth)

hector—to bully or pick on; *harass* (Gr. myth)

jovial—jolly, good-natured, fond of laughter (Rom. myth)

lethargy—sluggishness, *torpor, languor, lassitude* (Gr. myth)

malapropism—a hilarious misuse of words (Sheridan, *The Rivals*)

mentor—respected guide or counselor; teacher (Gr. myth)

mercurial—*volatile;* changing easily (Rom. myth)

mnemonics—the art of improving memory through association (Gr. myth)

muse—source of inspiration; a poet; v., *muse = to ponder or mull over* (Gr. myth)

narcissism—self-love; extreme egotism (Gr. myth)

nemesis—relentless pursuer of evildoers; any jinx or *bane* (Gr. myth)

quixotic—idealistic but impractical (Cervantes, *Don Quixote*)

stentorian—obnoxiously loud (Gr. myth)

tantalize—to torment or tease, often with something unobtainable (Gr. myth)

thespian—actor or actress (from Thespis, a Greek)

From the Animal World

asinine—stupid or ridiculous; lacking good judgment

bellwether—a leader whom others follow (from the belled sheep who leads his flock)

bovine—slow-moving, stolid, slow-witted, as cows and oxen

canine—referring to dogs or anything doglike

carnivorous—meat-eating

denizen—a normal inhabitant, either plant or animal

feline—like cats (big and small) in behavior, character, or appearance

herbivorous—plant-eating

prehensile—able to grasp quickly and naturally, as a monkey's prehensile tail grasps a branch (a *prehensile* mind grasps ideas easily)

ruminate—to ponder repeatedly, slowly, and thoughtfully, the way a cud-chewing animal deals with its food

simian—like apes or monkeys in character, behavior, and appearance

whelp—any youngster *(pup);* v., to give birth (dogs)

Roots

HOM, HOMO (L); ANTHROP (Gr)   MAN, HUMAN-KIND

the *homage* virtue deserves (honor, respectful tribute)

abominable *homicide* (killing of a human being)

a course in *anthropology* (study of humankind's origins)

a victim of *misanthropy* (hatred of people in general)

MAN, MANU (L)   HAND

a recent royal *mandate* (formal command or order)

emancipated the poor bird (set free, especially from captivity or bondage)

our *manifest* destiny (obvious, easy to recognize)

NOMEN, NOMIN (L); ONYM (Gr)   NAME

ancient botanical *nomenclature* (any system of naming)

a *nominal* fee for the job (in name only; insignificant)

famous *pseudonym,* Mark Twain (lit., false name; pen name)

— — — — — — — — — — — — — — — — — —

Depressing Adjectives

This list is a little longer than the rest. Spend some extra time today, or save a few words for Day 9 if you need to.

acrid—deeply bitter (comments); sharply pungent (smoke)

ambiguous—vague and unclear; lacking definition

apocryphal—of doubtful origin (an *apocryphal remark*)

arduous—demanding, difficult

banal—stale, overused, *trite, hackneyed* (opp. of *novel*)

belligerent—looking for a fight, *bellicose, feisty, pugnacious, truculent*

caustic—biting, corrosive, *incisive, cutting, trenchant, mordant*

contrite—sorrowful for some wrong; *penitent, remorseful*

credulous—innocent, *gullible, naive, ingenuous*

didactic—designed to teach; now often means boring or *pedantic*, like the behavior of a know-it-all

dogmatic—stubborn, strongly opinionated, *dictatorial, doctrinaire*

dubious—doubtful, questionable (opp. of *indubitable*)

erratic—on no set course, wandering, nomadic; *devious*

flagrant—conspicuous in a very negative way; glaring, gross

futile—hopeless

garrulous—extremely talkative, gabby, *loquacious* (opp. of *taciturn* or *reticent*)

heretical—against accepted teaching or practice (n., *heresy*)

inane—foolish and silly, *asinine*

infamous—famously bad, *notorious* (n., *infamy*)

insipid—boringly dull and bland, dopey

irascible—easily annoyed or angered, testy, grumpy, *choleric, splenetic*

lax—loose and unstructured; slack; *negligent* (opp. of *stringent*)

oblivious—unaware, as *oblivious of my existence*

ostentatious—noticeably showy in display, *pretentious*

parochial—limited in outlook or scope, narrow, restricted (opp. of *catholic = universal*)

pedestrian—everyday, common, ordinary, dull

pompous—self-important, often arrogant in manner; high-flown or ornate, as *pompous speech or writing*

prodigal—wildly extravagant or lavish in spending

prosaic—dull, *banal*, lacking originality

recalcitrant—tough to manage or control, *refractory,* unruly

redundant—needlessly repetitive; *tautological*

reprehensible—earning disapproval or blame; blameworthy

servile—lit., like a servant; very submissive

stagnant—not moving, *static,* stationary

stolid—showing no emotion, *impassive, phlegmatic; bovine*

terse—brief and to the point, *curt* even to rudeness

verbose—wordy (opp. of *pithy, succinct, concise*)

Roots

ORA (L)   SPEAK or PRAY

a lengthy, tiresome *oration* (formal speech or talk)

from the mouth of the *oracle* (giver of wise advice)

massive *orifice* of a whale (mouth; any opening through which things
   go)

PAS, PATH (Gr)   FEELING, SUFFERING, DISEASE

known for her *compassion* (*sympathy* plus a desire to help)

eyed the beets with *apathy* (lack of interest or feeling)

view his plight with *empathy* (a feeling exactly like another's; vicarious sharing of emotion)

his course in *pathology* (study of the nature of disease)

— —

Words from Science

This list is short, so today would be a good time to review your
flashcards from previous lists. (You *are* making flashcards, aren't you?)

anomaly—something different from the norm; irregularity or abnor-
   mality

antithesis—a direct opposite; *antipodes = exact opposites*

coalesce—to come together, join, mix, unite

doldrums—"the blues"; a state or place of inactivity, *listlessness,* or
   collapse

dormant—temporarily inactive, inert, or asleep; *latent*

hypothetical—for purposes of discussion, *theoretical* (n., *hypothesis
   = a supposition*)

ignition—the act of kindling or firing up (a motor or a person's mind
   or emotions)

incendiary—adj., highly exciting, *inflammatory,* as *an incendiary
   speech* (n., a bomb or explosive device)

inert—motionless, idle, static, dormant (n., *inertia*)

innocuous—harmless, *benign* (opp. of *noxious, malignant*)

metamorphosis—very noticeable change of form or character

mutable—changeable, not permanent (opp. of *immutable*)

skeptical—uncertain or doubtful; questioning

velocity—speed or rapidity of motion; rate of occurrence, especially when rapid, as *the velocity of change*

volatile—quick to show emotion; easily triggered or exploded

Roots

PED (L); POD (Gr)   FOOT

wanting to *expedite* shipment (speed up a process)

an *impediment* to progress (obstacle, anything in the way)

an *expedient,* but regrettable, idea (workable, often selfish way to achieve an end)

the speaker's *podium* (raised platform to stand on)

QUER, QUIR, QUIS (L)   ASK, SEEK

dissatisfied, *querulous* tone (whining, complaining)

an amused, *quizzical* look (questioning, teasing)

victim of an *inquisition* (official questioning, often excessively thorough)

REG, RIG, RECT (L)   RULE, RIGHT, STRAIGHT

a new, strict *regime* (method of government)

his *incorrigible* behavior (delinquent, unmanageable)

hoping to *rectify* the problem (to set right, correct)

— — — — — — — — — — — — — — — — — — —

Pleasant Verbs

adhere—to stick to, abide by (n., *adherent = believer*)

advocate—to talk in favor of, support, recommend (n., *advocate = a lawyer, or one who supports you*)

alleviate—to lessen the severity or intensity of something bad; to *allay, soothe, relieve, mitigate*

ameliorate—to make better, improve

articulate—to speak distinctly and well (adj., *articulate = well-spoken, persuasive*)

ascertain—to make certain, to find out for sure

augment—to add to, increase in size or amount

comply—to agree to, go along with (rules, ideas, wishes) (adj., *compliant = docile, tractable*)

conciliate—to calm someone's anger by agreeable behavior; to *appease, pacify, reconcile, mollify, placate*

condone—to overlook (an offense); to pardon or excuse

converge—to come together, meet

deter—to forestall, to "head off" or stop

discern—to see, as to *discern the campfire in the night;* to reason, conclude, or detect by more than sight alone; to note differences by careful discrimination

disseminate—to disperse or spread (ideas, knowledge) as though sowing seeds

emulate—to strive to equal; imitate, copy

enhance—to make better or more desirable

enthrall—to charm, entrance, as though by a spell

extol—to praise highly, even extravagantly

facilitate—to "smooth the way"; to make easier

flaunt—to show off, display proudly

heed—to pay attention to

innovate—to do something new; to be original

pacify—to calm, *appease, mollify, conciliate, placate*

preclude—to forestall (a bad outcome); to hinder, avert, *prevent*

rejuvenate—to give new life; to make youthful again

revere—to honor, worship, respect highly (n., *reverence*)

sanction—to authorize, *endorse,* approve (**Note:** pl. n., *sanctions = forceful measures to ensure compliance with law*)

scrutinize—to examine minutely (n., *scrutiny*)

solicit—to seek something (support, donations, customers)

temper—to moderate or adjust *(to temper discipline with love);* to strengthen through hardship *(tempered in war);* to soften *or* toughen metals during manufacture

venerate—to admire, revere, honor, worship (adj., *venerable = worthy of admiration*)

Roots

SCI (L)   KNOW

with a clear *conscience* (mental seat of moral judgment)
not being *omniscient* (all-knowing)
ESP—one form of *prescience* (foresight, foreknowledge)

STRING, STRICT (L)   TIE, BIND TIGHTLY

a *stringent* rule (rigid, strict)
her throat was *constricted* by fear (rigid, unrelaxed)
narrow *stricture* of belief (tight restraint or limit)

TANG, TING, TACT, TIG (L)   TOUCH, BORDER ON

a *tangible* difference (noticeable, perceptible)
contingent on student vote (dependent on)
fur with *tactile* appeal (ref. to the sense of touch)
contiguous garden plots (touching, bordering on)

— — — — — — — — — — — — — — — — — — — —

Potluck

abstract—without substance, *theoretical* (opp. of *concrete*)
barren—not fertile; lacking progeny (children, crops, etc.)
cognizant—aware, conscious of
concede—to yield, give in, or give way (n., *concession*)
cryptic—hard to decipher, puzzling, *enigmatic*
dichotomy—division into two groups or ideas at odds with one
    another, lit., cut in two
diffident—shy, lacking self-confidence (opp. of *arrogant*)
diverse—different, unlike, dissimilar, as *diverse careers*
enigma—complex puzzle, mystery, *conundrum*
expurgate—to abridge, cut; to censor for questionable material
fortuitous—happening by chance, accidental, not on purpose
germane—fitting and appropriate; *pertinent, relevant*
incontrovertible—absolute, beyond doubt, *indisputable*
inevitable—bound to occur, unavoidable
inexorable—not movable by any means; *relentless,* inflexible
innate—inborn, natural, inherent (talents, personality traits, physical
    appearance, fears, instincts)
intrinsic—internal, inherent (opp. of *extrinsic = external*)

irony—the use of words to convey meaning other than the literal meaning; an expression or happening implying its opposite; *sarcasm*

mundane—of the material world, as opposed to the spiritual; everyday, ordinary, dull, commonplace

nuance—subtle undertone of meaning; *nicety*

obscure—unclear, vague, faint; mysterious or enigmatic; remote, as *an obscure hideout;* ambiguous

paradox—a contradiction in terms; as *the occurrence of icy hail in summer is a paradox*

pervade—to *permeate,* to become part of something else as *smoke pervaded the air* (adj., *pervasive*)

relevant—important, significant (to what is being considered); *germane*

rhetoric—the skill of fine speaking and writing; also, pompous or hypocritical language, as *empty rhetoric*

superficial—on the surface; unimportant, insignificant

tortuous—winding, twisted, as *a tortuous mountain road (Don't confuse with torturous = cruelly painful)*

truncate—to cut short, curtail

vacillate—to waver among choices, to dither around

vicarious—felt or experienced through another person, as *I get a vicarious thrill watching Bob ski*

Roots

TERR (L)   LAND, EARTH

lovable Yorkshire *terrier* (lit., earth dog)

a *subterranean* animal (underground)

interment at Greengage (lit., into the earth; burial)

disinter the body (take out of the earth, dig up)

THE (Gr); DEI (L)   GOD

one prominent *theologian* (expert on religion)

most vocal *atheist* around (one denying God's existence)

as if she were a *deity* (a god; heavenly being)

VEN, VENT (L)   COME

convene the meeting (call to order; cause to come together

loves *The Ark of the Covenant* (pledge, promise, contract)

prior to their *advent* (arrival, coming)

— —

Word Groups Worth Knowing

Check out these word groups. Certain ideas and personality traits have given birth to many word sets.

To Soothe Injured Feelings or Fears

placate
mollify
pacify
conciliate

allay (fears, worries)
alleviate (pain, suffering)
calm
appease

Antonyms: aggravate, exacerbate, annoy, irritate

For Those Lacking Worldly Knowledge

naive
ingenuous
innocent

unsophisticated
unaffected
natural

Antonyms: sophisticated, urbane (men), street-smart, polished, affected

For the Unemotional

bovine
impassive
stolid

phlegmatic
stoic (mainly unemotional)
apathetic

Antonyms: volatile, emotional, sensitive, demonstrative

For Those like Scrooge

stingy
tight
parsimonious

niggardly
penurious
penny-pinching

Antonyms: generous, lavish, prodigal, philanthropic

Rigidly Set in Feelings or Behavior

obdurate
adamant
unyielding

inflexible
stubborn

Antonyms: flexible, accommodating, adaptable, pliable

For Clichés—Those Dull, Overused Expressions

trite   hackneyed
banal   stale

Antonyms: fresh, novel, inventive, original, new

For Thinkers

keen   perspicacious
perceptive   acute
discerning   sagacious
astute   judicious (wise)

Antonyms: obtuse, dense, dull, slow-witted

For Fighters

belligerent   aggressive
bellicose   feisty
truculent   pugnacious

Antonyms: pacific, peaceable, conciliatory

For Talkers

loquacious   chatty
gabby   prolix
garrulous   long-winded
verbose   effusive (gushy)

Antonyms: succinct, pithy, terse, concise, curt, reticent

Roots

VIA (L)   ROAD, WAY

deviate from tradition (swerve, take a different course)
a *devious* path (roundabout or remote)
having a *devious* mind (tricky, deceitful)
impervious to rain (lit., no way through, impenetrable)

VOC, VOKE (L)   CALL

music to *evoke* memories (call forth)
career that is *vocation* (job) and *avocation* (hobby)
revoke that order (lit., call back; rescind or take back)

Are you on Schedule?
Check the prep plan on pages vi and vii.

Successful tennis players are people whose muscles are so familiar with correct stroke motion that they would feel awkward moving in any other way. Good drivers subconsciously know, "Brake, shift, turn, accelerate, shift, straighten out," every time they go around a bend in the road. Success on the SAT math section is based on the same sort of familiarity. If, upon seeing a problem, you subconsciously know a path to its solution and the instructions for filling out the answer, you will do well. The bad news is that the only way to develop this sort of familiarity is to practice: hit a ball against a backboard 100 times, spend an afternoon parallel parking between two garbage pails, or *do math problems,* lots of them, of every type you might encounter on test day. The good news is that, with practice, anyone can develop familiarity.

Panic Plan for the SAT is a collection of exactly the types of problems you need to practice to succeed with the SAT. As you work through them, if you come across one type you don't recognize, go to a teacher or savvy friend and learn what you need to know. For the problems that you do recognize, use *Panic Plan* to redevelop your subconscious recognition of the problems, the topics they test, and the steps to their solutions.

For the rest of this introduction we'll review some generally helpful hints for solving SAT math problems. Then we'll analyze what types of problems are covered on the SAT. Finally, we'll present instructions for the three problem formats that appear on the SAT. This section is the most important if you're taking the SAT for the first time. By the time you take the SAT you should know its instructions cold. It would be a shame if you had to spend 5 extra minutes per test section rereading the fact that grid-in problems can never have a negative answer.

In case you missed it, there is a two-week lesson plan on the first page of this book. As you go through it, or your own schedule, you may find it helpful to keep a small notebook or 3×5 cards of new problems or tricks that you will want to refer back to as you study. Good luck!

Generally Helpful Hints

1. *If the arithmetic looks hairy, try to simplify the problem.* For example, simplify

$$\frac{1 \times 2 \times 3 \times 4 \times 5 \times 6}{180}$$

Divide top and bottom by 2:

$$= \frac{3 \times 4 \times 5 \times 6}{90}$$

Divide top and bottom by 3.

$$= \frac{4 \times 5 \times 6}{30}$$

Divide top and bottom by 30.

$$= \frac{4}{1}$$

$$= 4$$

I definitely did not say:

$$\frac{1 \times 2 \times 3 \times 4 \times 5 \times 6}{180}$$

$$= \frac{720}{180} = 4,$$

although it is true.

2. *If there's no picture for a problem and one would help, draw it; if there is a picture, add information to it.* Even if all you know is that two lines have the same length, put an x next to each.

3. *If a problem is presented in different units, such as inches and feet, remember to convert and work the problem in one unit.* Usually the smaller unit is the simpler one to work in.

4. *If a problem involves a lot of arithmetic, try to approximate the answer or look for patterns.* For example, which set is greater?

$$\left[\frac{1}{2} + \frac{1}{3} + \ldots + \frac{1}{10}\right] \text{ or}$$

$$\left[\left(\frac{1}{2}\right)^2 + \left(\frac{1}{3}\right)^2\right]$$

$$+ \ldots + \left(\frac{1}{10}\right)^2$$

The first is greater because

$$\frac{1}{2} > \left(\frac{1}{2}\right)^2, \frac{1}{3} > \left(\frac{1}{3}\right)^2,$$

and so on.

5. *When doing a geometry problem, draw information as you learn it.* Whenever you can figure out what an angle's measure is, write it directly on the figure. If two line segments have the same length, put a hash or some other identifying mark on those two lines so that you'll know that they're equal.

6. *The two-dimensional aspects of a geometric figure such as area grow in proportion to the square of the one-dimensional aspects.* For example, if the radius, diameter, or circumference of a circle is tripled, then the area grows by nine times. Likewise, if one linear aspect is halved, the area is quartered.

7. *Pick and plug.* A nice property of multiple-choice tests is that you have the answer right in front of you. Some questions, especially word problems, lend themselves readily to your picking each of the solutions one by one and trying them until you find the right one. This usually takes longer than solving the problem straightforwardly, but helps a lot when you're not sure how to attack a question.

8. *None of the above.* A good way to convince yourself that something is not necessarily true or that a value cannot be determined is to redraw the provided picture without disturbing the given information. On the SAT, do not assume that pictures are drawn to scale or that unstated information is true. For example, the right angles are preserved in both of these pictures, though the second could mislead you to believe that $\ell_1 \parallel \ell_2$.

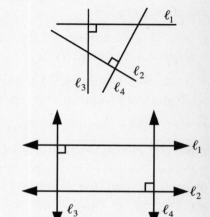

9. *Unless otherwise stated, all SAT geometry problems are two-dimensional.*

An Analysis of the SAT I

The SAT I math test is administered in three sections with the following characteristics:

- Math 1—30 minutes, 25 multiple-choice questions on arithmetic, algebra, and geometry

- Math 2—30 minutes, 25 questions: 15 quantitative comparisons and 10 student-produced answers (grid-ins)

- Math 3—15 minutes, 10 multiple-choice questions

Have you ever wanted to see a batch of very recent SAT I math questions? Since most people need to know what a test will be like in order to prepare for it and do their best, I dissected three recent SATs and two recent PSATs. Each test has 35 multiple-choice questions, 15 quantitative comparison questions, and 10 grid-ins. I sorted the problems into stacks representing the concepts being tested. I matched those stacks to the sections of this unit, as shown in the accompanying table. If you divide the frequency shown in the table by 5, you can estimate how often a given problem type appears on a single test.

But wait. *Most problems test multiple concepts.* It would be a mistake to assume that because eight problems involved mainly polynomials those were the only problems that touched on polynomials in these tests.

Instead, use this table as a guide for your study. Note the topics that make you nervous and focus your review.

Math Problem Distribution in Five Recent SATs and PSATs

Question Type	Frequency	Location in Unit 4
Day 1		
Basic Arithmetic	17	pp. 122–129
Arithmetic of Negatives	6	pp. 125–127
Factoring	6	pp. 127–128
Day 2		
Fractions	18	pp. 130–144
Day 3		
Ratios	12	p. 137
Percentages	12	pp. 138–139
Rate	13	p. 139
Decimals and Powers of 10	5	pp. 139–141
Day 4		
Exponents and Square Roots	18	pp. 144–148
Day 5		
Basic Geometry	22	pp. 149–168
Day 6		
Triangles	26	pp. 159–162
Quadrilaterals	16	pp. 162–164
Day 8		
Coordinate Geometry, Number Lines	16	pp. 168–173
Day 9		
Linear Equalities and Inequalities	18	pp. 174–179
Day 10		
Polynomials and Polynomial Equations	7	pp. 182–186
Two Equations with Two Unknowns	6	pp. 186–187
Word Problems	25	pp. 187–191
Day 11		
Odd, Evens, and Remainders	6	pp. 194–196
Average	13	pp. 196–198
Functions	6	pp. 198
Day 13		
Sequences	3	pp. 202–204
Probability	10	pp. 204
Pictorial Representations of Data	12	pp. 204–205
Time	2	pp. 205–206
Days 1–13		
Assorted Minor Topics	18	pp. 114–212
Total	280	

Check the prep plan on pages vi and vii.

The Three SAT Question Formats

There are three formats of questions on the math section of the SAT. They are multiple-choice, quantitative comparison, and grid-in. More than anything else, being familiar with these problem formats and knowing the directions for filling out their solutions will improve your performance on the SAT.

MULTIPLE-CHOICE PROBLEMS

The format for multiple-choice problems is fairly intuitive. The problem is presented to you in your booklet with five options, marked A through E. The answer key has five columns of ovals, one for each possible solution. You fill in the oval corresponding to the correct solution. For example, in your test booklet you see:

15. The average of four consecutive even numbers is equal to:

   (A) The first number
   (B) The second number
   (C) The third number
   (D) The fourth number
   (E) None of the above

In your answer booklet you will see:

15. Ⓐ Ⓑ Ⓒ Ⓓ Ⓔ

The correct solution is E, none of the above, so you will fill in the oval in the E column in row 15:

15. Ⓐ Ⓑ Ⓒ Ⓓ ⬤

Make sure you fill in the oval completely; otherwise, the automatic scoring system will miss your answer.

QUANTITATIVE COMPARISON PROBLEMS

Quantitative comparison problems present you with values in two columns, A and B. The instructions, which will be printed once at the beginning of the quantitative comparison section of your test, are as follows:

DIRECTIONS FOR QUANTITATIVE COMPARISON QUESTIONS

Questions 1-15 each consist of two quantities in boxes, one in Column A and one in Column B. You are to compare the two quantities and on the answer sheet fill in oval

- A if the quantity in Column A is greater;
- B if the quantity in Column B is greater;
- C if the two quantities are equal;
- D if the relationship cannot be determined from the information given.

AN E RESPONSE WILL NOT BE SCORED.

Notes:

1. In some questions, information is given about one or both of the quantities to be compared. In such cases, the given information is centered above the two columns and is not boxed.
2. In a given question, a symbol that appears in both columns represents the same thing in Column A as it does in Column B.
3. Letters such as x, n, and k stand for real numbers.

EXAMPLES

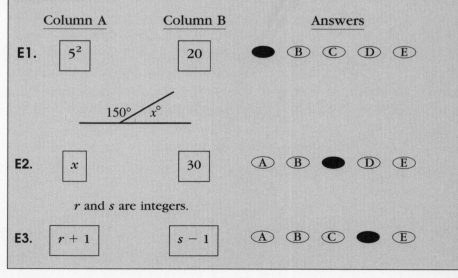

	Column A	Column B	Answers
E1.	5^2	20	● Ⓑ Ⓒ Ⓓ Ⓔ
E2.	x	30	Ⓐ Ⓑ ● Ⓓ Ⓔ
E3.	$r + 1$	$s - 1$	Ⓐ Ⓑ Ⓒ ● Ⓔ

$150°$ $x°$

r and *s* are integers.

GRID-IN PROBLEMS

Multiple-choice and quantitative comparison problem formats have the nice property that there are only four or five possible solutions. If you can disprove one or two possibilities you are left with a small set from which you can guess the correct solution. Recently, ETS, the folks who write the SAT, developed a new format called "student-produced response questions," commonly called grid-ins. The questions look the same except that you are not given possible solutions to choose from. Using a grid like the ones shown on the next page, you are to construct the solution from scratch. Because a grid can represent roughly 13,000 distinct solutions, this format is not conducive to guessing. The instructions for grid-in problems are on the next page.

Throughout this unit, one or two questions in each practice set are set up as grid-ins, so you'll get plenty of practice with them.

Arithmetic

BASIC ARITHMETIC

This section gives hints for doing basic arithmetic in a faster, more efficient manner and covers arithmetic with negative numbers and factoring integers into their prime components.

Addition, Subtraction, Multiplication, and Division

Arithmetic, the manipulation of numbers as opposed to, say, geometric figures or variables, manifests itself everywhere in the SAT. You must be able to perform the four basic arithmetic operations—addition, subtraction, multiplication, and division—both accurately and quickly. Because these are the basics, we'll forgo the definitions and start immediately with formulas and examples of SAT skills that you'll need to finish the test correctly *and* on time.

Directions for Student-Produced Response Questions

Each of the remaining 10 questions requires you to solve the problem and enter your answer by marking the ovals in the special grid, as shown in the examples below.

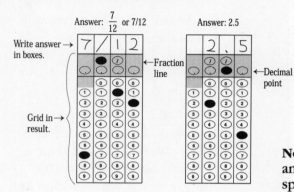

Note: You may start your answers in any column, space permitting. Columns not needed should be left blank.

- Mark no more than one oval in any column.
- Because the answer sheet will be machine-scored, **you will reveive credit only if the ovals are filled in correctly.**
- Although not required, it is suggested that you write your answer in the boxes at the top of the columns to help you fill in the ovals accurately.
- Some problems may have more than one correct answer. In such cases, grid only one answer.
- No question has a negative answer.
- **Mixed numbers** such as $2\frac{1}{2}$ must be gridded as 2.5 or 5/2.

  (if [2 1 / 2] is gridded, it will be interpreted as 21/2, not $2\frac{1}{2}$.)

- **Decimal Accuracy:** If you obtain a decimal answer, **enter the most accurate value the grid will accommodate.** For example, if you obtain an answer such as 0.6666 . . . , you should record the result as .666 or .667. **Less accurate values such as .66 and .67 are not acceptable.**

Acceptable ways to grid $\frac{2}{3}$ = .6666 . . .

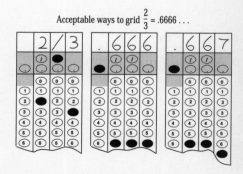

Formulas and Guidelines

- **Quick tests for divisibility:** A number is divisible by:

  2   if it ends in 2, 4, 6, 8, or 0

  3   if the sum of its digits is divisible by 3 (for example, 87 is divisible by 3 because $8 + 7 = 15$, which is divisible by 3)

  5   if it ends in a 0 or a 5

  10 if it ends in a 0

- **Fractions are shorthand for division.**

  $\frac{3}{5}$ is shorthand for $3 \div 5$.

- $a(b + c) = ab + ac$: Multiplication distributes over addition and subtraction. When you multiply a number, a in the definition above, by the sum or difference of a series of other numbers, b and c in the definition, you get the same result as if you first multiplied a by each of the numbers to be added or subtracted.

  Example:

  $$\frac{111 + 33 - 66}{3}$$

Distribute the 3 out of the numerator.

$$= \frac{3(37 + 11 - 22)}{3}$$

Cancel the 3s in the numerator and denominator.

$$= 37 + 11 - 22$$

$$= 26$$

- **When adding lists of positive numbers, look for pairs that add to 10. If there are negative numbers, find positive numbers that when added to the negatives yield 0.**

  Example:

  Simplify $3 - 7 + 2 + 3 + 4 + 8$.

  1. Notice that $3 + 4 - 7 = 0$, so you can cross out these three numbers leaving $2 + 3 + 8$.
  2. Pair off the 2 and 8 to leave $10 + 3 = 13$.

  Tens and 0's are easy and fast to add with a relatively low chance of error.

- **When you multiply a list of numbers, look for pairs whose product is a multiple of 10.**

Example:

Solve $5 \times 7 \times 4$.

1. First multiply the 4 and 5 to get 20.
2. Easily finish off the multiplication 20×7 to reach 140.

Problems to Watch For

- *When dividing two numbers, do it in steps, dividing both the dividend and the divisor by the same number.*

Example:

Simplify $720 \div 180$.

1. Divide both 720 and 180 by 10 to get $72 \div 18$.
2. Divide both by 3 to get $24 \div 6$ (72 is evenly divisible by 3 because $7 + 2 = 9$, which is evenly divisible by 3).
3. Divide both by 2 to get $12 \div 3$.
4. Solve the much simpler problem $12 \div 3 = 4$.

It does not matter in what order you do the simplification. You could just as easily begin by dividing by 2.

- *When you add something t times, it is the same as multiplying it by t.*

Example:

Solve $\dfrac{n^2 + n^2 + n^2}{3}$ for $n = 7$.

You could do this by saying $n^2 = 49$, so

$$n^2 + n^2 + n^2 = 49 + 49 + 49$$
$$= 147$$

and $147 \div 3 = 49$.

A much more efficient way to work the problem is to first combine the n^2's:

1. $\dfrac{n^2 + n^2 + n^2}{3} = \dfrac{3n^2}{3}$
2. $\dfrac{3n^2}{3} = n^2$
3. When $n = 7$, $n^2 = 49$.

Negative Numbers

Definitions

- **Absolute value ($|x|$):** The size of a number without regard to its sign. Absolute value is symbolized by vertical lines, as $|-3| = |3| = 3$.

- **Less than (<):** A number that is to the left of another number on the number line is less than the other number. For example, $-3 < 2$.

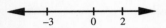

- **Greater than (>):** A number that is to the right of another number on the number line is greater than the other number. For example, $2 > -3$, as shown above.

Formulas and Guidelines

- **Adding with negatives:** To add two negatives, add them as though they were positives and negate the answer. To add a negative and a positive number, compute the *difference* of their absolute values. The sign of the result is the sign of the number with the greater absolute value. For example, when given the problem $-4 + 3$, think: the difference between 4 and 3 is 1, and 4, the negated number, has the greater absolute value, so $-4 + 3 = -1$.

- **Subtracting with negatives:** If a negative number follows a subtraction sign, change the subtraction to addition and change the negative to a positive.

For example,

$$-4 - (-3) = -4 + 3 = -1.$$

- **−1 = 1:** If you ever end up with a contradiction like $-1 = 1$ you probably divided by 0 somewhere.

- **Multiplying with negatives:**

Neg × neg = pos
Neg × pos = neg
Pos × neg = neg
Pos × pos = pos

More simply, if two numbers have the same sign, their product is positive; otherwise their product is negative. Notice that this directly implies that x^2 is positive for all x other than 0.

If you are having a hard time memorizing the table, pick any two numbers, say 1 and -1, and run a test: $-1 \times 1 = -1$, so neg × pos = neg and $-1 \times -1 = 1$, so neg × neg = pos.

- **Dividing with negatives:** This follows exactly the same rules as multiplying with negatives.

Problem to Watch For

- *Taking the rule about multiplication of signed numbers a step further, if you multiply a negative number by itself an even number of times the result is positive. If you multiply it by itself an odd number of times the result is negative. The following example appears in the quantitative comparison section of the test:*

Column A	Column B

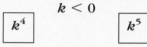

1. k is negative, so k^5 is negative and k^4 is positive.
2. Hence, $k^5 < 0 < k^4$ and the quantity in column A is greater.

Factoring

Factoring, per se, is usually tested in one question on an SAT. However, being able to factor a number into its prime factors is extremely useful for simplifying fractions and doing division.

Definitions

- **Factor:** An integer that evenly divides another number is said to be a factor of the other number. If $y = ab$, then a and b are factors of y.

- **Prime number:** A number greater than 1 whose only factors are 1 and itself. One prime number is 7, because the only numbers that evenly divide it are 1 and 7. Other prime numbers include 3, 5, 11, and 13.

- **Prime components:** The prime components of a number are the *unique* set of prime factors that when multiplied together yield the number. The prime components of 12 are 2, 2, and 3 because $12 = 2 \times 2 \times 3$. Note: 4 is not a prime component because it is not a prime number.

Guideline

- **Uniqueness of prime components:** Two numbers are equal if and only if their prime factors are the same.

Problems to Watch For

- *Some problems on the SAT give you the product of a set of variables and ask you to determine what the variables might be. This type of problem is often best solved by factoring the product into its prime components.*

Example:

The product of three integers greater than 1 is 30. What is the maximum difference between any two of the numbers?

1. Factoring 30 into its prime components yields 30 = 2 × 3 × 5, so we know exactly what the three numbers are.
2. The maximum difference between any two of 2, 3, and 5 is the greatest minus the least: 5 − 2 = 3.

- *When you have two equations and two unknowns and the unknowns are multiplied together, it is usually easier and faster to enumerate the factors of their product and guess the values of the unknowns than to solve the problem explicitly.*

Example:

The product of two positive numbers is 21 and their difference is 20. What is the greater number?

1. Set up the two equations:
$$xy = 21$$
$$x - y = 20$$
2. By factoring 21 you can guess that x and y are either 1 and 21, or 3 and 7.
3. You know 21 − 1 = 20, so the greater number must be 21.

PRACTICE PROBLEMS IN BASIC ARITHMETIC

Answers begin on page 282.

1. What is the sum of the integers between $-x$ and x inclusive when x is 3?

   (A) −3
   (B) −1
   (C) 0
   (D) 1
   (E) 3

2. How many unique pairs of positive integers can be multiplied together to yield 24?

   (A) 2
   (B) 3
   (C) 4
   (D) 6
   (E) 8

3. If $n = -1$ then $n^3 + n^2 =$

   (A) -2

   (B) -1

   (C) 0

   (D) 1

   (E) 2

The directions for quantitative comparison problems are on page 121.

Column A   **Column B**

$$x + 9 = 0$$

4. | x | | 9 |

$$a < m$$
$$am < 0$$

5. | 0 | | m |

---

6. | $2 + 4 + 6 + 8$ | | $1 + 3 + 5 + 7 + 9$ |

$$pw < 0$$

7. | p | | w |

$$y = -y$$

8. | y | | -1 |

The directions for grid-in problems are on page 123.

9. Rounded to the nearest integer, what is $620 \div 60$?

10. If $2 \times 3 \times 4 \times 5 \times 6 \times 7 = 6 \times a \times 42$, then $a =$

FRACTIONS

Next to basic arithmetic, fractions are the most tested topic on the SAT. We'll focus on fractions in this section and the next; however, you'll see them arise throughout the text in conjunction with all sorts of other problems.

Definitions

- **Fraction:** A fraction is short-hand for a division problem. The fraction $\frac{a}{b}$ is equivalent to $a \div b$. You can also think of a fraction as a part-whole relationship: $\frac{a}{b}$ means a parts of something that has a total of b parts.

- **Numerator:** The "top" of the fraction. In $\frac{a}{b}$, a is the numerator. Note that the numerator does not have to be a single number: In the expression $\frac{a+b}{c}$, the numerator is a sum.

- **Denominator:** The "bottom" of the fraction. In $\frac{a}{b}$, b is the denominator. The denominator does not have to be a single number either.

- **Inverse:** The inverse of b is $\frac{1}{b}$. When b is a fraction, the inverse is simply the fraction inverted. The inverse of $\frac{3}{5}$ is

$$\frac{1}{\frac{3}{5}} = \frac{5}{3}.$$

Formulas and Guidelines

If you're unsure of one of the following rules while taking the SAT, test it on two simple fractions.

- **Equivalence rule for fractions:**

$$\frac{a}{b} = \frac{ac}{bc} = \frac{a \div c}{b \div c}.$$

This rule is the most important fraction rule to remember during the SAT because it allows you to simplify a complex problem into one with easier calculations.

For example,

$$\frac{20}{25} = \frac{20 \div 5}{25 \div 5} = \frac{4}{5},$$

and

$$\frac{20}{25} = \frac{20 \times 4}{25 \times 4} = \frac{80}{100}.$$

- **Adding fractions:**

$$\frac{a}{c} + \frac{b}{c} = \frac{a+b}{c}.$$

Before you can add two fractions, the denominators must be the same. Also, note that the denominator does not change. To alter a problem so that the denominators of the addends are the same, apply the equivalence rule by multiplying the numerator and denominator of each fraction by the denominator of the other fraction:

$$\frac{a}{b} + \frac{c}{d} = \frac{ad}{bd} + \frac{cb}{db} = \frac{ad+cb}{bd}.$$

For example,

$$\frac{2}{3} + \frac{3}{4} = \frac{2\times4}{3\times4} + \frac{3\times3}{4\times3}$$

$$= \frac{8}{12} + \frac{9}{12} = \frac{17}{12}.$$

- **Subtracting fractions:** Follow the same rules as for addition.

- **Multiplying fractions:**

$$\frac{a}{b} \times \frac{c}{d} = \frac{ac}{bd}.$$

For example

$$\frac{2}{3} \times \frac{2}{5} = \frac{2\times2}{3\times5} = \frac{4}{15}$$

- **Dividing fractions:**

$$\frac{a}{b} \div \frac{c}{d} = \frac{a}{b} \times \frac{d}{c} = \frac{ad}{bc}.$$

When a fraction follows a division sign, invert the fraction and replace the division sign with one for multiplication.

For example,

$$\frac{2}{3} \div \frac{3}{4} = \frac{2}{3} \times \frac{4}{3} = \frac{8}{9}.$$

- **Fractions within fractions:**

$$\frac{\frac{a}{b}}{\frac{c}{d}} = \frac{ad}{bc}.$$

Remember, a fraction is shorthand for division, so $\frac{\frac{a}{b}}{\frac{c}{d}}$ is the same as $\frac{a}{b} \div \frac{c}{d}.$

Applying the rule for dividing fractions, you end up with

$$\frac{\frac{a}{b}}{\frac{c}{d}} = \frac{ad}{bc}.$$

For example,

$$\frac{\frac{2}{3}}{\frac{4}{5}} = \frac{2}{3} \times \frac{5}{4} = \frac{10}{12} = \frac{5}{6}.$$

- $a = \dfrac{a}{1}$: For example, $3 = \dfrac{3}{1}$.

- $\dfrac{1}{\frac{a}{b}} = \dfrac{b}{a}$: This follows directly from the two preceding rules and defines the inverse of the fraction.

For example,

$$\dfrac{1}{\frac{1}{2}} = \dfrac{2}{1} = 2.$$

- $\dfrac{a}{b + c}$, **in general, cannot be simplified:**

For example,

$$\dfrac{3}{3 + 4} = \dfrac{3}{7}.$$

There is no way to cancel the 3's.

The sign of the fraction:

	Example
$\dfrac{a}{b} = 0$ if and only if $a = 0$.	$\dfrac{0}{7} = 0$

	Example
$\dfrac{a}{b} < 0$ if $a < 0$ or $b < 0$, but not both.	$\dfrac{-3}{7} < 0$ and $\dfrac{3}{-7} < 0$

	Example
$\dfrac{a}{b} > 0$ if a and b are both positive or both negative.	$\dfrac{-3}{-7} = \dfrac{3}{7} > 0$

$b \neq 0$, ever, in $\dfrac{a}{b}$.

Notice that these rules are just like those for division and multiplication of real numbers.

- **Mixed fractions:**

$1\dfrac{2}{3}$ is shorthand for $1 + \dfrac{2}{3}$, which equals $\dfrac{3}{3} + \dfrac{2}{3} = \dfrac{5}{3}$.

Problems to Watch For

- *You will need to be able to simplify a problem using the equivalence rule again and again throughout the SAT.*

Example:
Simplify the expression

$$\dfrac{3}{4} \times \dfrac{5}{6} \div \dfrac{7}{3} \div \dfrac{6}{2} \times \dfrac{8}{3} \times \dfrac{1}{4}.$$

1. Invert fractions that follow a $\div$ sign:

$$\dfrac{3}{4} \times \dfrac{5}{6} \times \dfrac{3}{7} \times \dfrac{2}{6} \times \dfrac{8}{3} \times \dfrac{1}{4}.$$

2. By the rules for multiplication this equals

$$\dfrac{3 \times 5 \times 3 \times 2 \times 8 \times 1}{4 \times 6 \times 7 \times 6 \times 3 \times 4}.$$

3. Now begin to simplify using the equivalence rule. The first obvious number to divide out of the top and bottom is 3, leaving:

$$\frac{\cancel{3} \times 5 \times 3 \times 2 \times 8 \times 1}{4 \times 6 \times 7 \times 6 \times \cancel{3} \times 4}.$$

That's one less multiplication step you have to do and about 15 seconds of time saved.

Now, for the other cancellations:

4. Divide the top and bottom by 4. Notice how a 2 is left after the 8 is divided by 4.

$$\frac{5 \times 3 \times 2 \times \overset{2}{\cancel{8}}}{4 \times 6 \times 7 \times 6 \times \cancel{4}}$$

5. Divide the top and bottom by 6.

$$\frac{5 \times \cancel{8} \times \cancel{2} \times 2}{\cancel{6} \times 7 \times 6 \times 4}$$

6. Divide the numerator and denominator by 2.

$$\frac{5 \times \cancel{2}}{7 \times 6 \times \underset{2}{\cancel{4}}}$$

What's left after all of the possible cancellations are done is

$$\frac{5}{7 \times 6 \times 2} \text{ or } \frac{5}{84}.$$

- *If two fractions have the same denominator, the fraction with the larger numerator is larger.*

Also, if two fractions have the same numerator, the fraction with the larger denominator is smaller.

Example:

Column A	Column B
$\dfrac{5}{17} - \dfrac{3}{19}$	$\boxed{0}$

1. $\dfrac{5}{19} > \dfrac{3}{19}$ The two fractions have the same denominator; the fraction with the larger numerator is larger.

2. $\dfrac{5}{17} > \dfrac{5}{19}$ The two fractions have the same numerator; the one with the larger denominator is smaller.

3. $\dfrac{5}{17} > \dfrac{5}{19} > \dfrac{3}{19}$ Combine statements 1 and 2.

4. $\dfrac{5}{17} - \dfrac{3}{19} > 0$ Subtracting a smaller number from a larger number always gives a positive.

The quantity in column A is greater; the answer is A.

- *If you memorize the following facts, several SAT problems will go much more quickly:*

$$\frac{1}{2} + \frac{1}{2} = 1; \quad \frac{1}{4} + \frac{1}{4} = \frac{1}{2};$$

$$\frac{1}{8} + \frac{1}{8} = \frac{1}{4}; \text{ and so on.}$$

Example: $1 - \dfrac{1}{1-\frac{1}{2}} = ?$

1. Simplify the denominator of the large fraction:

$$1 - \frac{1}{2} = \frac{1}{2}.$$

This leaves

$$1 - \frac{1}{\frac{1}{2}}.$$

2. Recognize that $\dfrac{1}{\frac{1}{2}}$ is an inverse and equals 2, leaving $1 - 2$.

3. $1 - 2 = -1$.

- *Some problems ask you to do things with fractions of fractions. The "of" is shorthand for multiplication.*
Example: How much more is $\frac{1}{2}$ of $\frac{2}{3}$ than $\frac{3}{4}$ of $\frac{1}{3}$?

1. $\dfrac{1}{2}$ of $\dfrac{2}{3} = \dfrac{1}{2} \times \dfrac{2}{3} = \dfrac{1}{3}$, and

$$\frac{3}{4} \text{ of } \frac{1}{3} = \frac{3}{4} \times \frac{1}{3} = \frac{1}{4}.$$

2. The first exceeds the second by their difference, $\dfrac{1}{3} - \dfrac{1}{4}$.

3. $\dfrac{1}{3} - \dfrac{1}{4} = \dfrac{1 \times 4}{3 \times 4} - \dfrac{1 \times 3}{4 \times 3}$

$$= \frac{4}{12} - \frac{3}{12} = \frac{1}{12}.$$

- *Some of the quantitative comparison problems test whether you believe incorrectly that $x > \dfrac{1}{x}$. This is not always true: if $0 < x < 1$ then $\dfrac{1}{x} > 1$. Notice that 1 and -1 are the only values for which $x = \dfrac{1}{x}$.*

Example:

Column A	Column B

$$x = \frac{1}{y}$$
x and y are integers.

1. Because x is an integer and equal to $\dfrac{1}{y}$, then $\dfrac{1}{y}$ must also be an integer.

2. $\dfrac{1}{y}$ is only an integer for $y = 1$ or -1.

3. When y is 1, x is 1; and when y is -1, x is -1.

4. In both cases $x = y$, so both quantities are equal; the answer is C.

PRACTICE PROBLEMS IN FRACTIONS 1

Answers begin on page 283.

1. One half of the socks in a drawer are brown, $\frac{1}{4}$ of them are black, and $\frac{1}{5}$ of them are blue. If the rest of them are white, what fractional part of the socks are white?

    (A) $\frac{19}{20}$

    (B) $\frac{3}{11}$

    (C) $\frac{1}{20}$

    (D) $\frac{1}{11}$

    (E) $\frac{8}{11}$

2. If a $\frac{1}{4}$-inch piece of ribbon costs a nickel, then 1 foot of ribbon will cost:

    (A) $0.15
    (B) $0.20
    (C) $0.24
    (D) $0.48
    (E) $2.40

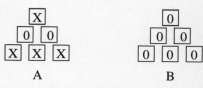

A   B

3. How many X cards would have to be taken from pile A and put into pile B for the fractional part of X cards to be the same in both piles?

    (A) None
    (B) 1
    (C) 2
    (D) 3
    (E) 4

4. In a race, runner B falls x inches farther behind runner A every y minutes. Express the distance runner B will be behind runner A in feet per hour.

    (A) $12xy$

    (B) $\frac{x}{12y}$

    (C) $\frac{12y}{x}$

    (D) $\frac{y}{5x}$

    (E) $\frac{5x}{y}$

5. The difference between

$7\frac{3}{4}$ feet and $5\frac{5}{6}$ feet in *inches* is:

(A) 12
(B) 12.5
(C) 18
(D) 23
(E) 25

---

6. Simplify $\dfrac{1}{\dfrac{1}{a}-\dfrac{1}{b}}$

$(a \neq 0, b \neq 0, a \neq b)$.

(A) $\dfrac{ab}{a-b}$

(B) $\dfrac{a-b}{ab}$

(C) $b - a$

(D) $\dfrac{ab}{b-a}$

(E) $\dfrac{b-a}{ab}$

The directions for quantitative comparison problems are on page 121.

Column A   **Column B**

7. $\dfrac{-8}{1}$ $\dfrac{1}{-8}$

Let $x \ \S \ n$ mean x inverted n times. For example:

$\dfrac{1}{2} \ \S \ 3 = 2$.

8. $\dfrac{3}{7} \ \S \ 101$ $\dfrac{7}{3}$

9. If $\dfrac{5}{x} = \dfrac{15}{9}$, then $x =$

---

10. Jim paints $\dfrac{1}{3}$ of a fence, Joan paints $\dfrac{1}{2}$ of what is left. What fraction of the fence is left unpainted?

OTHER TYPES OF FRACTIONS

This section covers ratios, percentages, rate, decimals, and powers of 10. For almost all ratio and percentage problems (and many decimal problems too), convert the problem to one that uses fractions. This simplifies problem solving, because everything that follows uses the same rules and there is only one set of rules to memorize.

Ratios

Definition

- **Ratio:** Remember that a fraction is a part-to-whole relationship. A ratio is a *part-to-part* relationship. *For their inheritance, Jessica receives $3 for every $2 that Jasmine receives* is written $3:2$. When you convert a ratio to a fraction you must add up all of the parts to determine the whole. In this example, Jessica receives $\frac{3}{3+2}$, or $\frac{3}{5}$, of the inheritance.

Formulas and Guidelines

- **Equivalence rule for ratios:** $x:y$ is the same as $ax:ay$; that is, you can multiply both parts of a ratio by the same number and the ratio will remain unchanged.

- **Conversion to fractions:** If the ratio of A to B to C is $a:b:c$, then A is $\dfrac{a}{a+b+c}$ of the total, B is $\dfrac{b}{a+b+c}$ of the total, and C is $\dfrac{c}{a+b+c}$ of the total.

Problem to Watch For

- *When you are given a ratio on an SAT, the problem is apt to test your ability to go from a part-part relationship expressed by a ratio to a part-whole relationship expressed by a fraction.*

Example: After taking 30 socks out of the dryer, Debbie noticed that the ratio of blue socks to brown socks to black socks was $2:3:5$. How many black socks were in the dryer?

1. There are a total of 30 socks.
2. The relationship of the number of black socks to the whole number of socks is $\dfrac{5}{2+3+5} = \dfrac{5}{10} = \dfrac{1}{2}$.
3. The total number of black socks is $\dfrac{1}{2} \times 30 = 15$.

Percentages

Definition

- **Percentage:** A percentage is a fraction whose denominator is 100. For example, $28\% = \dfrac{28}{100}$.

Formulas and Guidelines

- **Converting fractions to percentages:** To convert a fraction, $\dfrac{a}{b}$, to a percentage, $x\%$, set up the following equation: $\dfrac{a}{b} = \dfrac{x}{100}$. Multiplying both sides of the equation by 100, you get $x = \dfrac{100a}{b}$, so $\dfrac{a}{b} = \dfrac{100a}{b}\%$.

Example:

3 is what percent of 5?

First set up the equation

$$\frac{3}{5} = \frac{x}{100}.$$

Then solve for x:

$$x = \frac{300}{5} = 60.$$

So, $\dfrac{3}{5}$ equals 60%, or 3 is 60% of 5.

- **Converting percentages to fractions:** To convert $x\%$ to a fraction, simply write the fraction $\dfrac{x}{100}$ and simplify it. For example,

$$.5\% = \frac{.5}{100} = \frac{1}{200}.$$

- **x is $y\%$ of z:** This can be written mathematically as

$$x = \frac{y}{100}z.$$

Problems to Watch For

- *Percentages need not be between 0 and 100. Don't be misled into believing that your answer is wrong if it is greater than 100.*

Example:

What percent of 40 is 60?

1. Set up the equation

    $$\frac{x}{100} \times 40 = 60.$$

2. Multiply both sides by 100 and divide both sides by 40 to get $x = \dfrac{60 \times 100}{40}$.

3. Simplify to get $x = \dfrac{3 \times 50}{1} = 150$.

4. 60 is 150% of 40.

- *Know that*

    $$25\% = \frac{1}{4} \text{ and } 33\frac{1}{3}\% = \frac{1}{3}.$$

138

These equalities occur fairly often in the percentage questions.

Example:

Column A	Column B
$33\frac{1}{3}\%$ of 75	25% of 100

1. $33\frac{1}{3}\%$ of 75 is 25.
2. 25% of 100 is 25.
3. Hence, the two quantities are equal. Answer: C.

Rate

Definitions

- Rate = $\dfrac{\text{amount}}{\text{time}}$.
- Amount = rate × time.
- Time = $\dfrac{\text{amount}}{\text{rate}}$.

Formulas and Guidelines

- **Speed is a type of rate where the amount is a distance:** For example, we talk about miles per hour, $\dfrac{\text{miles}}{\text{hour}}$.
- **Treat speeds as fractions:** For example, 3 miles per hour is written $\dfrac{3\text{ miles}}{1\text{ hour}}$. Three miles is the amount, and 1 hour is the time.

Example: A plane travels x miles during the first 2 hours of a trip and y miles during the last 3 hours of the trip. What was the plane's average speed over the entire trip?

1. The amount (number) of miles the plane covered was $x + y$ miles.
2. The time it took the plane to cover the distance was $2 + 3 = 5$ hours.
3. The plane's average speed (rate of motion) was $\dfrac{x + y \text{ miles}}{5 \text{ hours}}$.

Decimals and Powers of 10

Definition

- **Decimal point:** A marker that separates the tenths and the units places in a number. For example, the number 123.45 equals 1 hundred, 2 tens, 3 units, 4 tenths, and 5 hundredths.

Formulas and Guidelines

- **Addition and subtraction of decimals:** These operations are just like addition and subtraction with integers, except that you need to line up the numbers using the decimal point.

Multiplication of decimals: Count the number of digits to the right of the decimal point in each of the numbers to be multiplied. Multiply the numbers, ignoring the decimal points. The sum of the number of digits to the right of the decimal points in each of the multipliers is the number of digits there should be to the right of the decimal point in the product.

For example, to find the product of 25.4 and 3.1:

25.4   (one digit to right of decimal point)

$\times$ 3.1   (one digit to right of decimal point)

254

762

78.74   (one + one = two digits to the right of the decimal point)

In a case where there are not enough digits, you must add zeros to the left of the product before putting in the decimal point.

- **To multiply a decimal by 10, move the decimal point one place to the right:** If there are no digits to the right of the decimal point, add a zero to the right of the last digit. (An integer has an implied decimal point after its last digit: $123 \times 10 = 123. \times 10 = 1230.$)

- **To divide a decimal by 10, move the decimal point one place to the left:** If there are no digits to the left of the decimal point, add a zero to the right of the decimal point. For example, $.3 \div 10 = .03$.

- $10^n = 1$ **with** n **zeros after it:** $10^3 = 1,000$.

- $10^{-n} =$ **a decimal point followed by** $(n - 1)$ **zeros and a 1:** $10^{-3} = .001$. Another way of looking at 10^{-n} is as the inverse of 10^n. So $10^{-3} = \dfrac{1}{10^3}$ $= \dfrac{1}{1,000} = .001$.

- **To convert a decimal to a fraction, count the number of digits to the right of the decimal point and call this** n: The numerator will be the number without the decimal point and the denominator will be a 1 followed by n zeros. For example, $2.345 = \dfrac{2,345}{1,000}$. Often, as is true in this case, you will be able to simplify the resulting fraction.

Problem to Watch For
- *Remember that* .1 *is just another name for* $\dfrac{1}{10}$.

Example:

Column A	Column B
$\boxed{.1}$	$\boxed{\dfrac{9}{100}}$

1. .1 is $\dfrac{1}{10}$.
2. Using the equivalence rule for fractions, $\dfrac{1}{10} = \dfrac{10}{100}$.

3. $\dfrac{10}{100} > \dfrac{9}{100}$ because their denominators are the same and $10 > 9$, so the answer is A; column A is greater than column B.

PRACTICE PROBLEMS IN FRACTIONS 2

Answers begin on page 284.

1. $8 \times .125 =$

   (A) 0
   (B) 1
   (C) .1
   (D) 8.125
   (E) .825

2. If $.2^2 = \sqrt{x}$, then $x =$

   (A) .2
   (B) .02
   (C) .04
   (D) 0.016
   (E) .0016

3. If $-0.6(0.4 - p) = 1.2(.8p + .7p)$, then $p =$

   (A) -5
   (B) $-.2$
   (C) .2
   (D) .5
   (E) None of the above

4. If $10n = 3.33333...$ and $n = .33333...$, then n can be rewritten as

   (A) $\dfrac{1}{3}$
   (B) $.3^2$
   (C) $\dfrac{3}{10}$
   (D) $\dfrac{1}{.3}$
   (E) None of the above

5. After picking 120 peaches, a woman eats 12 of them. What percent remains?

(A) 10
(B) 30
(C) 50
(D) 70
(E) 90

_____

6. If a boy must walk 12 miles to school and he has completed 75% of the trip, how many miles does he have left to go?

(A) 3
(B) 4
(C) 6
(D) 8
(E) 9

_____

7. A 60-gallon tank is 40% full of water. If the water is poured into a 40-gallon tank, what percent of the 40-gallon tank has been filled?

(A) 24
(B) 40
(C) 60
(D) 96
(E) 100

8. If 30% of a class consists of boys and there are 21 girls in the class, how many boys are there in the class?

(A) 30
(B) 9
(C) 60
(D) 42
(E) 10

_____

9. If the cost of a 4-minute telephone call is $0.24, then what is the cost of a 15-minute call at the same rate?

(A) $0.60
(B) $0.65
(C) $0.75
(D) $0.90
(E) $1.11

_____

10. In a scale drawing, 3 inches represents 9 feet. How many inches represents 1 foot 6 inches? (1 foot = 12 inches)

(A) .4
(B) .5
(C) .6
(D) 1
(E) 2

11 If $3:4$ is equivalent to $a:12$, then $a =$

(A) 1
(B) 9
(C) 11
(D) 12
(E) 14

_____

12. Michele, Ned, and Owen split the award for a contest in the ratio of $6:2:1$, respectively. If the total award was worth $72, then Ned received

(A) $9
(B) $18
(C) $16
(D) $48
(E) $8

_____

13. In a class of 25 students, 44% are boys. What is the ratio of boys to girls in the class?

(A) $11:1$
(B) $11:25$
(C) $11:14$
(D) $14:11$
(E) $25:14$

14. The length of a side of an equilateral triangle is what fraction of the perimeter of the triangle?

(A) $\dfrac{1}{6}$

(B) $\dfrac{1}{3}$

(C) 1

(D) $\dfrac{3}{1}$

(E) $\dfrac{60}{1}$

_____

15. Solve for x given in the equation $4{,}836 = 4x^3 + 8x^2 + 3x + 6$.

(A) 0
(B) 1
(C) 10
(D) 100
(E) 1,000

_____

16. 30% of 80 is what percent of 24?

143

17. In 15 years the ratio of my age to my father's age will be $1:2$. Five years ago, the ratio of my age to his was $1:4$. How old am I?

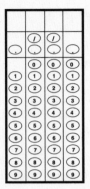

EXPONENTS AND SQUARE ROOTS

Except for their use of the radical sign ($\sqrt{}$), square roots are a type of exponent, and consequently the rules for manipulating the two are almost exactly the same.

Definitions

- a^n: n (the exponent) instances of a multiplied together.

$$\underbrace{a \times a \times a \times \ldots \times a}_{n \text{ times}}, \text{ for}$$

positive integer n.

- $\sqrt{b}$: The positive value that, when multiplied by itself, yields b. $\sqrt{b} = a$ implies that $a^2 = b$.

Formulas

- $a^n a^m = a^{n+m}$: For example, $2^3 \times 2^2 = 2^5 = 32$. If this is hard to memorize, think of n a's lined up next to m a's; how many do you have altogether?

- $a^n b^n = (ab)^n$: For example, $3^2 \times 2^2 = (3 \times 2)^2 = 6^2 = 36$. Imagine n a's and n b's lined up. By reordering the a's and b's, you have n pairs of them.

- $\sqrt{a}\sqrt{b} = \sqrt{ab}$: Remember that the radical sign follows the same rules as exponents. Notice how this can be used to simplify a square root:

$$\sqrt{12} = \sqrt{4 \times 3} = \sqrt{4}\sqrt{3}$$
$$= 2\sqrt{3}.$$

- $\dfrac{a^n}{a^m} = a^{n-m}$: For example, $2^3 \div 2^2 = 2^{(3-2)} = 2^1 = 2$.

If this is hard to memorize, think of a fraction with a numerator of n a's and denominator of m a's; then cancel m a's.

- $\dfrac{a^n}{b^n} = \left(\dfrac{a}{b}\right)^n$: For example,

$$\frac{16^2}{8^2} = \left(\frac{16}{8}\right)^2 = 2^2 = 4.$$

- $\dfrac{\sqrt{a}}{\sqrt{b}} = \sqrt{\dfrac{a}{b}}$: For example,

$$\dfrac{\sqrt{8}}{\sqrt{2}} = \sqrt{\dfrac{8}{2}} = \sqrt{4} = 2.$$

Note: There are no general rules for simplifying $a^n b^m$.

Also note: These rules for simplification do not apply to addition or subtraction, only to multiplication and division.

- $(a^b)^c = a^{bc}$: If you have a hard time visualizing this, think of c groups of b a's. For example, you can say

$$(2^2)^3 = 2^2 \times 2^2 \times 2^2$$
$$= 4 \times 4 \times 4 = 64$$

or $(2^2)^3 = 2^6 = 64$

or $(2^2)^3 = 4^3 = 64$

- **If a is positive, then a^n is always positive.**
- **If a is negative, then a^n is positive when n is even and a^n is negative when n is odd:** Remember that multiplying a negative by a negative yields a positive and multiplying a negative by a positive yields a negative.

Problems to Watch For

- *People often assume (incorrectly) that whenever one raises a number to a power the result is larger than the original number. This is not true, and there are questions on the SAT designed to test your understanding of this fact.* For example:

Column A	Column B
a and n are positive	

The answer is D, the relationship cannot be determined. If a is greater than 1, then multiplying it by itself makes the result grow larger. However, if a is between 0 and 1, then the more times you multiply it by itself, the smaller the result becomes. Remember that when you multiply by a fraction you are taking a part of the multiplicand, thereby making the result smaller.

- *Memorize the fact that $4^n = (2^2)^n = 2^{2n}$. When it appears in problems it makes them appear much tougher than they truly are.*

Example: Solve for k.

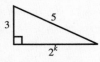

Note: Figure not drawn to scale.

Using the Pythagorean theorem (Need a reminder? See p. 160, then p. 161 for the Pythagorean triple, 3-4-5), you can set up the equation

$$(2^k)^2 = 5^2 - 3^2$$
$$2^{2k} = 4^2$$
$$2^{2k} = (2^2)^2 = 2^{2 \times 2}$$
$$2k = 2 \times 2$$
$$k = 2$$

- *You will be able to solve many problems much more quickly if you remember that exponents are shorthand for multiplication and consequently follow all of the rules of multiplication.*

Example: When $a = 3$, solve for

$$\frac{a^3 + a^4}{a + 1}.$$

1. Because exponents follow all of the rules for multiplication, you can distribute a^3 in the numerator to get
$$\frac{a^3(1 + a)}{a + 1}.$$

2. $1 + a$ and $a + 1$ cancel each other, so you are left with a^3.

3. Substituting 3 for a, you have $3^3 = 27$.

- *Finally, memorize the squares of 1 through 10 so that when you see a 64 on the exam you will immediately recognize the possibility that the solution somehow involves the fact that $8^2 = 64$.*

Example: Solve for positive x in the equation $(x + 5)^2 = 64$.

1. Because you recognize 64 as a perfect square, you can rewrite the equation to read $(x + 5)^2 = 8^2$.

2. Take the square root of both sides of the equation to get $x + 5 = 8$.

3. Solve the simple addition to reach $x = 3$.

PRACTICE PROBLEMS IN EXPONENTS AND SQUARE ROOTS

Answers begin on page 287.

1. If $\dfrac{1}{y} = \sqrt{.25}$, then y equals

    (A) $\dfrac{1}{4}$

    (B) $\dfrac{1}{2}$

    (C) 1

    (D) 2

    (E) 4

---

2. $4\sqrt{48} - 3\sqrt{12} =$

    (A) 5

    (B) 10

    (C) $\sqrt{3}$

    (D) $2\sqrt{3}$

    (E) $10\sqrt{3}$

---

3. $\left(\dfrac{1}{2}x^6\right)^2 =$

    (A) x^8

    (B) x^{12}

    (C) $\dfrac{1}{4}x^8$

    (D) $\dfrac{1}{4}x^{12}$

    (E) $\dfrac{1}{4}x^{36}$

4. $\sqrt{\dfrac{x^2}{4} + \dfrac{4x^2}{9}} =$

    (A) $\dfrac{x}{2} + \dfrac{2x}{3}$

    (B) $\dfrac{3x}{5}$

    (C) $\dfrac{x\sqrt{5}}{36}$

    (D) $\dfrac{5x}{36}$

    (E) $\dfrac{5x}{6}$

---

5. If $7x - 7y = 20$, then $x - y =$

    (A) $\dfrac{20}{7}$

    (B) -2

    (C) $\dfrac{-20}{7}$

    (D) 2

    (E) 20

6. One pipe can fill a pool in 8 hours, and a second pipe can fill the same pool in 12 hours. If both pipes work together, how long will it take to fill the pool?

(A) $4\frac{1}{5}$ hours

(B) $4\frac{2}{5}$ hours

(C) $4\frac{3}{5}$ hours

(D) $4\frac{4}{5}$ hours

(E) 5 hours

7. If $2^{x+2} = 32$, then x equals

8. If $3x - .3x = 54$, then $x =$

9. Simplify $\sqrt{0.121}$

10. Twin A leaves New York City, heading north at 35 miles per hour. At the same time, Twin B leaves New York City, heading south at 45 miles per hour. In how many hours will they be 640 miles apart?

Geometry

Although most people only study one year of geometry, it accounts for almost one third of the SAT (see p. 119 for a breakdown of the SAT by problem type). This means that knowing the information in the next three sections can earn you 200–300 points.

BASIC GEOMETRY

This section deals with angles and circles in a plane.

Angles

Definitions

- **Straight angle:** An angle whose measure is 180°. A line segment forms a straight angle.

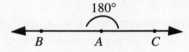

$\angle BAC$ is a straight angle.

- **Supplementary angles:** Two angles whose measures add to 180° are supplementary.

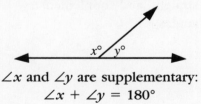

$\angle x$ and $\angle y$ are supplementary:
$\angle x + \angle y = 180°$

- **Right angle:** An angle whose measure is 90° is a right angle.
- **Perpendicular:** Two lines are perpendicular if they form a right angle.

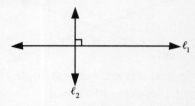

Note that ⌐ indicates an angle of 90°. $\ell_1 \perp \ell_2$ means line 1 is perpendicular to line 2.

- **Complementary angles:** Two angles whose measures add to 90° are complementary. If you split a right angle into two smaller angles, the smaller angles are complementary.

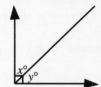

$\angle x$ and $\angle y$ are complementary:
$\angle x + \angle y = 90°$

- **Vertical angles:** Opposing angles formed by intersecting lines are vertical angles, which are equal.

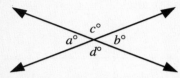

$\angle a$ and $\angle b$ are vertical angles and consequently equal. Likewise, $\angle c$ and $\angle d$ are vertical angles and equal.

- **Parallel lines (∥):** Two lines in a plane that never intersect are said to be parallel. The distance between parallel lines is constant over their entire length.

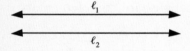

$\ell_1 \| \ell_2$ means line 1 is parallel to line 2.

Formulas and Guidelines

- **Transversal of parallel lines:** A line that intersects two parallel lines is a transversal.

Given that $\ell_1 \| \ell_2$, ℓ_3 is a transversal.

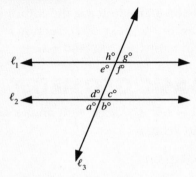

The eight angles formed by two parallel lines and a transversal adhere to the following rules:

Rule 1: $\angle a = \angle c = \angle e = \angle g$

Rule 2: $\angle b = \angle d = \angle f = \angle h$

Rule 3: Angles *a, c, e,* and *g* are *supplementary* to angles *b, d, f,* and *h.*

Notice that these rules agree with the definitions of vertical, straight, and supplementary angles.

Problem to Watch For

- *Problems involving parallel lines cut by a transversal may appear more difficult when the diagrams include extraneous lines or when the transversals do not continue past the parallel lines.*

Example:
Solve for x in the following diagram:

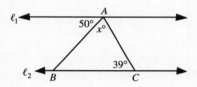

$\ell_1 \| \ell_2$

1. AB is a transversal, so $\angle ABC = 50°$.
2. The sum of the angles of a triangle is 180°, so $x° + 50° + 39° = 180°$.
3. $x = 180 - 50 - 39 = 91$.

Circles

Definitions

- **Circle:** The set of points a given distance from a single point. The single point is called the circle's *center*. The distance from the center to any point on the circle is called the *radius*. For example, a circle with radius 3 inches is the set of all points 3 inches from the center of the circle.

- **Degrees:** A circle is defined to sweep out an angle of 360 degrees.
- **Radius (r):** A line segment joining a circle's center and any point on the circle. Also, the length of that line segment.
- **Chord:** A line segment joining any two points on a circle.
- **Diameter (D):** A chord that passes through the center of the circle. Also, the length of that chord. Note that $D = 2r$ and is the longest chord.

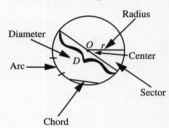

- **Pi (π):** $\pi \approx \dfrac{22}{7} \approx 3.14$. The ratio between every circle's circumference and its diameter:
$$\pi = \frac{C}{D}$$
- **Arc:** A contiguous piece of a circle.
- **Degrees in an arc:** The number of degrees in an arc is equal to the number of degrees in the angle formed by the radii drawn to the ends of the arc.
- **Sector of a circle:** The area like a pie slice enclosed by an arc and the radii to the endpoints of the arc.

- **Tangent:** (1) A line that shares exactly one point with a circle. (2) Two circles are tangent if they are tangent to a line at the same point.

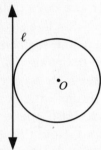

ℓ is tangent to O.

- **Inscribed:** A circle is inscribed within a square if each of the sides of the square is tangent to the circle. A square is inscribed within a circle if each of its vertices lies on the circle.

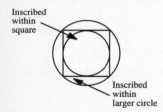

Inscribed within square

Inscribed within larger circle

Formulas

- **Circumference (*C*):** The perimeter of a circle.
  $C = \pi D = 2\pi r.$
- **Area of a circle (*A*):** $A = \pi r^2.$

- **Length of an arc:** The ratio of the number of degrees in an arc to the number of degrees in a circle, 360, is equal to the ratio of the length of the arc to the circumference of the circle.

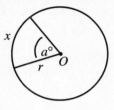

$$\frac{a}{360} = \frac{x}{2\pi r}$$

Circumference of circle = $2\pi r$.
Area of a sector: The ratio of the number of degrees in an arc to the number of degrees in a circle, 360, is equal to the ratio of the area of the sector the arc defines to the area of the circle.

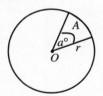

$$\frac{a}{360} = \frac{A}{\pi r^2}$$

Area of circle = πr^2.

Problems to Watch For

- *You must be able to recognize and relate the radius, diameter, and circumference of a circle and approximate the value of π.*

Example:

The circle centered at *P* is tangent to and passes through the center of the circle centered at *O*. What fraction of the larger circle's circumference best approximates the smaller circle's radius?

(A) $\dfrac{1}{2}$

(B) $\dfrac{1}{3}$

(C) $\dfrac{1}{4}$

(D) $\dfrac{1}{6}$

(E) $\dfrac{1}{12}$

Use capital letters to denote elements of the larger circle and lowercase to denote those of the smaller one. Keep the goal of the problem in mind, to relate *r* and *C*, and notice that the diameter of the smaller circle is the same as the radius of the larger circle to start with the equation:

1. $d = R$ Diameter small circle = radius of large circle.

2. $2r = \dfrac{D}{2}$ $d = 2r$ and $R = \dfrac{D}{2}$.

3. $2r = \dfrac{C}{2\pi}$ $D = \dfrac{C}{\pi}$.

4. $r = \dfrac{C}{4\pi}$ Divide both sides of the equation by 2.

5. $r \approx \dfrac{C}{12} = \dfrac{1}{12}C$,   Approximate π as 3.

The correct answer is (E).

- *Often word problems use this fact: If you say that a wheel is a circle, then the distance the wheel travels in one revolution is equal to its circumference.*

Example:
If a bicycle with wheels 2 feet in diameter were to go around a circular track with diameter 100 feet, how many revolutions would each of the wheels make per lap?

1. Circumference of the wheel $(C_w) = 2\pi$ ft.

2. Circumference of the track $(C_t) = 100\pi$ ft.

3. Number of revolutions =
distance around the track
divided by distance each
revolution of the wheel
covers.

4. Number of revolutions =
$\dfrac{C_t}{C_w} = \dfrac{100\pi}{2\pi} = 50.$

• *To test your ability to relate
rectangular and circular
measures, problems often use
the fact that tangents to circles
define right angles.*

Example:

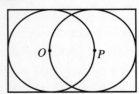

The circle centered at P passes
through O, and the circle
centered at O passes through P.
If the radius of circle O is 2
centimeters, what is the area, in
square centimeters, of the
circumscribed rectangle?

Because the circles share a
radius, OP, their radii, diameters, circumferences, and other
measures are the same.

1. Length of the rectangle
= diameter of the circles
= 4 cm.

2. Width of the rectangle
= 3 × radius of the circles
= 6 cm.

3. Area of the rectangle
= length × width
= 24 cm².

• *Problems with angles and triangles often involve circles because a tangent to a circle con-
veniently forms a right angle to
the radius. Furthermore, when
two radii of a circle are used to
form the sides of a triangle, the
triangle is guaranteed to be
isosceles because all radii of a
circle have the same length.*

Example:

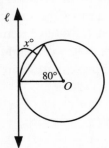

Line ℓ is tangent to the circle
with center O. What is x?

1. Notice that the two unknown angles of the
inscribed triangle are
opposite equal-length sides.
Why? Because the two sides
are radii of the same circle.
Call the degree measure of
each of these angles a. The
sum of the angles in a
triangle is 180°, so $2a + 80°$
$= 180°$, and subsequently a
$= 50°$. Write the angle
measures into the figure.

2. Line ℓ is a tangent to the circle; consequently it forms a right angle with the radius that intersects it. Draw in the right angle.

3. $x + 50 = 90$, the number of degrees in a right angle. So, $x = 40$.

PRACTICE PROBLEMS IN BASIC GEOMETRY

Answers begin on page 288.

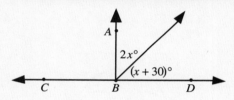

1. $BA \perp CD$. Solve for x.

   (A) 15

   (B) 20

   (C) 30

   (D) 40

   (E) 50

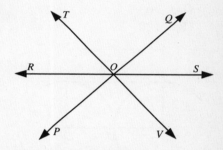

2. Lines PQ, RS, and TV intersect at O. If $\angle ROQ = 142°$ and $\angle TOS = 129°$, find the measure of $\angle POV$.

   (A) 38°

   (B) 51°

   (C) 89°

   (D) 91°

   (E) 189°

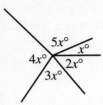

Note: Figure not drawn to scale.

3. From above, $x =$

(A) 24
(B) 48
(C) 72
(D) 96
(E) 120

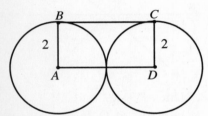

4. From the figure above, A and D are the centers of two equivalent circles. Find the area of rectangle $ABCD$ if AB and CD are both radii of the circles and have length 2.

(A) 1
(B) 2
(C) 4
(D) 6
(E) 8

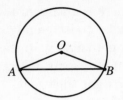

Note: Figure not drawn to scale.

5. The measure of $\angle OAB$ is 20°. If O is the center of the circle, then the number of degrees in $\angle AOB$ is

(A) 40
(B) 70
(C) 80
(D) 140
(E) 160

6. As shown in the figure above, two equivalent circles are drawn inside a third circle in such a way that they each intersect the third circle at only one point, and they share a common point at the center of the third circle. Find the area of the shaded region if the radius of the larger circle is 4.

(A) π
(B) 2π
(C) 4π
(D) $2\pi - 2$
(E) $\frac{1}{2}(4\pi - 2)$

7. A cylindrical roller is dipped in paint and then rolled for one complete revolution over a piece of paper. If the line of paint is 4 inches long, what is the radius, in inches, of the roller?

(A) $\dfrac{2}{\pi}$

(B) 2

(C) π

(D) 2π

(E) It cannot be determined from the information given.

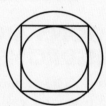

8. One circle is circumscribed around a square with side of length 2, and another circle is inscribed in the same square. Find the ratio of the area of the larger circle to that of the smaller circle.

(A) $4:1$

(B) $\sqrt{3}:1$

(C) $1.5:1$

(D) $\sqrt{2}:1$

(E) $2:1$

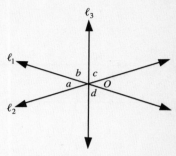

9. ℓ_1, ℓ_2, and ℓ_3 intersect at O. If $\angle b$ is twice the measure of $\angle a$ and $\angle a$ is half the measure of $\angle c$, find the measure of $\angle d$ in degrees.

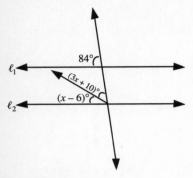

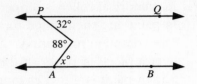

11. If $PQ \parallel AB$, solve for x.

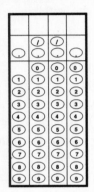

10. If $\ell_1 \parallel \ell_2$, solve for x.

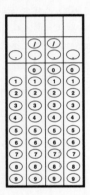

POLYGONS AND POLYHEDRONS

A polygon is a closed, multisided figure in a plane (for example, a triangle, a quadrilateral, . . .). A polyhedron is a closed, multisided figure in *three-dimensional space* (for example, a pyramid, a rectangular solid, . . .). Triangles, quadrilaterals, rectangular solids, and cubes are treated in this section.

Triangles

Definitions

- **Triangle (Δ):** A closed figure in a plane with 3 sides.

- **Equilateral Δ:** A triangle whose sides and angles are equal.

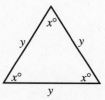

- **Isosceles Δ:** A triangle, 2 of whose sides and angles are equal.

- **Right Δ:** A triangle with 1 angle whose measure is 90°.

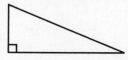

Formulas

- **The sum of the angles in a triangle is 180°.**
- **Opposite sides of equal angles are equal. Conversely, opposite angles of equal sides are equal.**

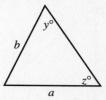

If $y = z$, then $a = b$. Conversely, if $a = b$, then $y = z$.

- **If ∠y is greater than ∠z, then the side opposite ∠y is greater than the side opposite ∠z.**

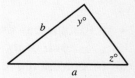

If $y > z$, then $a > b$. Conversely, if $a > b$, then $y > z$.

159

- **Pythagorean theorem ($a^2 + b^2 = c^2$):** In a right triangle, the square of the length of the *hypotenuse* (the side opposite the right angle) equals the sum of the squares of the lengths of the *legs* (other two sides).

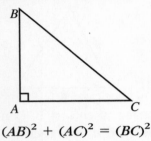

$$(AB)^2 + (AC)^2 = (BC)^2$$

- **Area of a triangle:** The *area* of a triangle equals one half the base times the height:

$$A = \frac{1}{2}bh.$$

  (a) Every triangle has three bases, as each of its sides can be considered a base.

(b) The height, or altitude, of a triangle is the distance, or length, from the base to the vertex opposite it.

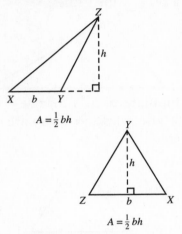

$$A = \frac{1}{2}bh$$

$$A = \frac{1}{2}bh$$

Note that the base is always perpendicular to the height.

- **30-60-90 triangle:** A *30-60-90 triangle* is one whose angles are 30°, 60°, and 90°.

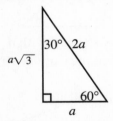

The ratio of the lengths of the sides of a 30-60-90 triangle is $1:\sqrt{3}:2$. Put another way, if the length of the side opposite the 30° angle is a, then the length of the side opposite the 60° angle is $a\sqrt{3}$, and the side opposite the right angle is $2a$.

Conversely, if the sides of a triangle are a, $2a$, and $a\sqrt{3}$, then the triangle is a 30-60-90 triangle.

Watch out for the case where a, from above, is $\sqrt{3}$, leaving sides of $\sqrt{3}$, 3, and $2\sqrt{3}$.

Problems to Watch For

- *The area of a right triangle is one half the product of the legs because the legs are the base and height of the triangle.*

Example:

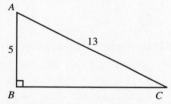

What is the area of $\triangle ABC$?

1. By the Pythagorean theorem, $BC = 12$.

2. Area $\triangle ABC = \left(\dfrac{1}{2}\right)(12)(5)$

   $= 30$.

- *Pythagorean triples: Certain sets of integers satisfy the Pythagorean theorem, and they often occur on the SAT. They include 3-4-5, 5-12-13, 8-15-17, and 7-24-25.*

Example:

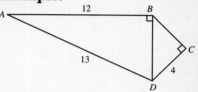

Note: Figure not drawn to scale.

What is the perimeter of *ABCD*

1. $\triangle ABD$ is a right triangle. So, by the Pythagorean theorem, $BD = 5$.

2. Again, using the Pythagorean theorem, $BC = 3$.

3. The perimeter of *ABCD* = $13 + 4 + 3 + 12 = 32$.

You could have done this problem by applying the Pythagorean theorem twice, but it is faster to recognize the Pythagorean triples.

- *Triangles whose angles measure 45°, 45°, and 90° occur often on the SAT because they are both right and isosceles triangles, and because one can form them by splitting a square along its diagonal.* Applying the Pythagorean theorem and the formula for the area of the triangle, if the length of a leg of a 45-45-90 triangle is a, then the length of the hypotenuse is $a\sqrt{2}$, and the area of the triangle is $\dfrac{1}{2}a^2$.

Example:

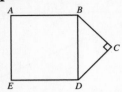

If the area of square *ABDE* is 4 and *BC = CD*, what is the area of Δ*BCD*?

1. Area *ABDE* = 4 implies *BD* = 2.
2. *BD* = 2 implies *BC = CD*

$$= \frac{2}{\sqrt{2}} = \frac{2\sqrt{2}}{\sqrt{2}\sqrt{2}} = \frac{2\sqrt{2}}{2}$$
$$= \sqrt{2}.$$

3. The area of a 45-45-90 triangle with legs of length $\sqrt{2}$ is $\frac{1}{2}(\sqrt{2})^2 = 1$.

• *Be familiar with 30-60-90 triangles. You need to memorize the ratio of the lengths of the sides of 30-60-90 triangles.*

Example:
What is the area of an equilateral triangle with side of length 4?

1. Draw the triangle and drop a perpendicular from a vertex to the opposite base.
2. Because of symmetry you have formed two 30-60-90 triangles.
3. The hypotenuse of each is 4, so the leg opposite the 60° angle is $2\sqrt{3}$ and the leg opposite the 30° angle is 2.

4. The area of each 30-60-90 triangle is
$$\left(\frac{1}{2}\right)(2)(2\sqrt{3}) = 2\sqrt{3}.$$

5. The area of the equilateral triangle is
$$(2)(2\sqrt{3}) = 4\sqrt{3}.$$

Quadrilaterals

Definitions

• **Quadrilateral:** A polygon with 4 sides in a plane.

• **Parallelogram:** A quadrilateral whose opposite sides are parallel.

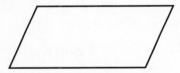

• **Rectangle:** A parallelogram whose 4 angles each measure 90°.

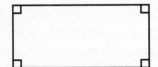

- **Square:** A rectangle whose sides have the same length.

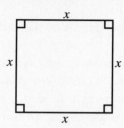

- **Rectangular solid:** Without getting too technical, think of a box. All of the angles formed by the edges are 90°.
- **Cube:** A rectangular solid, all of whose edges have the same length.

Formulas and Guidelines
- **The sum of the angle measures in a quadrilateral is 360°.**
- $A = lw$: The area of a rectangle is the product of its length and width.
- $A = s^2$: For a square, the length and the width are the same, so the area is the length of the side squared.
- **The perimeter of any object is the sum of the lengths of its sides.**
- $P_r = 2(l + w)$: For a rectangle, the perimeter is twice the sum of the length and the width.

- $P_s = 4s$: For a square, the perimeter simplifies to 4 times the length of a side.
- $V_r = lwh$: The volume of a rectangular solid (a box) is length $\times$ width $\times$ height.
- $V_c = s^3$: The volume of a cube is the length of its edge cubed.
- **Rectangular solids and cubes have 6 faces.**

Problems to Watch For
- *When determining how many rectangular solids of the same dimensions can fit into another, compute the ratio of their volumes.*

Example:
How many $2 \times 1 \times 3$ boxes can fit into a $4 \times 5 \times 6$ box?

1. The volume of the large box is $4 \times 5 \times 6$.
2. The volume of the small box is $2 \times 1 \times 3$.
3. The ratio of their volumes is
$$\frac{4 \times 5 \times \cancel{6}}{\cancel{2} \times 1 \times \cancel{3}} = \frac{4 \times 5}{1} = 20.$$

- *Know the perfect squares up to 100* (perfect squares are the squares of whole numbers): 1, 4, 9, 16, 25, 36, 49, 64, 81, 100.

Example:

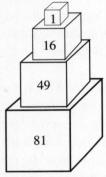

Note: Figure not drawn to scale.

The area of one face of each cube is given on that face. What is the height of the stack of cubes?

1. The face of a cube is a square. Given the area of a face of each cube, you can figure out the height of each cube.

2. The heights of the cubes from bottom to top are 9, 7, 4, and 1.

3. The height of the stack is $9 + 7 + 4 + 1 = 21$.

- *When a rectangle is inscribed within a circle, the diagonal of the rectangle is also a diameter of the circle.* (Remember that a square is a type of rectangle.)

Example: What is the area of a circle circumscribed about a square with perimeter 56?

1. *Draw* the picture!
2. Perimeter of square = 56.
3. Side of square = $56 \div 4$
   $= 14$.
4. Diagonal of square
   $= 14\sqrt{2}$.
5. Diameter of circle = $14\sqrt{2}$.
6. Radius of circle = $7\sqrt{2}$.
7. Area of circle = πr^2
   $= \pi(7\sqrt{2})^2 = \pi \times 49 \times 2$
   $= 98\,\pi$.

PRACTICE PROBLEMS IN POLYGONS AND POLYHEDRONS

Answers begin on page 289.

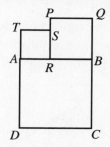

1. *ABCD* is a square whose area is 100. *PQBR* is a square of area 36. What is the area of square *TSRA?*

(A) 2
(B) 4
(C) 16
(D) 25
(E) 36

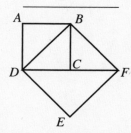

2. *ABCD* and *BFED* are both squares. If square *ABCD* has side 4, then *CF* =

(A) 2
(B) $2\sqrt{2}$

(C) 4
(D) $4\sqrt{2}$
(E) 8

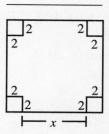

Note: Figure not drawn to scale.

3. Four square pieces are cut out of a square sheet of metal. If the original area of the metal sheet was $x^2 + 24x$, then the area of the sheet without the four pieces is

(A) 1
(B) 4
(C) 6
(D) 9
(E) It cannot be determined from the information given.

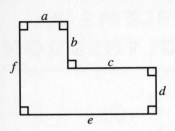

4. The area of the above figure is all of the following EXCEPT

(A) $ab + de$
(B) $af + cd$
(C) $fe - bc$
(D) $af + ed$
(E) $ab + ad + cd$

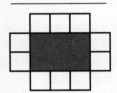

5. From the figure above, if each of the equally sized square tabs is folded up and a lid is put on to form a box, then the volume of the box in terms of s, the side of one of the squares, is:

(A) $10s^2$
(B) $6s^3$
(C) $6s$
(D) $10s^3$
(E) It cannot be determined from the information given.

6. What is the average degree measure of the angles of a triangle?

(A) 30
(B) 45
(C) 60
(D) 90
(E) It cannot be determined from the information given.

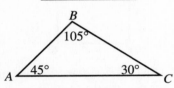

7. If AB from above equals $\sqrt{2}$, then the area of $\triangle ABC$ is

(A) $\dfrac{1}{2} + \dfrac{\sqrt{3}}{2}$
(B) $2\sqrt{2}$
(C) $1 + \sqrt{3}$
(D) $\dfrac{1}{2} + \dfrac{\sqrt{6}}{2}$
(E) $\dfrac{\sqrt{2}}{2} + \sqrt{3}$

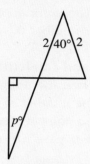

8. From the figure above, find p.

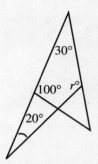

9. From the figure above, $r =$

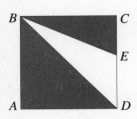

10. *ABCD* is a square, and *E* is the midpoint of *CD*. Find the percentage of the square that is shaded.

COORDINATE GEOMETRY

This section covers number lines and coordinate geometry.

Number Lines

Definitions

- **Number line:** A graphical representation of real numbers in which each point on a straight line corresponds to exactly one number.

- **Origin:** The point corresponding to the number 0.

Formulas and Guidelines

- $x < y$ **when** the point representing the number x **is to the left of** the point representing the number y **on a number line.**

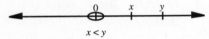

- **The distance between two points on a number line is proportional to the difference between the numbers the points represent.**
- **The midpoint of two points on a number line lies halfway between the points and corresponds to the average of the two numbers the points represent.**

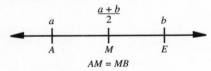

Problem to Watch For

- *Even though you may not know the actual lengths of sections on a line segment, you can often determine relative lengths. Ask yourself: Is the length of one section less than, greater than, or equal to the length of another? Often this information is enough to answer the problem.*

Example:

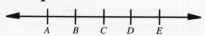

Note: Figure not drawn to scale.

In the figure, *B* is the midpoint of *AC* and *D* is the midpoint of *CE*. Which of the following statements is necessarily true?

I. *C* is the midpoint of *AE*.
II. *C* is the midpoint of *BD*.
III. The length of *BD* is half the length of *AE*.

1. *B* is the midpoint of *AC*, so *AB* = *BC*. Put an *O* on each of these line segments.
2. By the same reasoning, put an *X* on both *CD* and *DE*.
3. The length of *AC* is equal to two *O*s, while the length of *CE* is equal to two *X*s. These two are not necessarily equal, so *C* is not necessarily the midpoint of *AE* and statement I is not necessarily true.
4. By the previous reasoning, *C* is not necessarily the midpoint of *BD*, so statement II is not necessarily true.
5. The length of segment *BD* is an *X* plus an *O*, and the length of segment *AE* is two *X*s plus two *O*s. Whatever *X* and *O* are, the length of *BD* is half the length of *AE*, so statement III is the only one that is necessarily true.

Coordinate Geometry

Definitions

- **Coordinate axes:** You can think of the coordinate axes as a two-dimensional number line defining a plane on which each point is represented by a pair of numbers. The first dimension is a horizontal number line called the "*x*-axis." The second dimension is a vertical number line called the "*y*-axis."

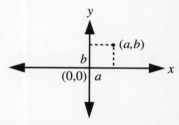

- **x-axis:** See "Coordinate axes."
- **y-axis:** See "Coordinate axes."
- **x-coordinate:** The first number in the pair representing a point.
- **y-coordinate:** The second number in the pair representing a point.
- **Origin:** The point on the coordinate axes represented by the pair (0,0).
- **Positive x-axis:** Those points on the *x*-axis that are to the right of the origin.
- **Positive y-axis:** Those points on the *y*-axis that are above the origin.

- **Negative *x*-axis:** Those points on the *x*-axis that are to the left of the origin.
- **Negative *y*-axis:** Those points on the *y*-axis that are below the origin.
- **Quadrants:** The four sections of the coordinate axes separated by the *x*- and *y*-axes. They are numbered from I to IV with Roman numerals as shown in the following diagram.

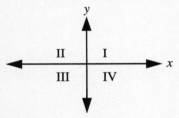

When:

x is:	and *y* is:	then:
positive	positive,	(*x,y*) is in Quadrant I.
negative	positive,	(*x,y*) is in Quadrant II.
negative	negative,	(*x,y*) is in Quadrant III.
positive	negative,	(*x,y*) is in Quadrant IV.
0	—,	(*x,y*) is on the *y*-axis.
—	0,	(*x,y*) is on the *x*-axis.

Formulas and Guidelines

- **All points on a horizontal line parallel to the *x*-axis have the same *y*-coordinate.**
- **All points on a vertical line parallel to the *y*-axis have the same *x*-coordinate.**

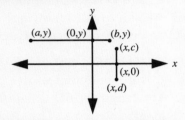

- **Midpoint of two points:** The midpoint of (x_1, y_1) and (x_2, y_2) is $\left(\dfrac{x_1 + x_2}{2}, \dfrac{y_1 + y_2}{2} \right)$.

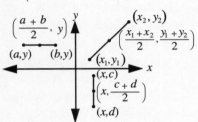

Notice how much simpler the equation is when the points lie on either a horizontal or vertical line.

- **Distance between two points:** The distance between the points (x_1, y_1) and (x_2, y_2) is

$$\sqrt{(x_2 - x_1)^2 + (y_2 - y_1)^2}.$$

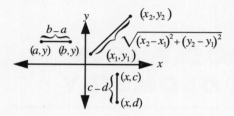

Notice how much simpler the equation is when the points lie on either a horizontal or vertical line.

- **The slope of a line** describes how steep an angle the line makes with the x-axis. The slope of a line that includes two points (x_1, y_1) and (x_2, y_2) is $\dfrac{y_2 - y_1}{x_2 - x_1}$. Note, it does not matter what two points on the line you choose to compute its slope—a line has a constant slope throughout. The slope of a horizontal line is zero, because all of its points have the same y-value. The slope of a vertical line is undefined because all of its points have the same x-value, which generates a zero in the denominator of the slope's definition.

Problem to Watch For

- *Squares often appear in problems dealing with coordinate geometry because the equations for the midpoint of two points and the length of a line segment simplify a great deal when the points lie on a horizontal or vertical line.*

Example:

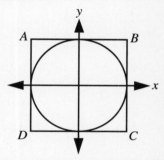

If the circle pictured above has area 16π and is centered at $(0,0)$ and *ABCD* is a square, find the x-coordinate of point B.

1. The area of a circle is given by the equation $A = \pi r^2$. Substituting 16π for A and solving for r, you get $r = 4$. Now you know that every point on the circle is 4 units from the origin.

2. Where the circle crosses the positive x-axis it must have coordinates $(4,0)$. The circle must cross the positive y-axis at the point $(0,4)$.

3. *B* is on a line parallel to the *y*-axis at (4,0), so its *x*-coordinate is 4. *B* is on a line parallel to the *x*-axis at (0,4), so its *y*-coordinate is also 4.

4. Putting these together, you determine that the coordinates of point *B* are (4,4).

PRACTICE PROBLEMS IN COORDINATE GEOMETRY

Answers begin on page 291.

Column A	Column B

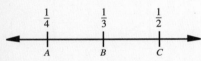

Note: Figure not drawn to scale.

1. | B | the midpoint of $\overline{AC}$ |

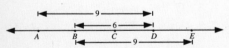

Note: Figure not drawn to scale.
$BD = 6$ $BE = 9$ $AD = 9$

2. | The length of $\overline{BC}$ | 3 |

3. The distance between points (3,4) and (*a,b*) is 5. Point (*a,b*) could be any of the following EXCEPT

(A) (0,0)
(B) (3,1)
(C) (−2,4)
(D) (3,9)
(E) (6,0)

4. If $x > y$, then point (*x,y*) can be in all of the following EXCEPT

(A) Quadrant I
(B) Quadrant II
(C) Quadrant III
(D) Quadrant IV
(E) the *x*- or *y*-axis

5. If the midpoint of AB is $(0,0)$, and if the coordinates of point A are (x,y), then the coordinates of point B are

(A) $(-x,-y)$

(B) $(-x,y)$

(C) $(x,-y)$

(D) (x,y)

(E) None of the preceding answers.

_____

6. If the distance between $(a,3)$ and $(b,9)$ is 10, then $|b - a| =$

(A) 4

(B) 12

(C) 8

(D) 64

(E) It cannot be determined from the information given.

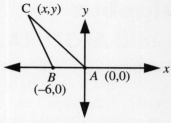

7. If the area of $\triangle ABC$ is 12, then the y-coordinate of C is

(A) -4

(B) 4

(C) -2

(D) 2

(E) It cannot be determined from the information given.

_____

8. A line including the points (x,y) and $(3,7)$ passes through the origin. What is the value of $\dfrac{y}{x}$?

Algebra
BASIC ALGEBRA

This section deals with linear equalities and linear inequalities. It is one of the longest and toughest sections in the book. Set aside extra time and go through all of the practice problems. If you don't understand a problem, check the short answers in the back of this unit. If you don't understand the answer, ask your teacher for help.

Linear Equations

At the very heart of algebra are the variable and the linear equality. We want to know what constant can be put in place of the variable to make the equality a true one. Algebraic problems rarely start out in the form $x = 5$, what is x? In fact they often begin as English descriptions. You have probably heard of the proverbial train that heads east from Chicago. . . .

Formulas and Guidelines

- **Your goal is to isolate the unknown variable,** that is, to end up with an equation that has the variable on one side of the equal sign and everything else on the other.
- **A linear equation is like a balance. As long as you** manipulate both sides of the equation in the same way, the equation remains the same.
- **There are 7 standard manipulations you can perform on equations: divide, multiply, add, or subtract an equal quantity on both sides; square both sides; take the square root of both sides; and invert both sides.**
- **Exceptions to the above rule: you can never divide by 0, and you can never take the square root of a negative number.**

Problems to Watch For

- *Do not mistakenly invert the sum of two fractions. Inversion works only on single fractions.*

Example:

Solve for m in the problem

$$\frac{1}{m} + \frac{1}{n} = \frac{1}{p}.$$

Multiply both sides by the common denominator mnp.

$$np + mp = mn$$

Get all of the m's on the same side by subtracting mp from both sides.

$$np = mn - mp$$

Use the distributive law.

$$np = m(n - p)$$

Divide both sides by $(n - p)$.

$$\frac{np}{n - p} = m$$

It would have been wrong to first try to invert both sides of the equation and get $m + n = p$. The SAT tests to make sure you know this.

- *Always keep in mind what is being asked.* For example: In the previous problem, if you were asked to solve for $\frac{1}{m}$, the steps you would take to solve the problem would be much simpler and much faster.
- *You need to recognize that $a - b = -1(b - a)$.*

Example:

Solve for w in the problem

$$\frac{5}{w - 6} + \frac{7}{6 - w} = 2.$$

Multiply the numerator and denominator of the second fraction by -1. (Remember: multiplying the numerator and denominator of a fraction by the same number does not change the value of the fraction.)

$$\frac{5}{w - 6} + \frac{-7}{w - 6} = 2$$

Add the fractions.

$$\frac{-2}{w - 6} = 2$$

Multiply both sides by $(w - 6)$.

$$-2 = 2w - 12$$

Add 12 to both sides.

$$10 = 2w$$

Divide both sides by 2.

$$5 = w$$

- *Solutions with fractions can have more than one form. If you're confident of your answer, try altering its form.*

Example:

$$2\frac{m}{a} - L = \frac{2m - aL}{a}.$$

- *You can often apply the distributive rule for multiplication over addition to get rid of parentheses and isolate the unknown variable.*

Example:

Solve for y in the problem

$$6(2y + 3) - 3(y + 1) = 3(y + 1) + 3.$$

Eliminate the parentheses.

$$12y + 18 - 3y - 3 = 3y + 3 + 3$$

Collect like terms on both sides of the equation.

$$9y + 15 = 3y + 6$$

Subtract $3y$ from both sides.

$6y + 15 = 6$

Subtract 15 from both sides.

$6y = -9$

Divide by 6 and reduce the fraction to lowest terms.

$$y = \frac{-9}{6} = -\frac{3}{2}$$

Linear Inequalities

A linear inequality is just like a linear equality except that the statement will have either a less than sign ($<$) or a greater than sign ($>$) instead of an equal sign. Being able to manipulate inequalities is extremely important on the SAT. Think about the directions to the quantitative comparison section of the test: you are to determine which column is greater, whether the two columns are equal, or whether the relationship between the two quantities is indeterminable. By knowing how to solve inequalities, you can manipulate quantitative comparison problems in such a way that they are easier to solve, yet the relationship between the values in the two columns is preserved.

Formulas and Guidelines

Each of these rules that follow can be checked with actual numbers, so if you're unsure of a rule during the test, run a quick check; try a negative number, 0, a positive number, and a number between 0 and 1 to cover the major cases.

- **Adding or subtracting a number from both sides of an inequality, whether it is negative or positive, does not change the direction of the sign:**

    $-4 < 2$, so $-4 + 5 < 2 + 5$.

- **Multiplying or dividing by a positive number does not change the direction of the inequality sign:**

    $-4 < 2$, so $-4 \times 5 < 2 \times 5$.

- **Multiplying or dividing by a negative number changes the direction of the inequality sign:**

    $-4 < 2$, so $\dfrac{-4}{-5} > \dfrac{2}{-5}$.

- Taking the square roots of both sides of an inequality does not affect the direction of the inequality sign (but remember, you cannot take the square root of a negative number):

$4 < 9$, so $\sqrt{4} < \sqrt{9}$, so $2 < 3$.

- **Squaring changes the direction of the sign if both values in an inequality are negative. If both values are positive, then it does not. If you don't know the sign of either value or the signs are different, then the effect of squaring is indeterminate.**

- **Inverting both sides changes the direction of the inequality sign if both values have the same sign. If they have different signs, their relationship remains unchanged:**

$-3 < 2$, so $-\dfrac{1}{3} < \dfrac{1}{2}$ and $2 < 3$, so $\dfrac{1}{2} > \dfrac{1}{3}$.

- $a < |x|$ **can be written as** $-x < a < x$.
- $a > |x|$ **can be rewritten as** $a < -x$ **or** $x < a$.
- **Transitivity:** If $a < b$ and $b < c$, then $a < c$. **Note:** If $a < b$ and $a < c$, you know nothing about the relationship between b and c.

Problems to Watch For

- *As trivial as it may sound, do not forget that* $p - r < p < p + r$ *for all positive* r.

Example:

Column A	Column B
p	q

$q < p - 3$

1. You know that $p - 3 < p$, so by transitivity: $q < p - 3 < p$.
2. Column A is greater than column B; the solution is A.

- *If* $x - y$ *is positive, then* $x > y$. *Likewise, if* $x - y$ *is negative, then* $x < y$.

Example:

Column A	Column B
x	y

$a \neq 0$

$x - y = a^2$

1. a^2 is positive for all a except 0, so $x - y > 0$.
2. $x - y > 0$ implies $x > y$. (You are really just adding y to both sides of the inequality.)
3. Column A is greater than column B; the solution is A.

- *Again, although it seems obvious, remember this key fact: All positive numbers are greater than all negative numbers.*

Example:

Column A	Column B

$$st < 0$$

$$0 < t$$

| s | t |

1. Remember the rules for negative numbers and multiplication? The only way that the product of two numbers can be negative is for one of them to be negative and the other positive.
2. Because $0 < t$, s must be the negative number, and t the positive.
3. All positive numbers are greater than all negative numbers, so the value in column B is greater than the value in column A; the answer is B.

- *To solve problems in which you are given several inequalities and asked to determine the relationship between two variables referred to in the inequalities, draw a diagram in which each variable is represented by a circle. To show the relationship $a < c$, draw a circle for a, a circle for c, and a line from a to c with an arrow pointing to c. It makes the diagram easier to read if you put the smaller variables to the left. A variable should not appear in the diagram more than once, so if a variable is referenced in more than one inequality, reuse the circle in the graph. After you have represented all of the inequalities in the diagram, any path from one circle to another that goes in the direction of the arrows indicates that the variable represented by the first circle is less than the variable represented by the second circle.*

Example:

Column A	Column B

$$a < c$$
$$a < d$$
$$d < b$$
$$d < c$$

a	b

1. One inequality at a time, build the diagram of relationships between the variables:

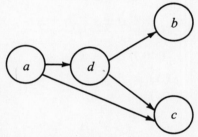

2. There is a path from a on the left to b on the right, so $a < b$. Hence, the answer is B.

• *Remember that a quantitative comparison problem is a lot like an inequality where you are trying to determine the relationship. If there is a lot of hairy arithmetic in each column, simplify using the manipulations that do not change the direction of the inequality sign. Do not waste your time, or chance making a mistake, by doing every bit of arithmetic.*

Example:

Column A	Column B
$\dfrac{38.14 \times 8}{6}$	$\dfrac{38.14 \times 7}{12}$

1. Divide both sides of the inequality by 38.14. This leaves $\dfrac{8}{6}$ on the left and $\dfrac{7}{12}$ on the right.

2. $\dfrac{8}{6}$ is clearly greater than 1 because $8 > 6$, and $\dfrac{7}{12}$ is clearly less than 1, so column B is less than column A. The answer is A.

PRACTICE PROBLEMS IN BASIC ALGEBRA 1

Answers begin on page 293.

1. Solve for x: $\dfrac{2x}{3} + \dfrac{5}{6} = \dfrac{x}{6}$

   (A) $\dfrac{5}{3}$

   (B) -1

   (C) $-\dfrac{5}{3}$

   (D) 1

   (E) -5

2. Solve for y:
   $4(y - 3) + 1 = 2(y + 4) - 3$

   (A) -5
   (B) 2
   (C) 8
   (D) 12
   (E) -8

3. If $\dfrac{1}{x + y} = 2$, then $y =$

   (A) $\dfrac{1}{2} - x$

   (B) $-x$
   (C) $1 - 2x$

   (D) $\dfrac{1}{2} + x$

   (E) $1 + 2x$

4. If $E = IR$, then $R =$

   (A) EI
   (B) $E - I$
   (C) $E + I$

   (D) $\dfrac{I}{E}$

   (E) $\dfrac{E}{I}$

5. If $\dfrac{p + q + r}{3} = \dfrac{p + q}{2}$,
   then $r =$

   (A) $q + p$
   (B) $2p + 2q$

   (C) $\dfrac{1}{2}(p + q)$

   (D) 1
   (E) 3

6. If $a + b = 3$,
   then $a + b - 6 =$

   (A) -3
   (B) 0
   (C) 3
   (D) 6
   (E) 1

7. If $a = b - c$ and $d = c - b$, what is the value of $d - a$ when $b = 4$ and $c = -4$?

   (A) 0

   (B) 8

   (C) −8

   (D) 16

   (E) −16

8. Solve for v if $\dfrac{3}{u} + \dfrac{4}{v} = 1$

   (A) $\dfrac{4u}{u-3}$

   (B) $\dfrac{12-4u}{3}$

   (C) $7 - u$

   (D) $\dfrac{1 - 4u}{3}$

   (E) $\dfrac{3u}{u-4}$

9. If $7x - 4y = 7$ and $x = \dfrac{3}{7}y$, then $x =$

   (A) −7

   (B) −5

   (C) −3

   (D) 5

   (E) 7

10. If $\dfrac{1}{x} > \dfrac{1}{5}$, then which of the following most accurately describes x?

   (A) $x < 5$

   (B) $x > 5$

   (C) $x \leq 5$

   (D) $0 < x < 5$

   (E) $0 \leq x \leq 5$

11. If $y \geq 4$, which of the following has the least value?

   (A) $\dfrac{4}{y + 1}$

   (B) $\dfrac{4}{y-1}$

   (C) $\dfrac{4}{y}$

   (D) $\dfrac{y}{4}$

   (E) $\dfrac{y + 1}{4}$

12. If a and b are positive and $a > b$, then which of the following is always true?

   (A) $\dfrac{b^2}{a^2} > \dfrac{b}{a}$

   (B) $\dfrac{a}{b} > \dfrac{a^2}{b^2}$

   (C) $\dfrac{b^2}{a^2} > 1$

   (D) $\dfrac{b^2}{a^2} > \dfrac{a^2}{b^2}$

   (E) $\dfrac{a^2}{b^2} > \dfrac{a}{b}$

13. If $|2x - 1| > 3$, then which of the following could *not* be a value of x?

   (A) 5
   (B) 3
   (C) -3.5
   (D) -1
   (E) 2^4

_____

14. If p and q are both positive and $q < p$, which of the following is *false*?

   (A) $-4q > -4p$

   (B) $\dfrac{q}{2} < \dfrac{p}{2}$

   (C) $5 - q < 5 - p$

   (D) $\dfrac{-p}{3} < \dfrac{-q}{3}$

   (E) $\dfrac{1}{q} > \dfrac{1}{p}$

_____

15. Solve for x: $4x - 6 \left(3 - \dfrac{1}{2}x\right) = 10$

MORE ALGEBRA

This section reviews polynomial arithmetic, polynomial equations, two equations with two unknowns, and word problems.

Polynomial Arithmetic

Definitions

- **Monomial:** A single number, variable, or product of numbers and variables, e.g., $3x^2y$.
- **Polynomial:** Two or more monomials that are added or subtracted, e.g., $3x^2y + 2z$.
- **Coefficient:** A multiplier that precedes a variable. In the expression $3x^2$, 3 is the coefficient.

Formulas and Guidelines

- **Distributive property:**
  $a(b + c) = ab + bc$: The distributive law is important because it allows you to convert parenthetical expressions to polynomials.
- **Addition and subtraction of polynomials:** When you add two polynomials you must consider each of their monomials independently, and then you may add only monomials whose variables are the same. For example,

  $(2xy + 3x) + (3xy + 4y)$
  $= 5xy + 3x + 4y.$

  There is no way to further simplify this expression.

- **Multiplication of polynomials:** From the distributive property above, you already know how to multiply a monomial by a binomial, $2x(z + w) = 2xz + 2xw$. If you are multiplying a binomial by a binomial, you must do two distributions:

$$(a + b)(c + d)$$

$$= (a + b)c + (a + b)d$$
$$= ac + bc + ad + bd$$

There are several special cases of this and a mnemonic device to help you.

- **FOIL:** This is short for First-Outer-Inner-Last. If you are multiplying two binomials (a polynomial with two monomials), multiply the first monomial of each binomial together, next the outer two, then the inner two, and finally the last two.

Example:

Find the product of $(3a + b)$ and $(c - d)$.

1. Write the binomials side by side and FOIL.

2. Add the partial products, making sure to treat d as a negative.

$$3ac + (-3ad) + bc + (-bd)$$

3. Get rid of the parentheses and change the appropriate signs. Notice that there are no similar terms so you cannot combine any terms.

$$3ac - 3ad + bc - bd$$

- $x^2 - y^2 = (x - y)(x + y)$: Try it using the FOIL rule.
- $(x + a)^2 = x^2 + 2ax + a^2$: Another application of FOIL.
- $(x - a)^2 = x^2 - 2ax + a^2$: Another.
- $(x - a)(x - b) = x^2 - (a + b)x + ab$: And another.

Problems to Watch For

- *Keep the negatives and positives straight when you're doing polynomial math.* It is easy to look at $(x - 5)$ and forget to treat the 5 as negative because it follows a subtraction sign.

183

Example:

Given $x^2 + (x - 5)(3 - x) = 0$, solve for x.

1. First, do the binomial multiplication by FOILing the polynomials to get $x^2 + (3x - x^2 - 15 + 5x) = 0$.

2. Collect the monomials that can be added together: $(x^2 - x^2) + (3x + 5x) - 15 = 0$.

3. Simplify the equation: $8x - 15 = 0$.

4. Do the arithmetic: $x = \dfrac{15}{8}$.

*   *Learn to recognize the special cases listed in the formula section. They will tip you off to the short way of doing a problem.*

Example:

What is $\dfrac{m^2 - n^2}{m + n}$ when $m = 17$ and $n = 15$?

1. Factor $m^2 - n^2$ into $(m - n)(m + n)$, and write the given equation as $\dfrac{(m - n)(m + n)}{m + n}$.

2. Simplify the fraction by dividing $m + n$ into the top and bottom to get $m - n$.

3. Substitute 17 for m and 15 for n, which results in $17 - 15 = 2$.

It would have been tedious and time-consuming if you did not recognize the common factors in the fraction and started by squaring 17 and 15.

Polynomial Equations

When you solve linear equations, your goal is to get the unknown on one side of the equation and everything else on the other. This is not possible in an equation such as $x^2 - 4x + 1 = -2$ and in general cannot happen when a variable is raised to a power and then added to itself. Instead, you must factor the polynomial into its linear (not raised to any power) constituents.

Definition

*   **Factor of a polynomial:** Just as 2 and 4 are factors of 8 because $2 \times 4 = 8$, $(x + 1)$ and $(x - 1)$ are factors of $(x^2 - 1)$ because $(x + 1)(x - 1) = (x^2 - 1)$.

Formulas and Guidelines

- **Zero product rule:** If $ab = 0$, then $a = 0$ or $b = 0$.
- **Solving a polynomial equation:** Get all of the monomials on one side of the equation, and leave a 0 on the other. Then factor the polynomial so you are left with the product of two binomials equaling zero. Using the zero product rule, you can deduce that one of the binomials must equal 0.

Example:

Given $x^2 - 4x + 1 = -2$, solve for x.

1. Collect all of the monomials on the left: $x^2 - 4x + 3 = 0$. This step is very important; otherwise, you won't be able to apply the zero product rule.
2. Factor the polynomial: $(x - 3)(x - 1) = 0$.
3. Using the zero product rule, you know that either $(x - 3) = 0$ or $(x - 1) = 0$. Solving these two linear equations, you get $x = 3$ or $x = 1$.

- **Factoring polynomials:**
  Remember that $(x - a)(x - b) = x^2 - (a + b)x + ab$. What you know about multiplication with positive and negative numbers can help you factor polynomials. Notice that:

1. The product of the constants a and b in the monomials is the constant in the polynomial.
2. The sum of the constants in the monomials is the opposite (negative) of the coefficient of the first-order term (the term with the variable raised to the first power).

For example: If you were asked to factor $x^2 + 2x - 24$, you would first note that the product of the constants in the monomials is -24, and then you would think that their sum is -2. The factors of -24 are:

-1 and 24	-6 and 4
-2 and 12	-8 and 3
-3 and 8	-12 and 2
-4 and 6	-24 and 1

The only pair that add to -2 are -6 and 4, so $x^2 + 2x - 24 = [x - (-6)](x - 4) = (x + 6)(x - 4)$.

- **Check your answers!** Remember that you're solving an equation, so if you stick your answers back into the original equation it should become a true statement and not something like $4 = 0$.

Two Equations with Two Unknowns

In the previous section you reviewed how to solve linear equations. This type of problem is also called one equation (only one equal sign) with one unknown (only one variable). An extension of this is two equations with two unknowns. There are two methods for solving this type of problem. Sometimes one is easier than the other, but both work all of the time.

Formulas and Guidelines
- **Combination method of solving two equations with two unknowns:** This method works best when the coefficient of one of the unknowns is the same in the two equations.

  1. Start with two equations with two unknowns, for example $3x + 2y = 33$ and $4x = 11 + y$.

2. Write the two equations one on top of the other:
$$3x + 2y = 33$$
$$4x = 11 + y$$

3. Manipulate the equations so like variables line up:
$$3x + 2y = 33$$
$$4x - y = 11$$

4. Manipulate the equations so that the coefficients in front of one of the variables are the same or opposite in the two equations. In this case, multiply both sides of the second equation by 2 so that the coefficients in front of y are 2 and -2:
$$3x + 2y = 33$$
$$8x - 2y = 22$$

5. If the matching coefficients are opposites, as they are here (-2 and 2), then add the two equations to generate a third:
$$11x + 0y = 55$$
If the coefficients were the same instead of opposites, then you would subtract the two equations. Keep in mind that *the goal is to get one of the coefficients to go to 0.*

6. The variable with the opposite coefficients (the y in this case) will drop out, so you have one equation with one variable, which you can manipulate and solve. In this case, you will get $x = 5$.

7. To solve for the other variable, substitute the value you find for the first variable into either of the original equations and solve the resulting equation. In this case, you will get $y = 9$.

- **Substitution method of solving two equations with two unknowns.** This method works best when the coefficient in front of one of the unknowns is 1 or -1.

  1. Start with two equations. Again take the example $3x + 2y = 33$ and $4x = 11 + y$.

  2. This time the first step is to use one of the equations to solve for one of the variables in terms of the other. Taking the second equation and manipulating it, you can find y as a function of x: $y = 4x - 11$.

3. Next, for every occurrence of y in the first equation substitute its value in terms of x as determined by the second equation, to yield: $3x + 2(4x - 11) = 33$.

4. Now you have reduced the problem to one equation with one unknown, which, with some manipulation, reduces to $11x = 55$ or $x = 5$.

5. Again you substitute the value of x back into either equation to find $y = 9$.

Word Problems

There is no one type of word problem. Word problems can involve concepts from arithmetic to probability. The common thread in all word problems is that you must first generate the equation before you can solve the problem. As you are setting up the equation, remember that *every equation needs an equal sign*. Once you have solved your equation, go back and check the answer. Answers to word problems are usually relatively quick and easy to check.

QUICK TIP

Here's how to solve a word problem:

Define what you are solving for and assign it a mnemonic variable name.

Taking one phrase at a time, set up the equation(s) that model(s) the problem.

Solve the equation(s).

Check your answer.

Problems to Watch For

- *The term "increased by" indicates that you should keep the original amount and add an additional amount. Do not forget to keep the original amount.*

Example:

Stephanie's company had a profit of $900 during its first month of operation. If its profits increased by $66\frac{2}{3}\%$ during the second month of operation, what are its second-month profits in dollars?

1. First, you are solving for second-month profits.

2. Set up the equation, one phrase at a time, recalling that $66\frac{2}{3}\% = \frac{2}{3}$:

(a) The profits of the first month are 900.

(b) The profits of the first month are increased by $\frac{2}{3}$:

$$900 + \left(\frac{2}{3}\right)900.$$

3. Solve the equation to get $900 + 600 = 1,500$.

4. Check the results: Is 1,500 two thirds more than 900? Yes. (If you had mistakenly omitted the original $900, your answer would be $600, which clearly is not an increase.)

- *Age problems are common on the SAT. If you give each person his or her own variable and work the problem phrase by phrase, you should have no difficulty setting up the appropriate equations.*

Example:

A father is four times as old as his daughter. Ten years ago he was only twice as old as his daughter will be in five years. How old was the father when his daughter was born?

1. Name the variables:

    (a) Call the father's age now F.

    (b) Call the daughter's age now D.

    (c) Because the question doesn't ask for F or D, call the answer A.

2. Set up the equations phrase by phrase:

    (a) $F =$ A father is

    (b) $F = 4D$ four times as old as his daughter.

    (c) $F - 10$ Ten years ago

    (d) $F - 10 =$ he was only

    (e) $F - 10 = 2(\ldots)$ twice

    (f) $F - 10 = 2(D + 5)$ as old as his daughter will be in five years.

    (g) $A = F - D$ How old was the father when his daughter was born?

3. Solve the equations $F = 4D$ and $F - 10 = 2(D + 5)$:

    (a) $4D - 10 = 2(D + 5)$
    Substitute $4D$ for F in the second equation.

    (b) $4D - 10 = 2D + 10$
    Distribute the 2 over the sum $(D + 5)$.

    (c) $2D = 20$
    Subtract $2D$ and add 10 to both sides.

    (d) $D = 10$
    Divide both sides by 2.

    (e) $F = 4D = 40$
    Go back to the original equation to solve for F.

    (f) $A = F - D = 40 - 10 = 30$
    Go back to the original equation to solve what was asked for.

4. Check your answer: 40 is four times 10, and $40 - 10 = 30$, which is two times $10 + 5 = 15$. All of the criteria for the problem have been met.

- *Forms of the verb "to be" indicate equality.* In step 2 of the previous example, circle each instance of the verb "to be" and notice how it corresponds to the insertion of an equal sign into the equations. The words "is," "was," and "will be" are examples of the verb "to be."

- *When one person gives something to another, the first person's total goes down and the other person's goes up.*

Example:

Chris and Andrea have $100 together. If Chris gives Andrea $10, she will have $20 more than he will. How much money did Chris start with?

1. You are solving for the amount Chris started with. Call it C. Call the amount Andrea started with A.

2. Set up the equations:
   (a) $C + A = 100$
       Chris and Andrea have $100 together.
   (b) $(C - 10) = (A + 10) - 20$
       If Chris gives Andrea $10, she will have $20 more than he will.

3. Solve the equations:
   (a) $C = A$
       Add 10 to both sides of the second equation.
   (b) $C + C = 100$
       Substitute C for A in the first equation
   (c) $C = 50$
       and solve.

4. Check the answer.
   (a) Chris and Andrea each have $50, which sums to $100.
   (b) If Chris gives Andrea $10, he will have $40 and she will have $60, which is $20 more than his $40.

- *If a person uses $\frac{a}{b}$ of something, then $\frac{b - a}{b}$ is left over. Notice that these two fractions added together equal 1. What is used plus what is left over equals the whole. When setting up a problem, keep track of whether you want to know how much was used or how much is left over.*

Example:

Jasper spends $\frac{1}{4}$ of his salary on rent and $\frac{1}{3}$ of what's left over on food. If Jasper's monthly salary is $1600, how much does he have left over after he pays for rent and food?

1. What's left over after Jasper pays his rent is $\frac{3}{4}$ (1600).

2. One third of that goes to food, so what is left over is $\left(\frac{3 - 1}{3}\right)\left(\frac{3}{4}\right)$(1600).

3. Simplify the expression before multiplying by fractions to get $\frac{1}{2}(1600)$.

4. $\frac{1}{2}(1600) = \$800$ is left over after Jasper pays for food and rent.

PRACTICE PROBLEMS IN BASIC ALGEBRA 2

Answers begin on page 294.

1. On a given day in February, the temperature in a town ranged from -12 to 19 degrees. What is the difference between the high and the low temperature for the day?

    (A) 7
    (B) 31
    (C) 21
    (D) -31
    (E) -21

2. If a woman is paid c dollars per hour for every hour she works up to 8 hours and is paid double for every hour she works after 8 hours, how many dollars will she be paid for working 13 hours?

    (A) $13c$
    (B) $\frac{13}{c}$

    (C) $\frac{c}{18}$
    (D) $18c$
    (E) $\frac{18}{c}$

3. A number is multiplied by another number. The product is then divided by the difference between the two numbers. What is the result?

    (A) $\frac{xy}{x-y}$
    (B) $\frac{x+y}{x-y}$
    (C) $\frac{x-y}{xy}$
    (D) $\frac{xy}{x+y}$
    (E) $\frac{x-y}{x+y}$

4. The volume of a box is 24 cubic inches. If its length is 3 inches and its width is 8 inches, what is its depth in inches?

(A) 0
(B) 1
(C) 2
(D) 3
(E) 4

_____

5. Bill had x dollars and he bought y apples for 16 cents each and z pears for 12 cents each. How many cents did he have left?

(A) $x - 16y + 12z$
(B) $100x + 6y + 12z$
(C) $x - 16y - 12z$
(D) $x - (y + z)$
(E) $100x - 16y - 12z$

_____

6. If 3 is subtracted from a certain number, then the result is 6 more than twice the number. Find the number.

(A) -3
(B) -9
(C) 3
(D) $\dfrac{9}{7}$
(E) $\dfrac{-9}{7}$

7. One third the sum of 13 and a certain number is the same as 1 more than twice the number. Find the number.

(A) $\dfrac{36}{5}$
(B) 12
(C) $\dfrac{12}{5}$
(D) 2
(E) -2

_____

8. Tom has a brother one third his age and a sister three times his age. If the combined age of all three children is five less than twice the oldest, how old is Tom?

(A) 3
(B) 6
(C) 9
(D) 1
(E) 12

_____

9. How many 32-cent stamps can be purchased for d dollars?

(A) $32d$
(B) $\dfrac{d}{32}$
(C) $\dfrac{32}{d}$
(D) $\dfrac{100d}{32}$
(E) $\dfrac{32}{100d}$

10. A woman left one fourth of her estate to her son and one third of her estate to her daughter. If she left the balance of $10,000 to charity, how large was her estate?

(A) $120,000
(B) $170,000
(C) $24,000
(D) $48,000
(E) $12,000

11. A woman buys a pound of steak for $3.00. If the meat loses one fourth of its weight when cooked, what is the cost per pound when it is served at the table?

(A) $2.25
(B) $3.00
(C) $3.75
(D) $4.00
(E) $4.50

12. A gas tank that is one third full requires 6 gallons to make it five sixths full. What is the capacity of the tank in gallons?

(A) 2
(B) 36
(C) 12
(D) 48
(E) 24

13. Four years ago my age was half of what it will be in eight years. How old am I?

14. One quarter of the students at a high school take algebra. One fifth of the students take geometry. The remaining 110 students do not take any math. How many students are there at the school?

15. A man goes to a bank with $4.00 and asks for change. He is given an equal number of nickels, dimes, and quarters. How many of each is he given?

16. The difference of the squares of two numbers is 9. The difference of the two numbers is 1. What is their sum?

17. Ten houses line one side of a street. The average space between the houses is 60 feet more than the average width of the houses. A sidewalk starts 60 feet before the first house and ends 60 feet after the last house. If the total length of the sidewalk is 3,206 feet, find the average width of the houses in feet.

COMMON ALGEBRAIC APPLICATIONS

This section is devoted to odd and even numbers and remainders, averages, and functions.

Odds, Evens, and Remainders

Definitions

- **Integer:** The numbers we use to count with, 0, 1, 2, 3, . . . , and their opposites, -1, -2, -3, . . .

QUICK TIPS

The knowledge you need to prove the five statements on page 196 is exactly what the SAT tests in the area of odd and even numbers.

To prove the second statement, $O \times O = O$, let the first odd number be $2n + 1$ and the second be $2m + 1$. Their product is

$$(2n + 1)(2m + 1)$$
$$= 4mn + 2n + 2m + 1$$
$$= 2(2mn + n + m) + 1$$

which is 2 times some number (admittedly a rather complex one) plus 1, one of the definitions of an odd number.

- **Remainder:** If, when a number x is divided into a number y, x goes into y a certain number of whole times with a bit left over that is less than x, the leftover amount is the remainder. For example, when 13 is divided by 5, 5 goes into 13 twice to get up to 10, with 3 left over. So 3 is the remainder.

- **Even number:** A number that is evenly divisible by 2, that is, a number that leaves no remainder when divided by 2. Even numbers always end in 0, 2, 4, 6, or 8.

- **Odd number:** A number that is not evenly divisible by 2. When an odd number is divided by 2, the remainder is always 1. Odd numbers always end in 1, 3, 5, 7, or 9.

Formulas and Guidelines

- **The remainder equation:** If dividing x by y has a remainder r, then you can set up the equation $x = ny + r$, where n is some integer and r is the remainder. For example, 13 divided by 5 has remainder 3, so you can set up the equation: $13 = 5n + 3$. In this case, $n = 2$. *When* y *evenly divides* x, r *is 0.*

- $E = 2n$: Any even number, E, can be written as the product of 2 and some other number. Remember, an even number is defined to be a number that is evenly divisible by 2.

- $O = 2n + 1$: Every odd number, O, can be written $O = 2n + 1$ for some n.

- **$2n$ is always even and $2n + 1$ is always odd, for any integer n.**
- **$E \times ? = E$:** An even number times any number is even.

  $O \times O = O$: An odd number times an odd is odd.

  $E + E = E$: An even plus an even is even.

  $E + O = O$: An even plus an odd is odd.

  $O + O = E$: An odd plus an odd is even.

If during the test you are unsure of one of these rules, just think of 1 and 2; 1 is odd, 2 is even, and 3 is odd, so an odd plus an even is odd.

Problems to Watch For
- *Concepts such as using something a certain number of times with an amount left over are a clue to you, as the problem solver, to try to apply the remainder equation.*

Example:
Betsy has a box of candy with fewer than 20 pieces of candy in it. If she splits the candy up evenly among herself and 3 friends, there is 1 piece left over. If she splits the candy evenly among her 3 friends but ex-cludes herself, there is still 1 piece left over. How many pieces of candy does Betsy have?

We use the remainder equation twice, once with Betsy and once without:

> With Betsy, pieces of candy $= 4n + 1$.

> Without Betsy, pieces of candy $= 3m + 1$.

Therefore, 1 less than the number of pieces of candy is divisible by both 3 and 4.

The only number less than 20 that is divisible by both 3 and 4 is 12.

So, the number of pieces of candy is 13.

Now go back and check your answer: When 13 pieces of candy are split among 3 people, there is 1 left over, and when 13 pieces of candy are split among 4 people, there is still 1 left over.

Average

Definitions
- **Average:** The sum of the quantities divided by the number of quantities. For example, the average of 1, 10, and 100 is the sum of 1, 10, and 100—or 111—divided by 3, which is 37.

QUICK TIP

If you're working on a multiple-choice question and are having trouble with the math, this is also a good time to try the "pick and plug" method of getting the answer.

There are only five possible solutions on the SAT, so try each of them. Quite often, if you are stumped on a problem like this, you can check the multiple-choice answers and find the one that fits.

- **Arithmetic mean:** Another name for *average.*

Formulas

- **Average** = $\dfrac{\text{Sum}}{\text{Number}}$, by definition of average.
- **Sum = Number × Average,** by simple algebraic manipulation.
- **Number** = $\dfrac{\text{Sum}}{\text{Average}}$, by simple algebraic manipulation.

Problems to Watch For

- *Not all problems that deal with averages ask you to solve for the average of a set of quantities. Often you will have to use the average to compute either the sum of the quantities, the value of an individual quantity, or the number of quantities.*

Example:

After he took his fourth quiz, Bill's average dropped from 78 to 75. What was Bill's last quiz grade?

1. The average of the first three quizzes is 78, so their sum is 78 × 3 = 234.
2. The average of all four of the quizzes is 75, so their sum is 75 × 4 = 300.
3. The difference is the score on the fourth quiz: 300 − 234 = 66.

- *Many people falsely believe that they cannot find a solution if they can't solve for every variable in a problem.*

Example:

The average of 5 numbers is 6, and the average of 3 of the 5 numbers is 4. What is the average of the other 2?

1. The average of the 5 numbers is 6, so their sum is 30, (6 × 5).

2. By the same logic, the sum of the first 3 numbers is 3 × 4 = 12.

3. So the sum of the last 2 numbers is 30 − 12 = 18.

4. Finally, 2 numbers whose sum is 18 have an average of 9.

5. Notice that you never did (and never could) solve for any of the individual numbers.

Functions

Definition

- **Function:** For the SAT, you should think of a function as a special symbol that tells you how to combine the numbers around it.

Guideline

- **Follow directions and use brute force:** For almost every math question on the SAT, there is a concept that makes the path to the solution much simpler. Not so with functions. The trick is to muddle through the problem, carefully following directions without being overwhelmed by the strange symbols.

Example:

The symbol $\begin{vmatrix} p & q \\ r & s \end{vmatrix}$ means $ps - rq$.

What is the value of $\begin{vmatrix} 2 & 3 \\ 5 & 4 \end{vmatrix}$?

Using the rule that was given to evaluate the problem, you get:

$$\begin{vmatrix} 2 & 3 \\ 5 & 4 \end{vmatrix} = \overset{p}{(2} \times \overset{s}{4)} - \overset{r}{(5} \times \overset{q}{3)}$$
$$= 8 - 15 = -7.$$

PRACTICE PROBLEMS IN ALGEBRAIC APPLICATIONS 1

Answers begin on page 295.

1. What is the average of $2x + 1$, $x + 5$, $1 - 4x$, $3x + 1$?

   (A) $2x + 1$
   (B) $2x + 4$
   (C) $\frac{1}{2}x + 2$
   (D) $\frac{x + 4}{4}$
   (E) $\frac{2x + 4}{4}$

2. Two members of a basketball team weigh 150 and 175 pounds. A third team member's weight is between the other 2. Which of the following cannot possibly be the average weight of the 3 players?

   (A) 159
   (B) 161
   (C) 163
   (D) 165
   (E) 167

3. The average of P and another number is A. The other number must be

   (A) $A - P$
   (B) $\frac{AP}{2}$
   (C) $2P - A$
   (D) $2A - P$
   (E) $\frac{2A + P}{2}$

4. The average grade of 10 students is x. If 5 other students each earned a grade of 84, what would be the average grade of the entire group?

   (A) $\frac{x + 84}{2}$
   (B) $\frac{x + 420}{5}$
   (C) $\frac{10x + 84}{15}$
   (D) $\frac{10x + 420}{15}$
   (E) None of the above

5. For all positive integers, if $(p,q \uparrow x,y) = py - qx$, then $(4,6 \uparrow 8,2) =$

   (A) -40
   (B) 56
   (C) 40
   (D) 44
   (E) 20

6. For all positive numbers x, if $\downarrow x = (x - 1)^2$, then $\downarrow \dfrac{3}{4} =$

   (A) $-\dfrac{1}{16}$

   (B) $\dfrac{1}{16}$

   (C) $-\dfrac{49}{16}$

   (D) $\dfrac{49}{16}$

   (E) None of the above

7. If $x \; O \; y$ means $y^2 - 2x^2$, then $2 \; O \; (-3) =$

   (A) -7
   (B) -1
   (C) 1
   (D) 5
   (E) None of the above

8. If $p \; \square \; q = \left(\dfrac{p - 1}{q + 1}\right)^2$, then $\dfrac{3}{2} \; \square \; \dfrac{2}{3} =$

   (A) $\dfrac{3}{10}$

   (B) $\dfrac{9}{10}$

   (C) $\dfrac{9}{100}$

   (D) 1

   (E) 9

9. If $x\uparrow = 3x$ and $x\downarrow = \dfrac{1}{3}x$, then $x\uparrow$ times $x\downarrow$ would equal

   (A) 1
   (B) x
   (C) $3x$
   (D) $\dfrac{1}{3}x$
   (E) x^2

10. Let $\lfloor x \rfloor$ denote the greatest integer less than or equal to x. For example, $\lfloor 3.4 \rfloor = 3$ and $\lfloor -1 \rfloor = -1$. What is the value of $\lfloor -2.3 \rfloor + \lfloor 2.3 \rfloor$?

    (A) 0
    (B) -1
    (C) 1
    (D) 2
    (E) 4.6

11. If $a \star b = a^2 b^3$, then $3 \star (-2) =$

   (A) -6
   (B) 24
   (C) -24
   (D) 72
   (E) -72

12. Frank can cut a lawn in $2\frac{1}{2}$ hours; Tom cuts the same lawn in $1\frac{3}{4}$ hours. What is the average length of time in hours that it takes the 2 of them to cut the lawn?

13. If $A \star B \star C = \dfrac{\dfrac{A}{B}}{C}$ for all positive integers, what is the value of $3 \star 4 \star 6$?

14. If $\boxed{\triangle y} = (y + 1)^2 - (y - 1)^2 + 1$, what is the value of $\boxed{\triangle 3}$?

15. If $\textcircled{p} = \dfrac{p}{4}$, for what value of p does $\textcircled{p} = 3$?

LESS COMMON ALGEBRAIC APPLICATIONS

This section treats sequences, probability, pictorial representations of data, and time.

Sequences

Definitions

- **Sequence:** An ordered list of objects or numbers.
- **Repeating sequence:** A sequence that can be characterized by a few elements that are repeated in a given order. For example, a decoration is made by hanging colored streamers from a rope. The colors form the pattern red, white, blue, red, white, blue, . . . The colors form a repeating sequence.

- **Consecutive integers:** A sequence of integers, such as 3, 4, and 5, without gaps.
- **Consecutive even integers:** A sequence of even integers, such as -6, -4, and -2, without gaps.
- **Consecutive odd integers:** A sequence of odd integers, such as -1, 1, 3, and 5, without gaps.

Formulas and Guidelines

- **Representing consecutive integers:** When a problem refers to unknown consecutive integers, let the smallest one be x, the next one be $x + 1$, and so on.
- **Representing consecutive even or odd integers:** When a problem refers to unknown consecutive even or odd integers, let the smallest one be x, the next one be $x + 2$, the next be $x + 4$, and so on. Notice that you use $x + 2 \ldots$ for both even and odd integers.
- **nth element rule for repeating sequences:** In a repeating sequence with n elements in the pattern, every element that occupies a position divisible by n is the same as the nth element. For example, given a decoration made by hanging colored streamers from a rope in the pattern red, white, blue,

red, white, blue, . . . , there are 3 colors in the base pattern, so every flag that occupies a position divisible by 3 is blue.

- **To solve a problem that asks you to find the nth object in a repeating sequence:**

1. **Isolate and count the number of elements in the pattern.**
2. **Find a number near n that is divisible by the number of elements in the pattern—you know what element that will be from the nth element rule.**
3. **Count off from the known element to the one you are asked to find.**

Example:

Determine what color the 100th flag is in the aforementioned streamer.

1. There are 3 elements, and the 3rd element is blue.
2. 102 is divisible by 3 (because $1 + 0 + 2 = 3$), so the 102nd streamer must be blue.
3. Counting backward, the 101st is white, and the 100th is red.

Problems to Watch For

- *If you are comfortable with keeping the meaning of your variables straight during a long problem, it is often easier to let the middle number in a sequence be a variable, say* x, *and the numbers around it be* x − 1, x + 1, x − 2, x + 2, . . .

Example:

The sum of 3 consecutive odd numbers is 33. What is the largest number?

1. Call the middle number m, the one less than it $m - 2$, and the one greater than it $m + 2$.
2. Setting up the equation with m as the middle number, you get: $(m - 2) + m + (m + 2) = 33$.
3. Simplify the left side of the equation: $3m = 33$ and solve to get $m = 11$.
4. Remember to go back and find the largest number, $m + 2$. The variable m stands for the middle one: $m + 2 = 11 + 2 = 13$.

- *If you are told that the difference between consecutive numbers in a sequence is constant, you should usually start the problem by determining the constant difference.*

Example:

The difference between consecutive numbers in the sequence 3, *a*, *b*, and 24 is constant. Find *b*.

1. It takes 3 steps to get from 3 to 24, and the difference between 3 and 24 is 21, so each step must be 7 long.
2. *a* is one step after 3, so $a = 3 + 7 = 10$.
3. *b* is one step after *a*, so $b = a + 7 = 10 + 7 = 17$.
4. Test the solution: The differences between 3 and 10, 10 and 17, and 17 and 24 are all 7, so you have satisfied the conditions placed by the problem.

Probability

Formulas and Guidelines

- **The probability that something will happen** is represented by the number of times the something happens divided by the number of times anything can happen. This is exactly the part-whole relationship that a fraction represents. For example, if there are 2 blue marbles and 4 red marbles in a bag, then the chance of reaching in and randomly choosing a blue marble is $\frac{2}{6}$,

2 blue marbles divided by 6 marbles total.

- **The probability that two independent events will occur is the product of their individual probabilities (not the sum!).** For example, if you were to pull a marble out of the aforementioned bag, put it back in the bag, and randomly choose a marble again, the chance that both marbles you chose were blue is $\left(\frac{2}{6}\right)\left(\frac{2}{6}\right) = \frac{4}{36} = \frac{1}{9}$.

Pictorial Representations of Data

Most information on the SAT is given to you in the form of mathematical statements or in words that translate into mathematical statements. However, one or two problems on each test present data in the form of a graph. Questions pertaining to the graph can involve concepts that range from arithmetic to probability. What is being tested is your ability to glean the information from the picture.

Except for pie charts, most graphs are two-dimensional with rows and columns. Each row and each column represents some value. *Where a row and a column meet correlates those two values.* The rows should have units that are explicitly labeled and so should the columns. Furthermore, the graph will often have a title, which explains the significance of where the rows and columns meet. If you are able to determine the title of a graph, what the rows represent, and what the columns represent, you will have an easier time interpreting the information in the graph.

Anatomy of a Graph

A problem based on the following graph is apt to ask a question about the batting average of a specific game or to compare a series of games.

Example:

In which game did the Beavers' batting average drop the most?

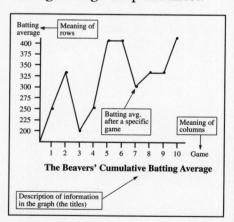

The Beavers' Cumulative Batting Average

Glancing quickly across, you will see that the steepest drop is from game 2 to 3; so in game 3 the Beavers' average dropped the most.

Time

Definitions
- **1 hour = 60 minutes**
- **1 minute = 60 seconds**
- **15 minutes = $\dfrac{1}{4}$ hour**
- **30 minutes = $\dfrac{1}{2}$ hour**

Formulas and Guidelines
- **Addition of times:**

1. Add the minutes together.
2. Add the hours together.
3. If the minutes are greater than 60, then
   (a) subtract 60 from the minutes, and
   (b) add 1 to the hours.
4. If the hours are greater than 12, then subtract 12 from the hours.

Example:

If you start bicycling at 12:40 and finish 50 minutes later, when will you be done?

1. 40 + 50 = 90 minutes
2. 12 + 0 = 12 hours

3. There are 90 minutes, which is greater than 60, so

    (a) $90 - 60 = 30$ minutes

    (b) $12 + 1 = 13$ hours

4. There are 13 hours, which is greater than 12, so $13 - 12 = 1$ hour

5. You are done at 1 hour and 30 minutes or 1:30.

• **Subtraction of times:**

1. Subtract the hours of the second time from the hours of the first.

2. Subtract the minutes of the second time from the minutes of the first.

3. If the resulting minutes are negative, then

    (a) add 60 to the minutes, and

    (b) subtract 1 from the hours.

4. If the resulting hours are negative, then add 12 to the hours.

Example:

If you want to watch a ball game beginning at 1:20 and have $1\frac{1}{2}$ hours of homework to do first, what is the latest time you can start doing your homework?

1. $1\frac{1}{2}$ hours is written 1:30 so you will need to solve $1{:}20 - 1{:}30 = x.$

2. $1 - 1 = 0$ hours

3. $20 - 30 = -10$ minutes

4. The resulting number of minutes is negative, so

    (a) -10 minutes $+ 60 = 50$ minutes

    (b) 0 hours $- 1 = -1$ hour

5. The resulting number of hours is negative, so -1 hour $+ 12 = 11$

6. You must start working by 11:50 to see all of the game.

PRACTICE PROBLEMS IN
ALGEBRAIC APPLICATIONS 2

Answers begin on page 297.

1. Josephine worked in the library for 45 minutes and then took a 5-minute break. If she continues this cycle throughout the day, what is the chance that someone would randomly walk into the library and find her working?

   (A) $\dfrac{1}{15}$

   (B) $\dfrac{1}{10}$

   (C) $\dfrac{1}{2}$

   (D) $\dfrac{9}{10}$

   (E) $\dfrac{14}{15}$

2. Donald is about to sit down and study at 7:45 P.M. First, he decides to saunter down to the refrigerator for 20 minutes and make a sandwich. As he's walking back to his desk, he stops at the den and stands in the doorway, catching 15 minutes of an "I Love Lucy" rerun. Finally, he settles down and works until 9:45. How long did he actually spend working?

   (A) 1:15
   (B) 1:25
   (C) 1:30
   (D) 1:45
   (E) 2:00

3. The sum of 5 consecutive odd integers exceeds 3 times the largest by 6. Find the sum of the integers.

   (A) 25
   (B) 30
   (C) 35
   (D) 40
   (E) 45

4. In a certain gym class the coach has the students line up and count off by fours. All of the ones are on Team A, the twos are on Team B, the threes are on Team C, and the fours are on Team D. On which team will the 53rd student be?

(A) Team A
(B) Team B
(C) Team C
(D) Team D
(E) Cannot be determined without knowing the total number of students.

Test No.	% Correct
1	90%
2	75%
3	95%
4	90%
5	85%

5. The above table shows the percent correct Olga received on each of five 60-question tests. What was the total number of questions Olga answered correctly during the five tests?

(A) 87
(B) 255
(C) 261
(D) 270
(E) 300

6. The image above is the face of a clock as it would be seen in a mirror. What is the time shown?

(A) 1:20
(B) 4:05
(C) 11:40
(D) 12:05
(E) 12:20

Column A	Column B

You reach into a jar filled with an equal number of pennies, nickels, dimes, and quarters, 600 coins total, and pull out a single coin.

7.

The probability that you will randomly grab a quarter	$\dfrac{25}{41}$

Column A   **Column B**

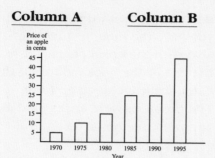

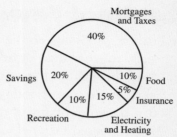

8.

The percentage increase in the price of an apple from 1970 to 1975	The percentage increase in the price of an apple from 1990 to 1995

9. The sum of 5 consecutive even integers is equal to 3 times the largest. What is the largest of the integers?

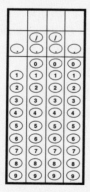

10. The pie chart shows Della's monthly budget as percentages. If her monthly income is $5000, how many dollars would she save each month if the electric and heating bills were reduced by 20%?

The Final Few

The last few problems on the SAT are usually tougher than those you'll find throughout the rest of the test. If you're not shooting for an 800, are unsure of any of the previously covered material, or just want to be finished, then don't bother with this section. If you have the time, feel comfortable with the concepts taught in the rest of the book, and want the extra challenge, then go for it. The problems here are as hard as any you'll see on an SAT.

PRACTICE WITH THE FINAL FEW

Answers begin on page 298.

1. The average of the remainders when 5 is divided into 5 consecutive positive integers is

    (A) 1
    (B) 2
    (C) 1.2
    (D) 3
    (E) 4

2. The function * is defined by the equation:

    $$x * y = \frac{x + y}{xy} \quad (xy \neq 0)$$

    I. $a * b = b * a$
    II. $(a * b) * c = a * (b * c)$
    III. $a * (b + c) = a * b + a * c$

    Of the properties listed, the ones that are true for all nonzero a, b, and c are

    (A) I only
    (B) I and II
    (C) II and III
    (D) I and III
    (E) I, II, and III

3. A square is drawn inside a circle in such a way that the diagonals of the square pass through the center of the circle, and the vertices of the square touch the circle's edge. If the square has side $a\sqrt{2}$, then the area of the circle is

(A) $\frac{1}{4}\pi a^2$

(B) $\frac{1}{2}\pi a^2$

(C) πa^2

(D) $\sqrt{2}\pi a^2$

(E) $2\pi a^2$

4. At a movie the cost of an adult's ticket is $1.50 and the cost of a student's ticket is $0.75. If 500 people see the show and spend a total of $450, how many of the people who saw the show were students?

(A) 100
(B) 200
(C) 300
(D) 400
(E) It cannot be determined from the information given.

5. In a town there are fewer than 30 unlicensed dogs. If $\frac{2}{5}$ of the unlicensed dogs are males and $\frac{3}{8}$ of the unlicensed male dogs are beagles, then how many unlicensed dogs are there in the town?

(A) 20
(B) 25
(C) 30
(D) 40
(E) It cannot be determined from the information given.

6. After the first two quarters at school, Buffy had an 87% average. What is the lowest average Buffy can have during the third quarter and still be able to have a 90% average for the year?

(A) 83
(B) 86
(C) 87
(D) 93
(E) 96

7. *G* girls share the cost of buying *P* pizzas at *D* dollars per pizza. *B* boys decide to join the girls. If no new pizzas are ordered and all of the boys and girls pay an equal share of the total cost of the pizzas, then how much less is each girl's share of the cost than it would have been if the boys hadn't come?

(A) $\dfrac{PDB}{G(B + G)}$

(B) $\dfrac{PD}{B + G}$

(C) $\dfrac{PD}{G}$

(D) $\dfrac{PD(B + G)}{BG}$

(E) $\dfrac{PD}{B}$

---

8. At a carnival a booth is set up with a chance game that costs 15 cents to play. The first person to play wins a penny, the second person a nickel, the third person a dime, and the fourth a quarter. The cycle is repeated infinitely with the fifth person winning a penny and so on. After 43 people have played the game, how much money has the booth made as a net profit?

(A) $2.06
(B) $2.19
(C) $3.00
(D) $4.30
(E) $6.45

---

9. If $x^2 + y^2 = 25$ and $xy = -5$, then $(x - y)^2 =$

(A) 15
(B) 20
(C) 25
(D) 30
(E) 35

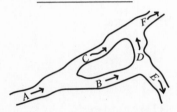

10. The river Paix flows in the directions indicated by the arrows on the map above. If $\dfrac{5}{8}$ of the water flowing from channel *A* takes channel *B*, and $\dfrac{3}{5}$ of the water from channel *B* takes channel *D*, then what percentage of the water takes channel *F*?

(A) 25%
(B) 33.3%
(C) 37.5%
(D) 62.5%
(E) 75%

UNIT 5

THE TEST SECTION

Are you on schedule?
Check the prep plan on pages vi and vii.

This unit allows you to put all of your new skills to work in more formal test situations. You should be watchful as you go through the various questions so that you can decide which require the most time, which the least, and so on. Also note which questions you handle least well, and *concentrate on bettering your approach to those.*

If you find specific problems that this book does not discuss, explain your difficulty to a helpful math or English teacher who is familiar with the SAT I or PSAT. Show the teacher your test materials and point out which problems give you fits; no doubt you two will devise a remedy. Most teachers want to aid students, but they can do so best when they're alerted to a specific need.

The first test consists of 40 actual problems from past SAT I exams. Because neither the math nor the verbal question section is the equivalent of a 30-minute test segment, do not worry about timing when working these problems. Notice instead how the questions are designed, what words are used to frame them, and how their level of difficulty compares with that of our Practice SAT questions. We believe you'll see that many actual SAT I questions are *simpler* than the practice questions we've written. We deliberately asked as much as possible from you on *our* test so that an actual SAT or PSAT would be a welcome surprise instead of a nasty shock.

The Practice SAT is designed to be as nearly like an actual SAT as possible. You'll have the six sections (three verbal and three math) that count toward your score on an actual SAT, plus an answer score section, an estimate of your theoretical SAT ranking based on the score you obtain on the test, and an evaluation to help you pinpoint your strengths and weaknesses.

PRACTICE WITH THE REAL THING: ACTUAL SAT QUESTIONS FOR STUDY

The following questions come from recent, actual SAT I exams (not from any published collection of SATs) and are used with the full permission of ETS. Answers are given on page 301.

- Do not race against time when working these questions.
- Analyze each question, noting how it is designed.
- If you are stumped on a question, decide why—and what you need to do to fix the problem.

ACTUAL SAT MATH QUESTIONS

Multiple-Choice Questions

In this section solve each problem using any available space on the page for scratchwork. Then decide which is the best of the choices given and fill in the corresponding oval on the answer sheet.

Notes

1. The use of a calculator is permitted. All numbers used are real numbers.
2. Figures that accompany problems in this test are intended to provide information useful in solving the problems. They are drawn as accurately as possible EXCEPT when it is stated in a specific problem that the figure is not drawn to scale. All figures lie in a plane unless otherwise indicated.

Reference Information

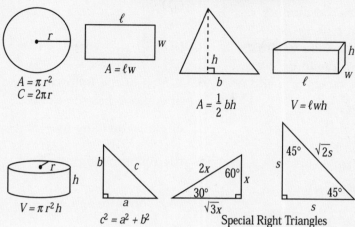

$A = \pi r^2$
$C = 2\pi r$

$A = \ell w$

$A = \frac{1}{2} bh$

$V = \ell wh$

$V = \pi r^2 h$

$c^2 = a^2 + b^2$

Special Right Triangles

The number of degrees of arc in a circle is 360.
The measure in degrees of a straight angle is 180.
The sum of the measures in degrees of the angles of a triangle is 180.

1. How many bottles, each holding 8 fluid ounces, are needed to hold 3 quarts of cider? (1 quart = 32 fluid ounces)

   (A) 8
   (B) 12
   (C) 14
   (D) 16
   (E) 18

$$\frac{4}{n}, \quad \frac{5}{n}, \quad \frac{7}{n}$$

2. If each of the fractions above is in its simplest reduced form, which of the following could be the value of n?

   (A) 24
   (B) 25
   (C) 26
   (D) 27
   (E) 28

3. The number p is 4 more than 3 times the number r. The sum of p and r is 10. Which of the following pairs of equations could be used to find the values of p and r?

(A) $p = 3r + 4$
  $p + r = 10$

(B) $p = 3r + 4$
  $pr = 10$

(C) $p = 3(r + 4)$
  $p + r = 10$

(D) $p + 4 = 3r$
  $p + r = 10$

(E) $p + 4 = 3r$
  $pr = 10$

4. If the vertices of a square are at $(-3, 4)$, $(3, 4)$, $(3, -2)$, and $(-3, -2)$, what is the area of the square?

(A) 12
(B) 16
(C) 24
(D) 25
(E) 36

5. If $x = yz$, which of the following must be equal to xy?

(A) yz
(B) yz^2
(C) y^2z

(D) $\dfrac{x}{y}$

(E) $\dfrac{z}{x}$

6. Which of the following operations has the same effect as dividing by $\dfrac{4}{3}$ and then multiplying by $\dfrac{2}{3}$?

(A) Multiplying by $\dfrac{1}{2}$

(B) Multiplying by 2

(C) Dividing by $\dfrac{1}{2}$

(D) Dividing by 3

(E) Dividing by 4

7. During a sale at a music store, if a customer buys one tape at full price, the customer is given a 50 percent discount on a second tape of equal or lesser value. If Linda buys two tapes that have full prices of $15 and $10, by what percent is the total cost of the two tapes reduced during this sale?

(A) 5%
(B) 20%
(C) 25%
(D) 30%
(E) 50%

8. If the sum of 4 consecutive integers is f, then, in terms of f, what is the least of these integers?

(A) $\dfrac{f}{4}$

(B) $\dfrac{f-2}{4}$

(C) $\dfrac{f-3}{4}$

(D) $\dfrac{f-4}{4}$

(E) $\dfrac{f-6}{4}$

9. In the equation $S = 3\pi r^2$, if the value of r is doubled, then the value of S is multiplied by

(A) $\dfrac{1}{2}$

(B) 2

(C) 3

(D) 4

(E) 8

10. One side of a triangle has length 6 and a second side has length 7. Which of the following could be the area of this triangle?

I. 13
II. 21
III. 24

(A) I only
(B) II only
(C) III only
(D) I and II only
(E) I, II, and III

Quantitative Comparison

Questions 11–15 each consist of two quantities. Determine their relationship and write

    A if the quantity in Column A is greater
    B if the quantity in Column B is greater
    C if the two quantities are equal
    D if the relationship cannot be determined from the information given.

AN E RESPONSE WILL NOT BE SCORED

Information that may help you in determining the relationship between the two quantities is centered above the two columns.

Column A	Column B

11. $\dfrac{3}{2} - \dfrac{1}{2}$ $\dfrac{7}{8} - \dfrac{1}{8}$

$$t + v = 76$$
$$t \neq 5$$

12. v 71

Column A	Column B

For all positive integers a and b, let $\overline{a \lfloor b}$ be defined as $\overline{a \lfloor b} = ab - (a + b)$.

13. $\overline{5 \lfloor 2}$ $\overline{2 \lfloor 5}$

$$6x - 2y < 0$$

14. x 0

$$\dfrac{x}{3} = \dfrac{y}{6}$$

15. $\dfrac{x + 1}{3}$ $\dfrac{y + 1}{6}$

Grid-In Questions

Directions for Student-Produced Response Questions

Each of the remaining 10 questions requires you to solve the problem and enter your answer by marking the ovals in the special grid, as shown in the examples below.

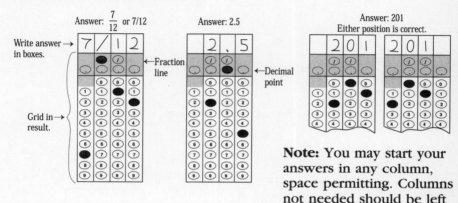

Note: You may start your answers in any column, space permitting. Columns not needed should be left blank.

- Mark no more than one oval in any column.
- Because the answer sheet will be machine-scored, **you will reveive credit only if the ovals are filled in correctly.**
- Although not required, it is suggested that you write your answer in the boxes at the top of the columns to help you fill in the ovals accurately.
- Some problems may have more than one correct answer. In such cases, grid only one answer.
- No question has a negative answer.

- **Mixed numbers** such as $2\frac{1}{2}$ must be gridded as 2.5 or 5/2.

(If [grid] is gridded, it will be interpreted as $\frac{21}{2}$, not $2\frac{1}{2}$.)

- **Decimal Accuracy:** If you obtain a decimal answer, **enter the most accurate value the grid will accommodate.** For example, if you obtain an answer such as 0.6666 . . . , you should record the result as .666 or .667. **Less accurate values such as .66 and .67 are not acceptable.**

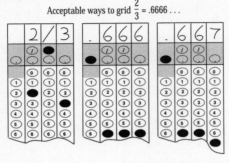

Acceptable ways to grid $\frac{2}{3}$ = .6666 . . .

17. If $(x + 2)^2 = 25$ and $x > 0$, what is the value of x^2?

50° $2x°$ ℓ

16. In the figure above, what is the value of x?

TRACK MEET AMONG SCHOOLS *A*, *B*, AND *C*

	First Place (5 points)	Second Place (3 points)	Third Place (1 point)
Event I	A		
Event II	A	B	
Event III			C

18. A partially completed score-card for a track meet is shown above. Schools *A*, *B*, and *C* each entered one person in each of the three events and there were no ties. What is one possible total score for School *C*? (Assume that all points are awarded in each event.)

19. A triangle has a base length of 13 and the other two sides are equal in length. If the lengths of the sides of the triangle are integers, what is the shortest possible length of a side?

20. In a stack of six cards, each card is labeled with a different integer 0 through 5. If two cards are selected at random without replacement, what is the probability that their sum will be 3?

ACTUAL SAT VERBAL QUESTIONS

Analogies

Each question below consists of a related pair of words or phrases, followed by five pairs of words or phrases labeled A through E. Select the pair that *best* expresses a relationship similar to that expressed in the original pair.

Example:

CRUMB : BREAD ::

    (A)   ounce : unit
    (B)   splinter : wood
    (C)   water : bucket
    (D)   twine : rope
    (E)   cream : butter

    Ⓐ ⬤ Ⓒ Ⓓ Ⓔ

1. RECUPERATE : SURGERY ::

  (A) restore : furniture
  (B) cleanse : alcohol
  (C) cure : illness
  (D) revive : faint
  (E) hospitalize : patient

2. SKETCH : ARTIST ::

  (A) secret : confidant
  (B) palette : painter
  (C) cell : prisoner
  (D) draft : writer
  (E) chisel : sculptor

3. YEARN : LONGING ::

  (A) beware : danger
  (B) rush : patience
  (C) enjoy : pleasure
  (D) suppress : rage
  (E) sleep : insomnia

4. WEDDING : MARRIAGE ::

  (A) birthday : cake
  (B) coronation : reign
  (C) graduation : diploma
  (D) promotion : job
  (E) decoration : bravery

5. REFUGEE : ASYLUM ::

  (A) astronaut : capsule
  (B) perfectionist : frustration
  (C) consumer : impulse
  (D) opportunist : advantage
  (E) director : stage

Sentence Completions

Each sentence below has one or two blanks, each blank indicating that something has been omitted. Beneath the sentence are five words or sets of words labeled A through E. Choose the word or set of words that, when inserted in the sentence, *best* fits the meaning of the sentence as a whole.

Example:

Medieval kingdoms did not become constitutional republics overnight; on the contrary, the change was _____.

  (A) popular
  (B) unexpected
  (C) advantageous
  (D) sufficient
  (E) gradual

  (A) (B) (C) (D) ⬤

6. The spacecraft has two _____ sets of electronic components; if one fails, its duplicate will still function.

  (A) divergent
  (B) identical
  (C) simulated
  (D) mutual
  (E) prohibitive

7. Trinkets intended to have only _____ appeal can exist virtually forever in landfills because of the _____ of some plastics.

  (A) arbitrary. .scarcity
  (B) theoretical. .resilience
  (C) ephemeral. .durability
  (D) obsessive. .fragility
  (E) impetuous. .cheapness

8. Although surfing is often _____ as merely a modern pastime, it is actually _____ practice, invented long ago by the Hawaiians to maneuver through the surf.

  (A) touted. .a universal
  (B) depicted. .an impractical
  (C) incorporated. .a leisurely
  (D) overestimated. .a high-spirited
  (E) dismissed. .a time-honored

9. Many linguists believe that our ability to learn language is at least in part _____, that it is somehow woven into our genetic makeup.

(A) innate
(B) accidental
(C) empirical
(D) transitory
(E) incremental

10. The student's feelings about presenting the commencement address were _____; although visibly happy to have been chosen, he was nonetheless _____ about speaking in public.

(A) positive. .insecure
(B) euphoric. .hopeful
(C) unknown. .modest
(D) ambivalent. .anxious
(E) restrained. .confident

Critical Reading

The two passages below are followed by questions based on their content and on the relationship between the two passages. Answer the questions on the basis of what is *stated* or *implied* in the passages and in any introductory material that may be provided.

Questions 11–20 are based on the following passages.
These passages present two perspectives of the prairie, the grasslands that covered much of the central plains of the United States during the nineteenth century. In Passage 1, a young English journalist writes about his visit to the prairie during a sightseeing tour in the 1840s. In Passage 2, an American writer describes the area near his childhood home of the early 1870s.

Passage 1

Line We came upon the Prairie at sunset. It would be difficult to say why, or how—though it was possibly from having heard and read so much about it—but the effect on me was disappointment. Towards the setting sun, there lay stretched out before my view a
5   vast expanse of level ground, unbroken (save by one thin line of trees, which scarcely amounted to a scratch upon the great blank) until it met the glowing sky, wherein it seemed to dip, mingling with its rich colors and mellowing in its distant blue. There it lay,

10 a tranquil sea or lake without water, if such a simile be admissible, with the day going down upon it: a few birds wheeling here and there, solitude and silence reigning paramount around. But the grass was not yet high; there were bare black patches on the ground and the few wild flowers that the eye could see were poor and scanty. Great as the picture was, its very flatness and
15 extent, which left nothing to the imagination, tamed it down and cramped its interest. I felt little of that sense of freedom and exhilaration that the open landscape of a Scottish moor, or even the rolling hills of our English downlands, inspires. It was lonely and wild, but oppressive in its barren monotony. I felt that in
20 traversing the Prairies, I could never abandon myself to the scene, forgetful of all else, as I should instinctively were heather moorland beneath my feet. On the Prairie I should often glance towards the distant and frequently receding line of the horizon, and wish it gained and passed. It is not a scene to be forgotten,
25 but it is scarcely one, I think (at all events, as I saw it), to remember with much pleasure or to covet the looking-on again, in after years.

Passage 2

In herding the cattle on horseback, we children came to know all the open prairie round about and found it very beautiful. On the
30 uplands a short, light-green grass grew, intermixed with various resinous weeds, while in the lowland grazing grounds luxuriant patches of blue joint, wild oats, and other tall forage plants waved in the wind. Along the streams, cattails and tiger lilies nodded above thick mats of wide-bladed marsh grass. Almost without
35 realizing it, I came to know the character of every weed, every flower, every living thing big enough to be seen from the back of a horse.

Nothing could be more generous, more joyous, than these natural meadows in summer. The flash and ripple and glimmer of
40 the tall sunflowers, the chirp and gurgle of red-winged blackbirds swaying on the willow, the meadowlarks piping from grassy bogs, the peep of the prairie chicken and the wailing call of plover on the flowery green slopes of the uplands made it all an ecstatic

world to me. It was a wide world with a big, big sky that gave
45   alluring hints of the still more glorious unknown wilderness
beyond.

Sometimes we wandered away to the meadows along the
creek, gathering bouquets of pinks, sweet william, tiger lilies, and
lady's slippers. The sun flamed across the splendid serial waves of
50   the grasses and the perfumes of a hundred spicy plants rose in
the shimmering midday air. At such times the mere joy of living
filled our hearts with wordless satisfaction.

On a long ridge to the north and west, the soil, too wet and
cold to cultivate easily, remained unplowed for several years.
55   Scattered over these clay lands stood small wooded groves that
we called "tow-heads." They stood out like islands in the waving
seas of grasses. Against these dark-green masses, breakers of blue
joint radiantly rolled. To the east ran the river; plum trees and
crabapples bloomed along its banks. In June immense crops of
60   wild strawberries appeared in the natural meadows. Their
delicious odor rose to us as we rode our way, tempting us to
dismount.

On the bare upland ridges lay huge antlers, bleached and
bare, in countless numbers, telling of the herds of elk and bison
65   that had once fed in these vast savannas. On sunny April days the
mother fox lay out with her young on southward-sloping swells.
Often we met a prairie wolf, finding in it the spirit of the wilderness. To us it seemed that just over the next long swell toward
the sunset the shaggy brown bison still fed in myriads, and in our
70   hearts was a longing to ride away into the "sunset regions" of our
pioneer songs.

11. In creating an impression of the prairie for the reader, the author of Passage 1 makes use of

   (A) reference to geological processes
   (B) description of its inhabitants
   (C) evocation of different but equally attractive areas
   (D) comparison with other landscapes
   (E) contrast to imaginary places

12. In line 10, the author includes the detail of "a few birds" primarily to emphasize the

   (A) loneliness of the scene
   (B) strangeness of the wildlife
   (C) lateness of the evening
   (D) dominance of the sky
   (E) infertility of the land

13. In line 20, "abandon myself" most nearly means

   (A) dismiss as worthless
   (B) isolate from all others
   (C) overlook unintentionally
   (D) retreat completely
   (E) become absorbed in

14. The author of Passage 1 qualifies his judgment of the prairie by

   (A) pointing out his own subjectivity
   (B) commenting on his lack of imagination
   (C) mentioning his physical fatigue
   (D) apologizing for his prejudices against the landscape
   (E) indicating his psychological agitation

15. In line 51, "mere" most nearly means

   (A) tiny
   (B) trivial
   (C) simple
   (D) direct
   (E) questionable

16. In Passage 2, the author's references to things beyond his direct experience (lines 44–46 and lines 68–71) indicate the

   (A) unexpected dangers of life on the unsettled prairie

   (B) psychological interweaving of imagination and the natural scene

   (C) exaggerated sense of mystery that is natural to children

   (D) predominant influence of sight in experiencing a place

   (E) permanence of the loss of the old life of the prairie

17. The contrast between the two descriptions of the prairie is essentially one between

   (A) misfortune and prosperity

   (B) homesickness and anticipation

   (C) resignation and joy

   (D) bleakness and richness

   (E) exhaustion and energy

18. In both passages, the authors liken the prairie to

   (A) a desert

   (B) an island

   (C) a barren wilderness

   (D) a large animal

   (E) a body of water

19. Both authors indicate that the experience of a beautiful landscape involves

   (A) artistic production

   (B) detached observation of appearances

   (C) emotional turmoil

   (D) stimulation of the imagination

   (E) fanciful reconstruction of bygone times

20. The contrast between the two passages reflects primarily the biases of a

   (A) grown man and a little boy

   (B) journalist and a writer of fiction

   (C) passing visitor and a local resident

   (D) native of Europe and a native of the United States

   (E) weary tourist and an energetic farm worker

Correct your answers by referring to the key on page 301. Which questions gave you trouble? Use your awareness of weak spots to guide your review.

PRACTICE SAT

Simulate test conditions as closely as possible—find a quiet spot where you won't be disturbed and sit yourself down at a desk or table for 2½ hours. *Set a timer* at the beginning of each section to the time noted there. Quit when the timer goes off, just as you would have to in a real test. If you finish before the timer goes off, you can review your work *on the current section only.*

When you have finished the entire test, check your answers against the answer key on page 302.

SECTION 1	TIME—30 MINUTES	25 QUESTIONS

In this section, solve each problem, and then choose the most appropriate answer from the choices given.

1. The cost of a 25¢ candy bar is raised 20 percent. What is the new cost of the candy bar?

    (A) 45¢
    (B) 40¢
    (C) 30¢
    (D) 25¢
    (E) 20¢

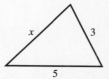

Note: Figure not drawn to scale.

2. Which of the following best describes x?

    (A) $3 < x < 5$
    (B) $x = 2$
    (C) $x = 4$
    (D) $2 < x < 8$
    (E) $2 < x < 5$

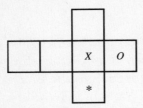

3. The above pattern can be folded into all of the following cubes EXCEPT

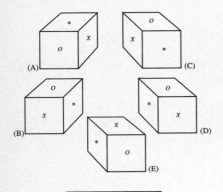

(A)

(B)

(C)

(D)

(E)

---

4. If $\dfrac{1}{2} + \dfrac{1}{8} - \dfrac{1}{4} - \dfrac{1}{6} = \dfrac{1}{x}$, then $x =$

(A) 0

(B) 1

(C) $1\dfrac{1}{2}$

(D) $\dfrac{5}{24}$

(E) $4\dfrac{4}{5}$

---

5. A \$50,000 inheritance has been left after a man has died. Before the money may be divided up, \$10,000 must be paid on outstanding debts. Of what is left, half is to be given to charity and the remainder is to be split evenly among 4 cousins. The amount each cousin receives is expressed by which of the following?

(A) $\dfrac{1}{2}(50{,}000 - 10{,}000) \div 4$

(B) $\left[\dfrac{1}{2}(50{,}000) - 10{,}000\right] \div 4$

(C) $\dfrac{1}{2}(50{,}000) - 10{,}000 \div 4$

(D) $\dfrac{1}{2}(4)(50{,}000 - 10{,}000)$

(E) $50{,}000 - \dfrac{1}{2}$
$(50{,}000 - 10{,}000) \div 4$

---

6. A desk-chair set costs \$9.89. If a dozen sets are purchased at once, the cost is reduced to \$9.14 per set. A school needs to buy 1 gross (12 dozen) sets. How much does it save by buying the sets by the dozen instead of singly?

(A) \$9.00

(B) \$18.00

(C) \$19.03

(D) \$24.00

(E) \$108.00

7. How many times between 12 noon and 12 midnight do the minute and hour hands of a clock line up exactly?

(A) 10
(B) 11
(C) 12
(D) 23
(E) 24

8. If 1 is added to each of the digits of 3,642, then the resulting number is

(A) 1 more than 3,642
(B) 4 more than 3,642
(C) 1,000 more than 3,642
(D) 1,111 more than 3,642
(E) 4,753 more than 3,642

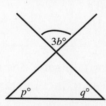

9. From the diagram above, the sum of p and q, in terms of b, equals

(A) $2b$
(B) $3b$
(C) $180 - b$
(D) $180 - 2b$
(E) $180 - 3b$

10. Over what interval(s) is the statement $x^3 > x^2$ true?

(A) All x
(B) $x > 0$
(C) $x > 1$ or $x < -1$
(D) $-1 < x < 1$
(E) $x > 1$

11. If $y = \dfrac{1}{x + 1}$, then what is x in terms of y?

(A) $\dfrac{1}{1 + y}$

(B) $\dfrac{1}{y - 1}$

(C) $\dfrac{1}{y}$

(D) $\dfrac{1 - y}{y}$

(E) $\dfrac{1}{y} - y$

12. The instructions on a can of orange juice concentrate state that the water should be mixed with the concentrate in the ratio of 3 to 1. If 12 liters of orange juice are needed, how many liters of concentrate need to be bought?

(A) 3
(B) 4
(C) 6
(D) 36
(E) 48

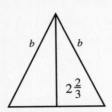

13. The area of the above isosceles triangle, with altitude $2\frac{2}{3}$, is 2. What is the base of the triangle?

(A) $\frac{2}{3}$

(B) $\frac{3}{2}$

(C) $\frac{3}{4}$

(D) $\frac{8}{3}$

(E) $\frac{3}{8}$

14. $(a - b)(b - a) =$

(A) $a^2 - 2ab + b^2$

(B) $a^2 - b^2$

(C) $a^2 + 2ab + b^2$

(D) $a^2 + 2ab - b^2$

(E) $-a^2 + 2ab - b^2$

15. The solution set of the equation $\sqrt{x} = x$ is

   I. -1

   II. 0

   III. 1

(A) II only

(B) III only

(C) I and III only

(D) II and III only

(E) I, II, and III

16. A cylinder is formed in such a way that a sphere of radius 2 can just fit inside. What is the volume of the cylinder?

(A) π

(B) 2π

(C) 4π

(D) 8π

(E) 16π

17. In a certain state one must pay a state income tax of 5%. The federal income tax instructions say that one may deduct 75% of the amount of one's state income tax. If a man was able to deduct $900 from his federal income tax because of his state income tax, what was his income?

(A) $3,375

(B) $6,000

(C) $7,200

(D) $13,500

(E) $24,000

18. Margaret has *d* dimes and *n* nickels totaling $3.00. If she has 40 coins altogether, which of the pairs of equations could be used to solve for the number of nickels and dimes Margaret has?

(A) $\begin{cases} x(d) + (40 - x)n = 300 \\ n + d = 40 \end{cases}$

(B) $\begin{cases} 300 - d = n \\ n + d = 40 \end{cases}$

(C) $\begin{cases} 5n + 10d = 300 \\ n + d = 40 \end{cases}$

(D) $\begin{cases} 40 - (n + d) = 300 \\ n + d = 40 \end{cases}$

(C) $\begin{cases} 2n + d = 300 \\ n + d = 40 \end{cases}$

19. In a prehistoric village, rocks, stones, and pebbles were used as money. The relative values of the "coins" were:

1 rock = 7 stones
1 rock = 49 pebbles

If a man used 6 rocks to purchase a hide that cost 5 rocks, 2 stones, and 3 pebbles, how much change was he owed?

(A) 1 rock, 5 stones, 4 pebbles
(B) 5 stones, 4 pebbles
(C) 4 stones, 4 pebbles
(D) 5 stones, 5 pebbles
(E) 6 stones, 5 pebbles

---

20. All of the following are implied by the equation $\dfrac{a}{b} = \dfrac{c}{d}$ EXCEPT

(A) $ad = bc$

(B) $\dfrac{a}{c} = \dfrac{b}{d}$

(C) $\dfrac{a - b}{b} = \dfrac{c - d}{d}$

(D) $\dfrac{a + b}{a - b} = \dfrac{c + d}{c - d}$

(E) $\dfrac{ad}{c} = \dfrac{bc}{d}$

21. The sum of three consecutive odd numbers is how many times as large as the middle number?

(A) 1

(B) $1\frac{1}{2}$

(C) 2

(D) 3

(E) 5

22. The set S contains the integers 1 through 9 inclusive. What is the value of the number of even numbers in S minus the number of odd numbers in S?

(A) -2

(B) -1

(C) 0

(D) 1

(E) 2

23. Four equilateral triangles are placed so they form one big equilateral triangle. How many times as large as the perimeter of a small equilateral triangle is the perimeter of the big equilateral triangle?

(A) 2

(B) $2\frac{1}{2}$

(C) 3

(D) $3\frac{1}{2}$

(E) 4

24. A 21-inch by 56-inch piece of material is to be cut up into equal squares. What is the largest length that the sides of the squares may be so that there is no extra material?

(A) 1

(B) 3

(C) 7

(D) 14

(E) 21

25. A job can be done in 25 hours by 6 people. How many people would be needed to do the same job in 8 or fewer hours?

(A) 16

(B) 17

(C) 18

(D) 19

(E) 15

Stop!

Do not go on to the next section of the test until you have set your timer.

SECTION 2   TIME—30 MINUTES   35 QUESTIONS

The following sentences need a word or words to complete their meaning. Choose the word or words that best fit the meaning of each sentence.

1. Life on La Digue, one of the smaller islands in the Seychelles group, goes on at a _____ pace; transport there is by ox cart, bicycle, or foot.

   (A) leisurely
   (B) jaunty
   (C) relentless
   (D) timeless
   (E) remarkable

2. Captain Jack's prompt, _____, and intelligent reactions were often necessary to save his ship and crew from disaster on their long voyage.

   (A) wise
   (B) decisive
   (C) swift
   (D) evasive
   (E) hereditary

3. The soft, rhythmic _____ of an owl's wings at night belies its _____ skill as a ruthless predator.

   (A) flap. .definite
   (B) beat. .dubious
   (C) motion. .unknown
   (D) whir. .formidable
   (E) singing. .scheming

4. Leukemia is a long and weary process of disease, _____ for a fortunate number of people, marching _____ toward death for a few.

   (A) vanquished. .inexorably
   (B) mitigated. .vainly
   (C) conquered. .peacefully
   (D) doomed. .swiftly
   (E) foretold. .inevitably

5. Once an enemy's true nature is _____, an opponent has some chance to _____ the situation and perhaps gain the upper hand.

   (A) superimposed. .recreate
   (B) exposed. .arbitrate
   (C) disguised. .ameliorate
   (D) veiled. .understand
   (E) manifest. .improve

6. The complexity of Doris Lessing's philosophical speculations sometimes obscures the _____, the clear purpose and vision, of her prose.

   (A) abstraction
   (B) singularity
   (C) irregularity
   (D) intricacy
   (E) lucidity

7. An oil painting that is offered as genuine must be _____ by reputable and acknowledged art historians before it is put up for sale in the best galleries.

   (A) authenticated
   (B) credited
   (C) coordinated
   (D) authorized
   (E) analyzed

8. To consolidate his reign Tsar Ivan the Terrible created the *oprichniki,* a ruthless palace guard loyal only to himself; they were the _____ of the nobility who always threatened his _____ rule.

   (A) pride. .vindictive
   (B) worst. .illegal
   (C) scourge. .tyrannical
   (D) founders. .benign
   (E) betrayers. .vulnerable

9. Unlike its original meaning, the word *sophistry* has acquired a negative _____, suggesting a _____ argument resulting from deceitful tactics artfully employed.

   (A) feeling. .famous
   (B) significance. .debatable
   (C) denotation. .mature
   (D) meaning. .forensic
   (E) connotation. .specious

10. Although he appeared _____ and timorous to his fellows, the rabbit Fiver in *Watership Down* proved his value to their community with repeated, _____ predictions.

    (A) pompous. .unwarranted
    (B) contentious. .fallacious
    (C) unstable. .unerring
    (D) untoward. .vague
    (E) audacious. .vacillating

The following questions are based on analogous relationships. Choose the lettered pair that most accurately reflects the comparison expressed by the pair in capital letters.

11. LACE : GOWN ::

   (A) frosting : cake
   (B) zipper : coat
   (C) paint : enamel
   (D) tongue : shoe
   (E) shag : carpet

12. CAPTAIN : TEAM ::

   (A) guard : forward
   (B) chef : menus
   (C) manager : policy
   (D) skipper : crew
   (E) overseer : concierge

13. HAWK : CLAWS ::

   (A) dinosaur : size
   (B) frontiersman : musket
   (C) equestrian : horse
   (D) analyst : statistics
   (E) skunk : spray

14. DISSENT : HARMONY ::

   (A) deplore : condition
   (B) flatter : servitude
   (C) deceive : reasons
   (D) mistake : identity
   (E) ridicule : acceptance

15. CLIENT : LAWYER ::

   (A) resident : apartment
   (B) patient : physician
   (C) devotee : opera
   (D) novice : expert
   (E) pupil : teacher

16. SPAT : ARGUE ::

   (A) inhibition : abandon
   (B) accord : embarrass
   (C) lull : insist
   (D) play : select
   (E) examination : inspect

17. TRESPASS : PROPERTY ::

   (A) ignore : license
   (B) elude : police
   (C) intrude : privacy
   (D) extract : essence
   (E) demolish : building

18. DANCER : LITHE ::

   (A) bookkeeper : meticulous
   (B) gymnast : ambidextrous
   (C) musician : corpulent
   (D) manager : autocratic
   (E) hurdler : adamant

19. FAT : CONGEAL ::

   (A) hide : shield
   (B) blood : coagulate
   (C) water : liquidate
   (D) food : nourish
   (E) metal : temper

20. AUGUR : FUTURE ::

(A) knight : medieval
(B) poet : ages
(C) vanguard : pack
(D) historian : past
(E) harbinger : evil

21. SPRY : DEBILITY ::

(A) wary : caution
(B) humorous : discernment
(C) benevolent : charity
(D) lucid : incoherence
(E) honest : candor

22. STUDENT : SAVANT ::

(A) tyro : master
(B) archer : centaur
(C) expert : connoisseur
(D) knight : errant
(E) recipient : philanthro-
pist

23. WASTREL : DISSIPATION ::

(A) warrior : exploitation
(B) hedonist : asceticism
(C) coward : retribution
(D) diva : imitation
(E) recluse : isolation

The passage below is followed by questions based on its content. Questions should be answered on the basis of what is *stated* **or** *implied* in the passage.

The following passage is a conversation between a young actress and a friend of hers. The time is the 1890s and the place is New York City. The actress, Carrie, has had some success in the theater and is about to become a celebrity.

Line   The music ceased and he arose, taking a standing position before
        her, as if to rest himself.
            "Why don't you get into some good, strong comedy-drama?"
        he said. He was looking directly at her now, studying her face.
5   Her large, sympathetic eyes and pain-touched mouth appealed to
        him as proofs of his judgment.
            "Perhaps I shall," she returned.
            "That's your field," he added.
            "Do you think so?"
10   "Yes," he said; "I do. I don't suppose you're aware of it, but
        there is something about your eyes and mouth which fits you for
        that sort of work."
            Carrie was thrilled to be taken so seriously. For the moment,
        loneliness deserted her. Here was praise which was keen and
15   analytical.
            "It's in your eyes and mouth," he went on abstractedly. "I
        remember thinking, the first time I saw you, that there was
        something peculiar about your mouth. I thought you were about
        to cry."
20   "How odd," said Carrie, warm with delight. This was what
        her heart craved.
            "Then I noticed that that was your natural look, and tonight
        I saw it again. There's a shadow about your eyes, too, which
        gives your face much this same character. It's in the depth of
25   them, I think."
            Carrie looked straight into his face, wholly aroused.
            "You probably are not aware of it," he added.

She looked away, pleased that he should speak thus, longing to be equal to this feeling written upon her countenance. It
30 unlocked the door to a new desire.

She had cause to ponder over this until they met again— several weeks or more. It showed her she was drifting away from the old ideal which had filled her in the dressing rooms of the Avery stage and thereafter, for a long time. Why had she lost it?
35 "I know why you should be a success," he said, another time, "if you had a more dramatic part. I've studied it out—"

"What is it?" said Carrie.

"Well," he said, as one pleased with a puzzle, "the expression in your face is one that comes out in different things. You
40 get the same thing in a pathetic song, or any picture which moves you deeply. It's a thing the world likes to see, because it's a natural expression of its longing."

Carrie gazed without exactly getting the import of what he meant.
45 "The world is always struggling to express itself," he went on. "Most people are not capable of voicing their feelings. They depend upon others. That is what genius is for. One man expresses their desires for them in music; another in poetry; another one in a play. Sometimes nature does it in a face—it makes the
50 face representative of all desire. That's what has happened in your case."

He looked at her with so much of the import of the thing in his eyes that she caught it. At least, she got the idea that her look was something which represented the world's longing. She took
55 it to her heart as a creditable thing, until he added:

"That puts a burden of duty on you. It so happens that you have this thing. It is no credit to you—that is, I mean, you might not have had it. You paid nothing to get it. But now that you have it, you must do something with it."
60 "What?" Carrie asked.

"I should say, turn to the dramatic field. You have so much sympathy and such a melodious voice. Make them valuable to others. It will make your powers endure."

Carrie did not understand this last. All the rest showed her
65 that her comedy success was little or nothing.

"What do you mean?" she asked.

"Why, just this. You have this quality in your eyes and mouth and in your nature. You can lose it, you know. If you turn away from it and live to satisfy yourself alone, it will go fast
70 enough. The look will leave your eyes. Your mouth will change. Your power to act will disappear. You may think they won't, but they will. Nature takes care of that."

He was so interested in forwarding all good causes that he sometimes became enthusiastic, giving vent to these preachments.
75 Something in Carrie appealed to him. He wanted to stir her up.

"I know," she said, absently, feeling slightly guilty of neglect.

"If I were you," he said, "I'd change."

The effect of this was like roiling helpless waters. Carrie
80 troubled over it in her rocking chair for days.

"I don't believe I'll stay in comedy so very much longer," she eventually remarked to Lola, her friend.

"Oh, why not?" said the latter.

"I think," she said, "I can do better in a serious play."
85 "What put that idea in your head?"

"Oh, nothing," she answered; "I've always thought so."

Still, she did nothing—grieving. It was a long way to this better thing—or seemed so—and comfort was about her; hence the inactivity and longing.

24. The speaker implies that "strong comedy-drama" (line 3) is

(A) the kind of theater that will make Carrie wealthy

(B) theater that is well suited to Carrie's beauty and talents

(C) the limit for Carrie's talents beyond which she could expect little success

(D) his only chance to impress Carrie and obtain her favor

(E) the most appropriate style of life for a woman like Carrie who could never be accepted as a lady

25. Which of the following is the most plausible inference to make based on the statement in lines 5-6?

(A) The speaker is intelligent but somewhat conceited.

(B) Carrie is trying to beguile the speaker with her good looks.

(C) The speaker is clearly revealing his own self-deception.

(D) Carrie has suffered some personal anguish caused by the speaker.

(E) Carrie and the speaker are both rehearsing a scene from a play.

26. Carrie feels the speaker's comments to be "keen and analytical" (lines 14–15) primarily because

(A) she is accustomed to hearing excellent criticism of her work

(B) she knows she is speaking with a highly educated and informed professional

(C) the speaker's comments confirm her own opinions about the quality of her work

(D) her innocent vanity is flattered by such favorable judgments

(E) her own ambition and drive need this kind of positive support in order for her to succeed

27. Carrie's real talent as an actress that so appeals to the speaker is apparently her ability to project an image of

(A) threatened innocence and virtue

(B) a seductive beauty and temptress

(C) a highly skilled manipulator

(D) towering pride and achievement

(E) universal qualities of kindness and generosity

28. Which of the following best states what Carrie's "heart craved" (line 21)?

(A) Sincere attention from an attractive man

(B) Assurance that she would never fail

(C) Intelligent public relations and promotion

(D) Better opportunities and offers to perform

(E) Admiration and strong ego support

29. The man speaking to Carrie assumes that she

(A) needs him to be her agent and manage her career

(B) lacks the necessary self-knowledge to create opportunities for herself

(C) will be easy to take advantage of when his chance arrives

(D) is impressed with his power of critical intelligence

(E) really wants only to get married and have a family

30. The "feeling written upon her countenance" (line 29) is best described as one of

(A) glamour and sophistication

(B) grief and abandonment

(C) pathos and vulnerability

(D) ambition and willfulness

(E) languor and self-satisfaction

31. The man's comments about Carrie in lines 54–59 affect her in which of the following ways?

(A) She is momentarily deflated because her previous success is now diminished.

(B) She is immediately excited and feels compelled to travel a new path in her career.

(C) She is perplexed and wishes to obtain more counsel and advice before she moves on.

(D) She is upset and rejects the man's comments as an effort to subvert her self-confidence.

(E) She is genuinely flattered but too modest to accept the praise.

32. The man implies that unless Carrie cultivates those artistic talents he sees in her (lines 67–72), she will

(A) grow restless and eventually leave the theater

(B) suffer increasingly nasty reviews from her critics

(C) be in defiance of nature and become vulnerable to God's anger

(D) lose control over her own future

(E) lose her talents altogether

33. In line 79, the word "roiling" most nearly means

(A) heating excessively

(B) turning around

(C) stirring up

(D) poisoning

(E) purifying

34. The author's chief purpose in the passage is to

    (A) evoke sympathy for the energetic and thoughtful man

    (B) clarify and highlight one particular trait of Carrie's

    (C) subtly reduce Carrie's image to that of a lonely, alienated woman

    (D) portray a potential romantic relationship between two young people

    (E) depict a bully engaged in humiliating an innocent young woman

35. Carrie's final response to the man's suggestions for her future career (lines 81–87) implies that she is

    (A) an indecisive person with little self-confidence and faith in her future

    (B) totally reliant on friends and coworkers for advice and support

    (C) the most astute judge of her prospects and talents

    (D) a very disciplined, reflective person who will take only known risks

    (E) an unintelligent, indolent person who lives only in the present

Stop!

Do not go on to the next section of the test until you have set your timer.

SECTION 3   TIME—30 MINUTES   25 QUESTIONS

There are two types of problems in this section. Questions 1–15 are quantitative comparison questions. Questions 16–25 are grid-in problems. Instructions are provided at the beginning of each section.

SUMMARY DIRECTIONS FOR COMPARISON QUESTIONS

Answer:

    A if the quantity in Column A is greater;
    B if the quantity in Column B is greater;
    C if the two quantities are equal;
    D if the relationship cannot be determined from the information given.

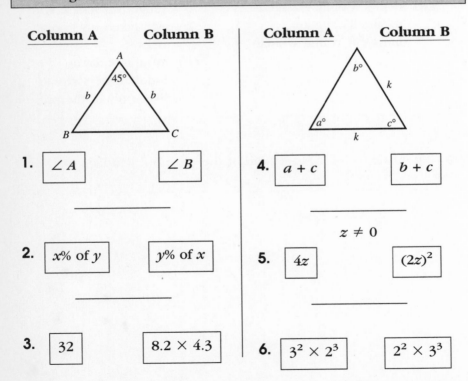

Column A	Column B	Column A	Column B
1. $\angle A$	$\angle B$	**4.** $a + c$	$b + c$
2. $x\%$ of y	$y\%$ of x	**5.** $4z$	$(2z)^2$
3. 32	8.2×4.3	**6.** $3^2 \times 2^3$	$2^2 \times 3^3$

$z \neq 0$

Column A	Column B

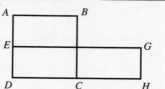

The area of square *ABCD* is equal to the area of rectangle *EGHD.*

7.

The perimeter of square *ABCD*	The perimeter of rectangle *EGHD*

_____

8.

Volume of a cylinder with diameter 2 and height 4	Volume of a rectangular solid with dimensions $2 \times 2 \times 4$

_____

Questions 9 and 10 refer to the following definition:

$$a!b = \frac{1}{a} + \frac{1}{b} \qquad (ab \neq 0)$$

9.

$a!b$	$\dfrac{a + b}{ab}$

Column A	Column B

$$x!y + 9 = 0$$

10.

$x!y$	9

11.

The distance from the point (a,a) to the point (p,q) on the coordinate axes	The distance from the point (a,a) to the point (q,p) on the coordinate axes

While walking from town A to town B, a man meets another man who has 12 wives, each of whom is carrying 10 sacks, each of which contains 4 cats. When returning from town B to town A, the man meets a woman who has 16 husbands, each of whom is carrying 6 sacks, each of which contains 5 dogs.

_____

12.

The number of cats the man met going from A to B	The number of dogs the man met returning from B to A

Column A	Column B

13. $(x + y)^2 - (x - y)^2$ | $4xy$

$4 \le a \le 14$
$7 \le b \le 12$

14. The maximum value of $\dfrac{b}{a}$ | 2

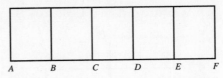

Note: Figure not drawn to scale.

A row of apartments is represented by the boxes above. A surveyor wants to measure the width of each apartment. He finds that

$AD = CF = 12$ and $BD = CE = 8$

Column A	Column B

15. CD | 4

Summary Directions for Student-Produced Response Questions

Each of the remaining 10 questions requires you to solve the problem and enter your answer by marking the ovals in the special grid on page 307.

Note: You may start your answers in any column, space permitting. Columns not needed should be left blank.

- Mark no more than one oval in any column.
- Because the answer sheet will be machine-scored, you will receive credit only if the ovals are filled in correctly.
- Although not required, it is suggested that you write your answer in the boxes at the top of the columns to help you fill in the ovals accurately.
- Some problems may have more than one correct answer. In such cases, grid only one answer.
- No question has a negative answer.
- Mixed numbers such as $2\frac{1}{2}$ must be gridded as 2.5 or 5/2.
- Decimal Accuracy: If you obtain a decimal answer, enter the most accurate value the grid will accommodate. For example, if you obtain an answer such as 0.6666 . . . , you should record the result as .666 or .667. Less accurate values such as .66 or .67 are not acceptable.

16. A 64-ounce bottle of concentrated detergent costs $7.20. The same size bottle of regular detergent costs $4.88. If one needs half an ounce of concentrated detergent or a whole ounce of regular detergent to wash a load of laundry, how many cents does one save per wash using the concentrated detergent?

17. If a car can go 30 miles on a gallon of gas, how many gallons are required to go 100 miles?

_____

18. The average height of three students is between 5 foot 8 inches and 5 foot 10 inches. If two of the students are exactly 6 feet tall, what is a possible height of the third student, in inches?

19.

2	a	b
c	d	3
e	1	f

A 3×3 table is filled in, as pictured above, such that each of its rows, columns, and diagonals sum to 15. What is the sum of all 9 entries in the table?

20. The points $(0,0)$, $(a,3)$, and $(3,b)$ all lie on a line. What is the value of ab?

21. Chicken is selling for $1.50 per pound. If Elizabeth buys two pounds with a coupon for 50 cents off the total price, how much does she pay per pound for the chicken? Give your answer in dollars without the dollar sign.

Column A   **Column B**

22. a $\dfrac{a}{2}$

The above square and rectangle have the same area. Denote the perimeter of the square P_s and the perimeter of the rectangle P_r. If $P_s = nP_r$, what is n?

23. What is the smallest positive number that may be represented in an SAT I/PSAT grid?

24.

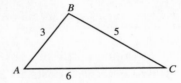

A circle is formed by spinning triangle ABC around point A. If its area is πx, what is x?

25.

$N = \{2, 4, 6\}$
$D = \{3, 6, 9\}$

What is the positive square root of the difference between the largest and smallest fractions that can be formed by choosing one number from set N to be the numerator and one number from set D to be the denominator?

Stop!

Do not go on to the next section of the test until you have set your timer.

SECTION 4   TIME—30 MINUTES   30 QUESTIONS

The following sentences need a word or words to complete their meaning. Choose the word or words that best fit the meaning of each sentence.

1. Many team members were abrupt, even _____ at times, about responding to suggestions from their young, inexperienced swimming coach.

   (A) pleasant
   (B) curt
   (C) uninterested
   (D) hesitant
   (E) unaware

2. The size and simplicity of an Indian tepee or wigwam lead us to conclude that it was built more for _____ than for _____.

   (A) tradition. .feasibility
   (B) liveability. .comfort
   (C) custom. .efficiency
   (D) practicality. .ostentation
   (E) pretense. .appearance

3. In general, _____ behavior on the part of administration aggravates an already tense worker problem rather than _____ it.

   (A) humorless. .worsening
   (B) responsible. .soothing
   (C) autocratic. .alleviating
   (D) diplomatic. .condoning
   (E) meretricious. .maximizing

4. Ignoring the power and _____ of domineering, even occasionally despotic, foreign governments could _____ the demise of our own.

   (A) pride. .continue
   (B) ambition. .herald
   (C) thrust. .forestall
   (D) prestige. .enhance
   (E) colonialism. .enjoin

5. While certain herbicides appear _____ to farmers deeply concerned with profit and loss, their effect has been to _____ the bird population dependent on formerly weedy hedgerows and ditches.

(A) beneficial. .decimate
(B) applicable. .augment
(C) attractive. .dishearten
(D) prohibitive. .enhance
(E) mandatory. .restructure

6. "I'm sure Jackie didn't intentionally _____," his older sister said quickly, "because he rarely even _____!"

(A) prognosticate. .hurries
(B) castigate. .bothers
(C) equivocate. .categorizes
(D) prevaricate. .fibs
(E) deliberate. .hesitates

7. Lawmakers eager to promote a piece of legislation no doubt feel _____ whenever their bill _____ committee.

(A) thwarted. .languishes in
(B) exasperation. .races through
(C) uplifted. .bogs down in

(D) satisfaction. .is deposited in
(E) exhilaration. .is studied in

8. Known for _____ rather than garrulity, Mrs. Brown was nonplussed when nominated to be president, a position that frequently demanded _____.

(A) amiability. .gravity
(B) fastidiousness. .precision
(C) reticence. .eloquence
(D) obsequiousness. .courtesy
(E) incoherence. .clarity

9. Though purists say it is _____ to suggest "splitting" an infinitive with an adverb, e.g., *to radically alter,* we need to _____ each inherited grammatical guideline to decide whether or not it suits our evolving language.

(A) redundant. .evaluate
(B) distasteful. .peruse
(C) heresy. .scrutinize
(D) expeditious. .establish
(E) incongruous. .ponder

The following questions are based on analogous relationships. Choose the lettered pair that most accurately reflects the comparison expressed by the pair in capital letters.

10. STREAM : CRAYFISH ::

   (A) grass : zebra
   (B) heavens : planet
   (C) garden : flower
   (D) ground : mole
   (E) water : fowl

11. DATA : COMPUTER ::

   (A) fodder : cattle
   (B) source : well
   (C) idea : title
   (D) bridle : horse
   (E) language : study

12. GLUT : SATIATION ::

   (A) force : condemnation
   (B) cheer : reparation
   (C) work : remuneration
   (D) height : exultation
   (E) anger : sensation

13. PROGENITOR : HEIR ::

   (A) noble : serf
   (B) forebear : descendant
   (C) adjudicator : decision
   (D) precursor : author
   (E) sponsor : candidate

14. TURNCOAT : VILIFY ::

   (A) viper : slay
   (B) pickpocket : describe
   (C) murderer : confound
   (D) podiatrist : confirm
   (E) terrorist : attest

15. PARAPHRASE : CLASSIC ::

   (A) define : data
   (B) bowdlerize : literature
   (C) analyze : refutation
   (D) persevere : annals
   (E) castigate : epoch

Each passage below is followed by questions based on its content. Questions should be answered on the basis of what is *stated* or *implied* in the passage.

Line The central mystery of the Celtic religion, and the ceremonial
rituals which embodied its essence, will always be elusive. For
many the Celtic mystique, with its romantic emphasis on the fairy
and the spirit-world, has obscured the spirituality of these warrior
5   peoples and the fact that they even had a religion. The ancient
oral tradition that perpetuated the laws, legends and the tribal
teachings, through the trained memories of a group of poets and
priests, made the act of writing unnecessary. And, much like the
prohibitions laid on the Celtic warrior heroes, which predestined
10   their lives and actions, the taboo on writing continued as long as
the old religion lasted.

        The earliest remnants of Celtic culture in Central Europe are
usually dated between 800 and 450 BC and assigned to the
Hallstatt culture, after the metal artifacts found in a cemetery at
15   Hallstatt in Austria, a centre for salt and copper mining. The later
Celtic phase, the La Tène, named after a village site in Switzer-
land, continued in Continental Europe until Roman times. The
style of ornament associated with the La Tène culture, with its
wild, imaginative but formalized decoration of floral patterns and
20   abstract symbols, was still the dominant characteristic of Celtic
metalwork, stonecarving and manuscript illumination in Britain
and Ireland a thousand years later.

        The Celts emerged from the Rhinelands of Central Europe as
a distinctive group of clans or tribes between 1000 and 500 BC.
25   Their language, religion, social organization and customs were
different from those in the Mediterranean south, or further east by
the Danube. In general the Celts seem to have many affinities
with Indo-European warrior groups who had overrun the Indus
Valley civilizations a millennium or so earlier. A number of archaic
30   linguistic forms, such as *raja,* king (Latin *rex,* Irish *ri,* and Gallic
-rix) or *rigu,* queen, as well as many others connected with
sacred customs and social organizations, are shared by Indo-
European languages in Asia and Europe. Cultural affinities

between the Celts and India can be also traced in the animal
35 rituals in which the spirit of the new king or queen is rendered
incarnate with that of a bull or horse; in the act of fasting to gain
recognition for a grievance; in the position of women and the fact
they were accorded parity with men (Boadicea in Britain and the
legendary Maeve in Ireland) in the warrior class; in metric forms,
40 which in the *Rig Veda,* oldest and most important of the sacred
books, are similar to some early Irish and Welsh verse; and in the
close relationship between teacher and pupil which is still such a
feature of Indian religious life and which was an essential part of
the Celtic oral tradition.

16. The passage is primarily concerned with the

(A) artifacts left by various Celtic cultures

(B) oral tribal teachings of two separate but related Celtic cultures

(C) dominant characteristics of Celtic art

(D) similarities between Indo-European warrior groups and the Celts

(E) elusive ceremonial rituals of the Celtic people

17. The passage suggests that Celtic culture is "elusive" (lines 1–2) primarily because

(A) there are relatively few artifacts of the Celts

(B) Celtic traditions were mingled with those of Wales and Ireland

(C) other related groups of warrior peoples added their beliefs to those of the Celts

(D) few archaeologists and historians have been properly trained to sift the available material for facts

(E) the Celts left no written records

18. In line 13, the phrase "assigned to" most nearly means
    (A) allotted for
    (B) set apart for
    (C) designated as
    (D) ascribed to
    (E) transferred to

19. The word *raja* is mentioned in line 30 as an example of a linguistic form that
    (A) has influenced modern linguistic forms despite its antiquity
    (B) is similar in Latin, Gallic, and Irish
    (C) is shared by some Asian and European languages
    (D) was used by Indo-European warrior groups in the Indus Valley
    (E) was used by the Celts but not by their neighbors to the east and south

20. Which one of the following is NOT mentioned in the passage as a cultural affinity between the Celts and India?
    (A) The position of women
    (B) Animal rituals involving a bull or horse
    (C) Ceremonial feasts as acts of recognition
    (D) Forms of language
    (E) Metric forms

21. It can be inferred that the Celtic verse mentioned in lines 39–41 differs from such Indian sacred texts as the *Rig Veda* in that the Celtic verse
    (A) is older than the Indian sacred texts
    (B) was passed down orally while the Indian sacred texts were written
    (C) contains fewer archaic Indo-European linguistic forms than do the Indian sacred texts
    (D) displays less complex schemes of rhyme and rhythm than do the Indian sacred texts
    (E) does not concern itself with religious or spiritual themes

Line   Ruins of Greek construction abound in the Mediterranean region,
       but as a matter of perspective one must realize that all written
       records of ancient Greece are exceedingly scarce. It is difficult to
       estimate how much Greek literature has survived in any form, but
5   it almost certainly must be less than 1 percent. Very few of the
       surviving works are in their original form, almost all are corrupted
       by careless copying over many centuries, and few contain much
       information that would permit dating them even indirectly.
       Nevertheless, it is clear that ancient Greece was the scene of
10   much geological thinking . . . and that many of the seminal ideas
       eventually found their way into printed books.
            The fragmentary kaleidoscope of Greek science records
       isolated glimpses of important geological understanding. In the
       sixth century B.C., the Pythagoreans were the first to teach that
15   the Earth was round because it cast a round shadow on the moon
       in eclipses. Eratosthenes (ca. 276–ca. 195 B.C.), the second
       director of the Museum Library in Alexandria, devised a method
       of measuring the diameter of the Earth's sphere. He observed that
       on the summer solstice, the longest day of the year, the sun stood
20   at an angle of one-fiftieth of a circle from vertical in Alexandria,
       but was directly overhead in Syene (now Aswan). He had no
       accurate way of measuring the north-south distance between the
       two places (the length of the meridian), but he made a reasonable
       estimate and calculated a remarkably accurate value for the
25   Earth's diameter. Later commentators have pointed out the
       obvious sources of error in his estimate, but that does not
       diminish the brilliant simplicity and fundamental grandeur of the
       experiment. There is some uncertainty about the units he used,
       but his result appears to be only about 20 percent larger than
30   modern determinations.
            Extending his calculations to include some doubtful sun-
       angle determinations and rough distance estimates, Eratosthenes
       then attempted to establish a coordinate grid for the whole
       ancient world. The result was a distinct improvement in the
35   world map of the day, but the unreliability of the data was
       recognized and severely criticized by the astronomer Hipparchus
       of Bithynia (?–after 127 B.C.). In categorically rejecting conclu-
       sions based on inadequate data, Hipparchus was being very

40 scientific, but in failing to concede that an inspired guess is better
than no information at all he set geography back a fair distance. It
was this same Hipparchus who pioneered the quantitative
approach to astronomy and developed the precession of the
equinoxes. Almost all of his original writings are lost and his work
is known mostly from references to it in Ptolemy's *Almagest,*
45 written about three centuries after Hipparchus died.

        Herodotus of Halicarnassus (?484–?425 B.C.), the great
historian of Greek antiquity, concerned himself mainly with
political and military history, but he had traveled as far as the
Black Sea, Mesopotamia, and Egypt and made accurate geological
50 observations. He was aware that earthquakes cause large-scale
fracturing and thus may shape the landscape. . . . He noted the
sediment carried by the Nile and estimated the amounts of
deposition from the annual floods in the Nile Valley and the
growth of the great delta. "Egypt . . . is an acquired country, the
55 gift of the river," he wrote, and throughout those discussions he
displayed a remarkable understanding of the vastness of geologic
time.

22. The reference to the "ruins of Greek construction" in line 1 serves primarily to

(A) provide a concrete example of the ancient Greeks' technical abilities

(B) introduce the relationship between Greek architecture and Greek geology

(C) highlight the influence of Greek culture throughout the Mediterranean region

(D) establish a contrast between the large number of ruins and the scarcity of written documents

(E) show that the ancient Greeks' intellectual legacy has endured better than have their physical monuments

23. The author calls ancient Greek geological ideas "seminal" in line 10 to suggest that these ideas

(A) contained the seeds of later development

(B) were fragmented or incomplete

(C) seem amorphous or unformed

(D) revealed primitive thought

(E) displayed the Greeks' carelessness

24. The passage as a whole is primarily concerned with explaining

(A) the differences in methodology between two Greek geologists

(B) how ancient Greek geology has affected modern geological thinking

(C) some of the remarkable achievements of early Greek geologists

(D) why the written records of ancient Greek science are so fragmentary

(E) why the ancient Greeks were fascinated with geology

25. The author views the achievements of Eratosthenes with

(A) professional detachment
(B) slight skepticism
(C) respect and qualified admiration
(D) amusement and deep interest
(E) condescension

26. It can be inferred from the passage that the astronomer Hipparchus was NOT

(A) scientific in his approach
(B) particularly flexible or intuitive
(C) pioneering in his approach
(D) published in his time
(E) critical of other scientific studies

27. Which of the following is cited in the passage as being true of the work of Hipparchus?

(A) It helped to establish that the earth was round.
(B) It was criticized in its day by Eratosthenes of Alexandria.
(C) It was primarily concerned with astronomy rather than with geology.

(D) Its conclusions were nearly always based on accurate and reliable data.
(E) Its existence is corroborated in a work written centuries after Hipparchus's death.

28. Which of the following is most likely to have been an objection raised by Hipparchus to Eratosthenes' research?

(A) Eratosthenes could not accurately measure the distances between the sites of his sun-angle measurements.
(B) Eratosthenes failed to take the precession of the equinoxes into account in making his calculations.
(C) Eratosthenes used estimated values when he should have taken accurate measurements.
(D) Eratosthenes' coordinate grid was based on a measurement of the earth's diameter that was too large.
(E) Eratosthenes' calculations were faulty.

29. According to the passage, Greek geological information was

I. almost all lost
II. of little value for today's scientists
III. surprisingly accurate and often grand in scope
IV. acquired after much thought and calculation
V. carefully dated and logically explained

(A) I, III, and V
(B) II and IV
(C) III and V
(D) I, III, and IV
(E) I, II, and V

30. In calling Egypt "an acquired country" (line 54), Herodotus was referring to the way in which

(A) Herodotus had added Egypt to the list of countries whose geography he had studied
(B) earthquakes had changed Egypt's natural borders to increase its territory
(C) Egypt's military might have enabled it to annex parts of other countries
(D) the Nile's predictable floods enabled Egypt's economic prosperity
(E) the Nile had added sediment to the great delta to increase Egypt's land mass

Stop!

Do not go on to the next section of the test until you have set your timer.

The two passages below are followed by questions based on their content and on the relationship between the two passages. Answer the questions on the basis of what is *stated* or *implied* in the passages and in any introductory material that may be provided.

The passages below are about the Maori people of New Zealand. The first passage, written in 1770, is from the log of Captain James Cook, who explored the southern Pacific around that time. The second is a general account of the Maoris written by another Englishman about 1900, more than a century later.

Passage 1

Line   The natives of this country are a strong, raw-boned, well-made active people rather above than under the ordinary size, especially the men. Those who do not disfigure their faces by tattooing and scarifying have in general very good features. The men
5   generally wear their hair long, combed up and tied upon the crown of their heads; some of the women wear it long and loose upon their shoulders, old women especially.

They seem to enjoy a good state of health and many of them live to a good old age. Many of the old and some of the middle
10   aged men have their faces marked and tattooed with black, and some few we have seen have had their backs and thighs and other parts of their bodies marked, but this is less common.

The women have very soft voices and may by that alone be known from the men. The making of cloth and all other domestic
15   work is wholly done by them, and the more laborious work such as building boats, houses, and tilling the ground, fishing, etc. by the men.

Whenever we were visited by any number of them that had never heard or seen anything of us before, they generally came
20   off in the largest canoes they had, some of which will carry 60, 80, or 100 people. They always brought their best clothes along with them which they put on as soon as they came near the ship.

25 In each canoe were generally an old man, in some two or three; these used always to direct the others, were better clothed and generally carried a halberd or battle ax in their hands or some such like thing that distinguished them from the others. As soon as they came within about a stone's throw of the ship, they would lay by and call out to us to come ashore with them so they could kill us with their spears which they would shake at us.

30 At times they would dance the war dance, and at other times they would trade and talk to us and answer such questions as were put to them with all the calmness imaginable. Then again, they would begin the war dance, shaking their paddles and spears and making strange contortions at the same time. As soon as they
35 had worked themselves up to a proper pitch, they would begin to attack us with stones and darts and oblige us, whether we would or no, to fire upon them. Musketry they never regarded unless they felt the effect, but great guns they did because these threw stones farther than they could comprehend. After they found that
40 our arms were so much superior to theirs and that we took no advantage of that superiority, and a little time given them to reflect upon it, they ever after were our good friends.

The Maoris are far happier than we Europeans; being wholly unacquainted not only with the superfluous but the necessary
45 conveniences so much sought after in Europe, they are happy in not knowing the use of them. They live in a tranquillity which is not disturbed by the inequality of condition: the Earth and sea of their own accord furnish them with all things necessary for life. They covet not magnificent houses, house-hold stuff, etc.; they
50 live in a warm and fine climate and enjoy a very wholesome air, so that they have very little need of clothing and this they seem to be fully sensible of, for many to whom we gave cloth, etc., left it carelessly upon the sea beach and in the woods as a thing they had no manner of use for. In short, they seemed to set no value
55 upon anything we gave them.

Passage 2

Among the most industrious of Polynesian races, the Maoris have always been famed for wood-carving; and in building, weaving, and dyeing they had made great advances before whites arrived. They are also good farmers and bold seamen. In the Maori wars
60 they showed much strategic skill, and their knowledge of fortification was very remarkable. Every Maori was a soldier, and war was the chief business and joy of this life. Tribal wars were incessant. The weapons were wooden spears, clubs and stone tomahawks. The women were allowed a voice in the tribe's
65 affairs, and sometimes accompanied the men into battle.

Ferocious as they were in war, the Maoris are generally hospitable and affectionate in their home life, and a pleasant characteristic, noticed by Captain Cook, is their respect and care of the old. They buried their dead, the cemeteries being orna-
70 mented with carved posts. Their religion was a nature worship intimately connected with the veneration of ancestors. There was a belief in the soul, which was supposed to dwell in the left eye. They had no doubt as to a future state, but no definite idea of a supreme being.
75 While they had no written language, a considerable oral literature of songs, legends, and traditions existed. Their priest-hood was a highly trained profession, and they had schools which taught a knowledge of the stars and constellations, for many of which they had names.
80 Many Maoris are natural orators and poets, and a chief was expected to add these accomplishments to his prowess as a warrior or his skill as a seaman. They have been called the Britons of the south, and their courage in defending their country and their intelligence amplify the compliment. By the New Zealanders,
85 they are cordially liked.

1. Which of the following is the most apt reading of the phrase "above than under" (line 2)?

   (A) more than less
   (B) nearer than farther
   (C) taller than shorter
   (D) heavier than lighter
   (E) stronger than weaker

2. Which of the following phrases is assumed, and not written, between "fishing, etc." and "by the men" (lines 16–17)?

   (A) is assigned
   (B) and such actions
   (C) or war-making
   (D) is mostly done
   (E) not women, but

3. The natives' behavior when first encountering the European seamen appeared to the seamen to be

   (A) puzzling and contradictory
   (B) clever and humorous
   (C) sinister and malevolent
   (D) heroic and gallant
   (E) friendly and hospitable

4. In line 37, "regarded" most nearly means

   (A) looked at
   (B) appreciated
   (C) understood
   (D) liked at all
   (E) noticed

5. The author implies that the Maoris became "good friends" of the seamen because the Maoris

   (A) had a judicious sense of reality
   (B) needed the seamen's knowledge
   (C) admired the seamen's energy
   (D) were forced to obey the seamen
   (E) admired the generosity of the seamen

6. The author suggests the Maoris are happier than Europeans because they

   (A) are healthier and stronger
   (B) lack guns and cannon
   (C) seem not to be acquisitive
   (D) have made war into a sport
   (E) have no commerce or money

7. In line 47, the phrase "inequality of condition" most nearly means

   (A) differences in inherited talents
   (B) social, class, and economic distinctions
   (C) physical variations in health
   (D) different historical and geographical back-grounds
   (E) degrees of wealth and poverty

8. In line 71, "veneration" most nearly means

   (A) flattering explanation of
   (B) deep reverence for
   (C) biological preservation of
   (D) easy appreciation for
   (E) supernatural fear of

9. The phrase "a future state" (line 73) is best understood to mean

   (A) modern England
   (B) colonial New Zealand
   (C) an advanced culture
   (D) protracted states of war
   (E) life after death

10. The phrase "amplify the compliment" (line 84) is best interpreted to mean

   (A) makes the Maoris as fine a society in their way as the Britons are in their own way
   (B) extends the worth of the Maoris' natural aggressiveness and tendencies to make war
   (C) enlarges the meaning of their ceremonies for the dead and their ancestor worship
   (D) that, compared with the Maoris, the Britons are deficient in courage and intelligence
   (E) that, though respected by the New Zealanders, the Maoris are a threat to British law and ethics

11. Passage 1 differs from Passage 2 primarily in which of the following aspects?

(A) The extent to which logical analysis is employed
(B) The persuasive goals of the authors
(C) Subject matter and facts
(D) Style of language and tone
(E) Authors' assumptions about culture

12. Compared to Passage 2 in terms of style, Passage 1 is

(A) sentimental and lyrical
(B) pointed and persuasive
(C) a closely reasoned argument
(D) an urgently stated sermon
(E) relaxed and discursive

13. The information about the Maoris in Passage 1 would seem to be more reliable than the information in Passage 2 because

(A) Passage 1 is longer than Passage 2
(B) the author of Passage 2 is not as friendly as the author of Passage 1
(C) the author of Passage 1 was with the Maoris when he wrote about them
(D) the author of Passage 2 offers fewer facts than does the author of Passage 1
(E) the author of Passage 2 was writing at a later date than was the author of Passage 1

Stop!

Do not go on to the next section of the test until you have set your timer.

SECTION 6   TIME—15 MINUTES   10 QUESTIONS

In this section, solve each problem, and then choose the most appropriate answer from the choices given.

1. A number that is divisible by both 6 and 8 is also divisible by

   (A) 5
   (B) 9
   (C) 11
   (D) 16
   (E) 24

2. On a certain island there are liars and truth-tellers. Liars must always lie and truth-tellers must always tell the truth. A visitor comes across a native and asks him if he always tells the truth. The native responds, "I always tell the truth." The native could be

   (A) a truth-teller
   (B) a liar
   (C) either a truth-teller or a liar
   (D) neither a truth-teller nor a liar
   (E) None of the above.

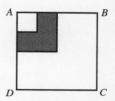

3. The three squares pictured above share a common vertex at *A*. The interior squares each have another vertex at the center of another one of the squares. What is the ratio of the area of the shaded region to the area of the unshaded region?

   (A) $\dfrac{3}{4}$
   (B) $\dfrac{3}{8}$
   (C) $\dfrac{3}{12}$
   (D) $\dfrac{3}{13}$
   (E) $\dfrac{3}{16}$

4. On a long street the houses are numbered in jumps of 6. That is, the first house has a street number 6, the second 12, and so on. What is the sum of the last digits of the street numbers of the 83rd, 84th, 85th, 86th, and 87th houses?

(A) 15
(B) 20
(C) 25
(D) 85
(E) 90

5. A man can paint m meters of fence in h hours and 15 minutes. What is his average speed in meters per hour?

(A) $h\left(1 + \dfrac{1}{4}\right)m$

(B) $\dfrac{m}{h + 15}$

(C) $\dfrac{m}{h + \dfrac{1}{4}}$

(D) $\dfrac{h + 15}{m}$

(E) $\dfrac{h + \dfrac{1}{4}}{m}$

6. A car is driven 2 miles across town. If the radius of a wheel on the car is 1 foot, how many revolutions has the wheel made?

(5,280 feet = 1 mile)

(A) $\dfrac{5,280}{\pi}$

(B) $\dfrac{10,560}{\pi}$

(C) $\dfrac{2,640}{\pi}$

(D) 5,280

(E) 10,560

7. The operation $\boxed{x}$ indicates that one should subtract 2 from x and then multiply the result by 2. The operation $\boxed{x}$ indicates that one should multiply x by 2 and then subtract 2 from the product.
$\circledx - \boxed{x} =$

(A) -2
(B) 0
(C) 2
(D) 4
(E) It cannot be determined from the information given.

8. $\left(x - \dfrac{1}{x}\right)^2 + 4 =$

   (A) 4

   (B) 5

   (C) $x^2 - \left(\dfrac{1}{x}\right)^2 + 4$

   (D) $x^2 + \left(\dfrac{1}{x}\right)^2$

   (E) $\left(x + \dfrac{1}{x}\right)^2$

9. On a street corner there are two flashing lights, a red one and a blue one. The red one flashes three times per minute, and the blue one flashes twice per minute. If the lights start off flashing at the same time, how often do they flash together?

   (A) once every 6 seconds

   (B) once every 10 seconds

   (C) once every minute

   (D) once every 2 minutes

   (E) once every 6 minutes

10.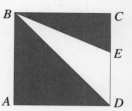

In this figure, ABCD is a square with area 2. If $\overline{DE}$ is twice as long as $\overline{EC}$, what is the area of $\triangle BED$?

   (A) 1

   (B) $\dfrac{1}{3}$

   (C) $\dfrac{2}{3}$

   (D) $\sqrt{2}$

   (E) $\dfrac{\sqrt{2}}{3}$

Stop!

Do not go on to the next section of the test until you have set your timer.

ANSWER SECTION

ANSWERS TO PRACTICE ANALOGIES

Practice Analogies 1
(pp. 16–17)

1. **The correct answer is (D).** verse : song :: bicuspid : teeth (Part of a whole.)

2. **The correct answer is (C).** fish : school :: geese : gaggle (Implied comparison. A group of fish is called a school just as a group of geese is termed a gaggle.)

3. **The correct answer is (A).** fortitude : heroine :: talent : artist (Person related to defining characteristic.)

4. **The correct answer is (E).** food : hunger :: water : thirst (Implied comparison. Lack of food leads to hunger just as lack of water leads to thirst.)

5. **The correct answer is (A).** studio : art :: conservatory : music (Implied comparison. First the place; then the subject studied or practiced in that specific place.)

6. **The correct answer is (E).** scalpel : incision :: plow : furrow (Implied comparison. A scalpel makes an incision, or cut, in the skin just as a plow makes a furrow, or cut, in the soil.)

7. **The correct answer is (B).** media : news :: government : laws (Implied comparison. A major function of the media is to provide news just as a major function of the government is to provide laws.)

8. **The correct answer is (E).** enervate : exhaustion :: assimilate : uniformity (Cause and effect or result. To be enervated leads to exhaustion as to be assimilated leads to uniformity.)

9. **The correct answer is (D).** accord : dissension :: gentility : coarseness (Antonyms. Also, the lack of accord may result in dissension just as the lack of gentility may result in coarseness.)

10. **The correct answer is (C).** tortuous : path :: convoluted : prose (Implied comparison. A winding, twisted path is referred to as tortuous, just as winding, twisted prose is termed convoluted.)

Practice Analogies 2
(pp. 17–18)

1. **The correct answer is (A).** orchestra : pit :: skaters : rink (A specific group related to its most typical location.)

2. **The correct answer is (D).** monarchy : government :: sonata : music (One of a kind.)

3. **The correct answer is (E).** article : newspaper :: scene : play (Part of a whole.)

4. **The correct answer is (C).** grandeur : scale :: harmony : balance (Implied comparison. The quality of grandeur depends on a thing's scale as the quality of harmony depends on a thing's balance.)

5. **The correct answer is (E).** stars : constellation :: particles : solution (Parts of a whole.)

6. **The correct answer is (E).** eager : zealous :: generous : prodigal (Degree.)

7. **The correct answer is (C).** clumsy : movement :: inarticulate : speech (Implied comparison. Poor, incoherent movement is termed clumsy just as poor, incoherent speech is called inarticulate.)

8. **The correct answer is (D).** malign : vilification :: satirize : mockery (Cause and effect or result.)

9. **The correct answer is (A).** connoisseur : discrimination :: monk : asceticism (Person related to characteristic practice.)

10. **The correct answer is (D).** edify : enlightenment :: persuade : accord (Cause and effect or result.)

Practice Analogies 3
(p. 19)

1. **The correct answer is (A).** tiger : ferocious :: deer : timorous (Animal related to its most logical trait.)

2. **The correct answer is (C).** honey : hive :: wine : cask (Product and customary storage location before marketing.)

3. **The correct answer is (E).** radiance : glimmer :: midday : dawn (Degree. Radiance is much brighter than a glimmer just as midday is much brighter than dawn.)

4. **The correct answer is (C).** pioneer : apathy :: disciple : rebellion (Implied comparison. A pioneer could never be accused of apathy—lack of interest or enthusiasm—just as a disciple—a devout follower—could never be accused of rebellion.)

5. **The correct answer is (C).** law : regulation :: outline : structure (Cause and effect or result.)

6. **The correct answer is (C).** difficult : arcane :: tenuous : impalpable (Degree. Arcane is the extreme of difficult, just as impalpable—unable to be touched, felt, grasped—is an extreme of tenuous.)

7. **The correct answer is (A).** child : mature :: bud : burgeon (Implied comparison of natural development—a child matures just as a bud burgeons into a flower, leaf, or shoot.)

8. **The correct answer is (A).** caricature : character :: clown : person (Implied comparison. A caricature is a ridiculous distortion of a character as a clown is a ridiculous distortion of a person.)

9. **The correct answer is (D).** incise : hack :: embrace : seize (Implied comparison. Incising is a more refined way of cutting than hacking is, just as embracing is more refined than seizing.)

10. **The correct answer is (D).** sloth : torpid :: ant : assiduous (Animal related to its most logical or expected characteristic.)

Practice Analogies 4
(p. 20)

1. **The correct answer is (C).** bee : swarm :: spectator : throng (Part of a whole.)

2. **The correct answer is (E).** drench : sprinkle :: squander : spend (Degree.)

3. **The correct answer is (D).** sleep : fitful :: thought : chaotic (Implied comparison. Disturbed sleep is fitful sleep, just as disturbed thought is chaotic—muddled, in other words.)

4. **The correct answer is (A).** perseverance : success :: curiosity : knowledge (Cause and effect or result. One logically leads to the other on both sides of this analogy.)

275

5. **The correct answer is (A).** heed :
advice :: rejoice : good fortune
(Implied comparison. We're
expected to heed—pay attention—to advice just as we're
expected to rejoice at good fortune.
Don't fall for other idiomatic
expressions, such as (D), which fail
to complete the comparison set up
in the original pair.)

6. **The correct answer is (D).**
ruminate : plan :: guess : think
(Implied comparison. Ruminating is
a rudimentary or preliminary kind of
planning just as guessing is a
rudimentary kind of thinking.)

7. **The correct answer is (C).**
obligatory : optional :: incessant:
sporadic (Antonyms.)

8. **The correct answer is (E).**
narcotic : dull :: unguent : soothe
(Product related to its effect or
purpose.)

9. **The correct answer is (B).**
constitution : amendment :: will :
codicil (Implied comparison. On
both sides, what is in the second
slot alters the document in the first
slot.)

10. **The correct answer is (B).**
emulsion : disintegrate :: congregation : individualize (Implied comparison. When an emulsion falls
apart, it disintegrates, just as when a
congregation falls apart, it individu-
alizes.)

Are you making flashcards of words that give you fits?

ANSWERS TO ANTONYM EXERCISE

Antonyms A (p. 24)

1. *Zeal* is the opposite of *apathy.*

2. *Vigorous* is the opposite of *decrepit.*

3. *Burgeon* is the opposite of *atrophy.*

4. *Paucity* is the opposite of *plethora.*

5. *Resist* is the opposite of *capitulate.*

Antonyms B (p. 24)

1. *Sophisticated* is the opposite of *ingenuous.*

2. *Exuberant* is the opposite of *staid.*

3. *Biased* is the opposite of *indifferent.*

4. *Obtuse* is the opposite of *discerning.*

5. *Disdain* is the opposite of *revere.*

Antonyms C (p. 25)

1. To *talk pleasantly* is the opposite of to *rant* (and rave).

2. *Esteem* is the opposite of *ignominy.*

3. *Confound* is the opposite of *elucidate.*

4. *Embroil* is the opposite of *extricate.*

5. *Sincerity* is the opposite of *hypocrisy.*

Antonyms D (p. 25)

1. *Irreplaceable* and *vital* are opposites of *expendable.*

2. *Extant* is the opposite of *defunct.*

3. *Sparse* is the opposite of *copious.*

4. *Broad-minded* is the opposite of *provincial.*

5. *Definite* is the opposite of *ambiguous.*

Antonyms E (p. 25)

1. *Prejudiced* is the opposite of *impartial.*

2. *Opulent* is the opposite of *meager.*

3. *Laud* is the opposite of *denounce.*

4. *Adopt* is the opposite of *repudiate.*

5. *Guile* is the opposite of *candor.*

ANSWERS TO PRACTICE SENTENCE COMPLETIONS

Practice Sentence Completions 1 (pp. 34–36)

1. **The correct answer is (D).** inestimable (This word is defined after the blank.)

2. **The correct answer is (B).** ambivalent. .diversity (Everything after the semicolon shows that James is of two minds about joining a fraternity, and the first blank must describe this state; only answer (B) and possibly answer (A) fill this requirement. The second blank must offer a contrast to being with people just like James—like-minded, in other words. The question is of people types, not education, so answer (A) does not work.)

3. **The correct answer is (C).** compromise. .disparate (Logic points to *disparate* for the second blank; the first blank must be filled by a word describing how people with differences can meet and solve problems. Answer (D) is way off the mark.)

4. **The correct answer is (B).** credulous. .succumb to (The first blank narrows the choice to (A) or (B); *credulous* means *gullible, easily fooled.* One can't *adhere to* a scheme, so that leaves (B) *succumb to,* or *give in to.*)

5. **The correct answer is (B).** a volatile (The word chosen must be a direct opposite of the name *Patience;* note *at odds with her name,* plus the entire predicate.)

6. **The correct answer is (B).** incompatible. .witty repartee (Logic requires a negative word for the first blank, because this sentence contrasts the attitude of a serious artist with that of people who give endless parties. Idiomatic usage then requires *witty repartee* for the second blank, as the people are being *regaled* (delightfully entertained).)

7. **The correct answer is (C).** paradox. .inhibited (This sentence requires an understanding of the word *paradox,* which the sentence goes on to illustrate. The second blank demands a negative word; thus, answer (B) may be tempting, but it is not as precise as answer (C), nor does it work idiomatically.)

8. **The correct answer is (C).** chaotic. .tranquillity (The first blank needs a negative word to contrast with a positive word that goes with *and peaceful* in the second blank. Only answer (C) offers that contrast.)

9. **The correct answer is (E).**
susceptible. .efficacy (A sentence of contrast: the first blank narrows the choices to (C) and (E), but *inevitability* isn't a logical choice of word to refer to *miracles*.)

10. **The correct answer is (A).**
terseness. .profusion (This sentence contrasts literary styles, the lean versus the fat. Other answers may be momentarily tempting, but none set up the exact contrast except answer (A).)

Practice Sentence Completions 2 (pp. 37–39)

1. **The correct answer is (B).**
enriched (The rest of the sentence provides an implied definition. Note the word *distinguished*.)

2. **The correct answer is (E).**
lax. .bribed (The kind of security that makes escapes common could only be (C), (D), or (E). Guards who are easily *converted* or *investigated* wouldn't necessarily help someone escape, but those who are easily *bribed* (E) certainly would.)

3. **The correct answer is (B).**
incongruous (This sentence of stark contrasts joined in one person requires a word that describes this odd state, not a judgment call as offered by answers (C), (D), and (E).)

4. **The correct answer is (C).**
canny. .acumen (Contrast requires that the first blank be filled by an opposite of *young, ingenuous;* the second blank must explain why opponents are often *surprised.* Answer (A) is weak all around.)

5. **The correct answer is (A).**
attest. .unabated (Sentence sense and general knowledge require answer (A).)

6. **The correct answer is (D).**
prehensile. .precocious (The first clause points to a word meaning *to grasp quickly and well,* for which *prehensile* is the perfect choice; the word required in the second blank is extremely similar, and it is defined in the sentence.)

7. **The correct answer is (B).**
dearth. .inundated with (Contrast requires a negative word in the first blank, especially called for by the verb *suffered;* the second blank must complete the meaning of *reams of information.* Answer (E) is weak, off the mark.)

8. **The correct answer is (E).**
altruism. .narcissism (The first blank must be a word that coordinates well with *generosity,* because the two words are joined by *and;* the contrast, however, requires an opposite in the second blank, and *narcissism* is the most specific, given the phrase *in her own name.* Her new charity is an extremely selfish-looking thing to her associates.)

9. **The correct answer is (C).**
ascetic. .avaricious (Only answers (A), (B), and (C) can be considered for the first blank, and, of those choices, only answer (C) has a negative word in the second blank, and it's the perfect word, as it must be an opposite to *no need of worldly goods.*)

10. **The correct answer is (E).**
obsolescent. .myopic (Logic requires a word meaning *old, outdated,* or *obsolete* in the first blank; only answer (E) is possible. *Myopic,* meaning nearsighted, completes the contrast.)

Practice Sentence Completions 3 (pp. 40–42)

1. **The correct answer is (C).** problem-solving skills (Answer (B) merely repeats *logic* in the sentence and is not as specific as answer (C).)

2. **The correct answer is (E).** didactic (Definition of required word in sentence.)

3. **The correct answer is (A).** lackluster. .incapable (Sentence logic requires two negative words.)

4. **The correct answer is (B).** mollified (*Mollified* means *placated* and refers to someone whose anger or insult has been alleviated, as by an apology.)

5. **The correct answer is (D).** sanguinity. .debacle (Comparison requires a word meaning *optimism* in the first blank and a word referring to the effect of investments going sour in the second blank. Answer (A) shows a weak word, *process*, in its second slot.)

6. **The correct answer is (B).** catholic. .demagogue (Contrast requires an antonym of *parochial* (narrow, limited) in the first blank. The second blank is followed by a definition of *demagogue*, pointing to it as the perfect answer choice.)

7. **The correct answer is (A).** combat. .isolation (Sentence logic and idiomatic usage allow only the word *combat* in the first blank; the words *alone* and *solitary* mandate choosing *isolation*.)

8. **The correct answer is (C).** reluctant. .inaccurately reflect (The word *although* sets up a sentence with contrasting clauses, further emphasized by the verb *feared*. Answer (C) is the only logical choice.)

9. **The correct answer is (E).** fortuitous (This word is what the sentence goes on to define.)

10. **The correct answer is (B).** a formidable. .revolutionizing (Another sentence of contrast: The first blank requires a negative word and the second, a positive one. Only (B) and maybe (D) meet this requirement, and *revolutionizing* is a much better way of describing what a "remarkable machine" does than is *codifying*.)

Practice Sentence Completions 4 (pp. 43–45)

1. **The correct answer is (B).** a modest (Key words: *viewers did not flock/only*)

2. **The correct answer is (D).** demanding (Key words: *economics textbook/yet/read attentively*)

3. **The correct answer is (D).** distort (Key words: *rather than/just so that*)

4. **The correct answer is (C).** truth (Key words: *Although* (sets up contrast)/*honestly*)

5. **The correct answer is (E).** metamorphosis. .ruthless (Key words: *considerate* (requires sharply contrasting word for second blank)/*underwent a total/bent on evil*)

6. **The correct answer is (A).** harsh reality. .idealistic goals (Key words: *moral good/imagination*)

7. **The correct answer is (D).** relentless. .tenacity (Key words: *determination/conquer*)

8. **The correct answer is (D).** an enigma (Key words: *to puzzle*)

9. **The correct answer is (D).** innate. .cultivate (Key words: *in a structured environment/wasteful* (sets up contrast))

10. **The correct answer is (B).** modicum. .chimera (Key words: *more than/not/but/an actual man*)

ANSWERS TO CRITICAL READING QUESTIONS

Practice Critical Reading 1
(pp. 74–76)

1. **The correct answer is (C).** The phrase "Transported to the Indies" modifies the noun phrase that comes right after it, "his live blood."

2. **The correct answer is (D).** See lines 6–11, especially "interior vitality," line 16.

3. **The correct answer is (C).** See lines 7–8, "those summers had *dried up* all his physical superfluousness."

4. **The correct answer is (B).** See the description in lines 12–15.

5. **The correct answer is (A).** You could substitute this phrase for "endued with" in the passage.

6. **The correct answer is (A).** The author describes Starbuck in positive terms but is aware of Starbuck's weaknesses.

7. **The correct answer is (E).** The other seamen are contrasted with Starbuck.

8. **The correct answer is (D).** See lines 27–34.

9. **The correct answer is (B).** See the second paragraph, especially lines 35–38.

10. **The correct answer is (D).** Starbuck seems to have learned to be cautious (lines 44–49) from these deaths.

11. **The correct answer is (E).** See lines 58–64.

12. **The correct answer is (E).** See lines 58–64.

13. **The correct answer is (C).** If you have any doubt, reread the last paragraph.

14. **The correct answer is (D).** The author has shifted from the particular man Starbuck to men in general.

Practice Critical Reading 2
(pp. 79–82)

1. **The correct answer is (B).** You have to read the whole paragraph to determine that the author considers being old and ignorant a "critically important" misery.

2. **The correct answer is (C).** See lines 2–4.

3. **The correct answer is (D).** See lines 4–5.

4. **The correct answer is (E).** See lines 7–9.

5. **The correct answer is (A).** Examples of figures of speech: the mind as a treasury in line 12; "foolish old age" as "a barren vine" and as a fool's university in lines 13–14; life as sweet as a summer day in lines 21–23.

6. **The correct answer is (D).** Antisthenes is saying that his studies taught him to talk with himself— that having something to think about is like having someone to talk to.

7. **The correct answer is (E).** See lines 16–17.

8. **The correct answer is (B).** See lines 43–50.

9. **The correct answer is (A).** See lines 52–56.

10. **The correct answer is (D).** See lines 49–50.

11. **The correct answer is (B).**
Forging "the anchors of the mind" (line 67) is the more rigorous or logical work of the mind, while "spinning the gossamers" is more delicate or creative.

12. **The correct answer is (E).** In line 70, being "full of life and fire" is contrasted to being a "stunted ascetic."

13. **The correct answer is (C).** Both authors are writing about education, the way to knowledge and learning.

14. **The correct answer is (C).** See particularly lines 4-7, 15-16, and 20-27 in Passage 1 and the final paragraph of Passage 2.

15. **The correct answer is (B).** Both authors reveal the strength of their opinions in the first paragraphs of their passages.

Practice Critical Reading 3
(pp. 84-85)

1. **The correct answer is (A).** The first paragraph discusses the simple nervous systems of simple animals in order to set up the discussion of the workings of more complex neural systems, which is the subject of the passage as a whole.

2. **The correct answer is (D).** See lines 20-23, which explain the opposite actions of axons and dendrites.

3. **The correct answer is (D).** Read the last sentence of the passage.

4. **The correct answer is (B).** The axon membranes are exposed to the "extracelluar medium"—the surrounding environment outside the cell.

5. **The correct answer is (B).** Note lines 26-30, which explain the contrast between vertebrate and invertebrate glial cell sheaths.

Practice Critical Reading 4
(pp. 87-88)

1. **The correct answer is (C).** See lines 27-30, which express Stein's dissatisfaction with his country's leadership.

2. **The correct answer is (D).** This interpretation is supported by the man's actions as recounted in this passage.

3. **The correct answer is (A).** See lines 4-8. Answer (B) is too narrow, as it could not include the immense war indemnities incurred as the war progressed.

4. **The correct answer is (B).** See lines 19-21.

5. **The correct answer is (E).** Note lines 41-45.

Practice Critical Reading 5
(pp. 90-91)

1. **The correct answer is (C).** See lines 1-2 and 9-14.

2. **The correct answer is (D).** See lines 7-9.

3. **The correct answer is (D).** This is the main argument advanced in the second and third paragraphs.

4. **The correct answer is (C).** For I and II, see lines 20-24; for IV, lines 30-34.

5. **The correct answer is (A).** The legislation must have been written down in order to be "offered to the states" (line 4).

Practice Critical Reading 6
(p. 93)

1. **The correct answer is (D).** M. Renard addresses the "Judge" (line 8) and speaks of his "witnesses" (line 18).

2. **The correct answer is (A).** At Mme. Renard's first outburst, M. Renard spoke to himself but not to her (line 6). When he teased her and she got angry, he was again silent (line 17). He also says he "felt" her final comment, though he did nothing (line 30).

3. **The correct answer is (A).** They felt indignant because the "little man" had stolen their fishing spot and wounded because he was catching what they considered to be their fish.

4. **The correct answer is (B).** See lines 24-25, 27-29, and 33-35.

5. **The correct answer is (D).** M. Renard is wordy, but he conveys his feelings movingly. Choice (C) might draw you, but note that M. Renard recounts events in precise chronological order.

ANSWERS TO MATH QUESTIONS

Practice Problems in Basic Arithmetic
(pp. 128-129)

1. The correct answer is (C). Whatever x is, $-x + x = 0$.

2. The correct answer is (C). Start with 1 and, using the tests for divisibility, enumerate all of the possible factors:

   $1 \times 24 = 24$
   $2 \times 12 = 24$
   $3 \times 8 = 24$
   $4 \times 6 = 24$

   5 is not a factor of 24. You needn't check any numbers greater than 6, because any number greater than 6 would go into 24 fewer than 4 times, and you've already enumerated all of the positive integers less than 4.

3. The correct answer is (C). -1 multiplied by itself an odd number of times is -1. Multiplied by itself an even number of times, it is 1, so $n^3 + n^2 = -1 + 1 = 0$.

4. The correct answer is (B). Don't leap at this problem and say $x = 9$. x is -9, so column B contains the larger quantity.

5. The correct answer is (B). The quantity am is less than 0, so either a is negative and m is positive or vice versa. a is less than m, so a must be the negative number and m the positive number. All positives are greater than 0, so column B contains the greater quantity.

6. The correct answer is (B). $2 < 3$, $4 < 5$, $6 < 7$, and $8 < 9$. Each addend in column A is less than a corresponding addend in column B, so we know that the total in column A must be less without doing any addition.

7. The correct answer is (D). Although you know that of p and w one is negative and one is positive, you can't determine which is which.

8. The correct answer is (A). The only time $y = -y$ is when $y = 0$. To prove this to yourself, add y to both sides of the equation, get $2y = 0$, and solve for y.

9. The correct answer is 10. $620 \div 60$ is the same as $62 \div 6$, which is the same as $31 \div 3$, which is 10 with a remainder of only 1.

10. The correct answer is 20. $2 \times 3 = 6$, and $6 \times 7 = 42$, so dividing each side of the equation by these factors leaves $4 \times 5 = a$, or $a = 20$.

Practice Problems in Fractions 1
(pp. 135–141)

1. The correct answer is (C). Since the brown socks, the blue socks, the black socks, and the white socks put together make up all of the socks in the drawer, the sum of all the different fractional parts must equal 1.

Algebraically, this can be stated $\frac{1}{2} + \frac{1}{4} + \frac{1}{5} + w = 1$, where w stands for the fractional part of the socks that are white. By subtracting $\frac{1}{2}$, $\frac{1}{4}$, and $\frac{1}{5}$ from both sides of the equation you are left with $w = \frac{1}{20}$. Getting answer (B), (D), or (E) means you are probably adding the denominators to get the sum of the fractions. Answer (A) is the fractional part of the socks that are *not* white.

2. The correct answer is (E). Don't disregard answer (E) just because it is so different from the others. If you get it as an answer, keep it. Divide the 12 inches of ribbon by the size of one piece $\left(\frac{1}{4} \text{ inch}\right)$ to get the number of pieces it contains. Then multiply that number by 5 (since each costs a nickel) to get the answer $2.40. Algebraically, you have $\left(12 \div \frac{1}{4}\right) \times .05$.

3. The correct answer is (D). Do this problem one card at a time. That is, take an X card from pile A and put it in pile B. Then find what fractional part of each pile the X cards make up. Do this until the fractional part of X cards is the same for each pile. Once the fractional parts are equal, go back and count how many X cards you moved. After taking one X card from A and putting it in pile B, the fractional part of X cards in pile A is $\frac{3}{5}$ and the fractional part of X cards in pile B is $\frac{1}{7}$. Notice that the "size" of the whole changes when you move cards. After moving the third X card, the fractional part of X cards in pile A is $\frac{1}{3}$ and in pile B is $\frac{3}{9}$. Since $\frac{1}{3} = \frac{3}{9}$, 3 is the answer.

4. The correct answer is (E). The distance that runner B falls behind is given by the fraction $\frac{x \text{ in.}}{y \text{ min.}}$. Since you want the answer in terms of feet and hours, you must multiply by unit fractions. $\frac{1 \text{ ft.}}{12 \text{ in.}}$ and $\frac{60 \text{ min.}}{1 \text{ hr.}}$ are the two unit fractions you use. The multiplication looks like:

$$\frac{x \text{ in.}}{y \text{ min.}} \times \frac{1 \text{ ft.}}{12 \text{ in.}} \times \frac{60 \text{ min.}}{1 \text{ hr.}}$$

The inches and the minutes drop out leaving you with $\frac{60x \text{ ft.}}{12y \text{ hr.}}$. By dividing the top and bottom by 12, you can simplify the equation to $\frac{5x}{y}$ feet in 1 hour.

5. The correct answer is (D). The steps for doing this problem are (1) change the mixed numbers to fractions; (2) find the difference between the distances in feet; and (3) convert the feet to inches with the unit fraction $\dfrac{12 \text{ in.}}{1 \text{ ft.}}$.

6. The correct answer is (D). Do not make the mistake of inverting $\dfrac{1}{a} - \dfrac{1}{b}$ and getting $a - b$. You must first change the denominator into a *single fraction* before you may invert it. To do this, find the difference between $\dfrac{1}{a}$ and $\dfrac{1}{b}$. It should come out to $\dfrac{b - a}{ab}$. Now you may invert the fraction in the denominator and get $\dfrac{ab}{b - a}$ for an answer.

7. The correct answer is (B). $\dfrac{-8}{1} = -8$, and $\dfrac{1}{-8} = -\dfrac{1}{8}$. On the number line, $-\dfrac{1}{8}$ is to the right of -8, so $-\dfrac{1}{8}$ is the greater number.

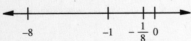

8. The correct answer is (C) If you invert a number an even number of times, you get back to the original number, so $\dfrac{3}{7} \,\S\, 100 = \dfrac{3}{7}$. If you invert a number an odd number of times, it's the same as inverting it once, so $\dfrac{3}{7} \,\S\, 101 = \dfrac{7}{3}$.

9. The correct answer is 3. Cross multiplying is the quickest way to work this problem. To save even more time though, instead of going from $5 \times 9 = x \times 15$ to $45 = 15x$, divide both sides by 5 *before* multiplying. This leaves $9 = 3x$, a fairly easy equation.

10. The correct answer is $\left(\dfrac{1}{3}\right)$. The trick here is remembering that Joan paints $\dfrac{1}{2}$ of what is left, *not* $\dfrac{1}{2}$ of the fence. You must first figure out how much of the fence is left before you can determine how much Joan paints. Subtracting $\dfrac{1}{3}$ (the amount Jim paints) from 1 gives the amount left, $\dfrac{2}{3}$. Half of $\dfrac{2}{3}$ is $\dfrac{1}{3}$. Subtracting the part Jim paints and the part Joan paints from 1 gives the part that is left unpainted. $1 - \dfrac{1}{3} - \dfrac{1}{3} = \dfrac{1}{3}$, so $\dfrac{1}{3}$ is the fractional part left unpainted.

Practice Problems in Fractions 2 (pp. 141–144)

1. The correct answer is (B). With this problem either you can convert the decimal to a fraction and then do the multiplication, or you can just do the multiplication with decimals. Doing the multiplication with decimals looks like

$$
\begin{array}{r}
.125 \\
\times\ 8 \\
\hline
1.000
\end{array}
$$

There are three digits in front of the decimal, so the answer must be 1.000, or just 1, answer (B).

2. The correct answer is (E). Squaring the .2 gives you $.04 = \sqrt{x}$. Do not stop here and put answer (C). Square both sides of the equation to get $.04^2 = x$. Multiplying out $.04 \times .04$ leaves $.0016$, answer (E).

3. The correct answer is (B). This is a problem in juggling equations, except the numbers used are decimals. The first thing to do is multiply both sides by 10. This changes the $-.6$ to -6 and the 1.2 to 12. From here you can divide both sides by 6, leaving $-(0.4 - p) = 2(.8p + .7p)$. Adding the .8p and the .7p and getting rid of the parentheses on both sides of the equation gives $p - .4 = 3p$. Subtract p from both sides, and then divide by 2. You're left with $-.2 = p$, answer (B). If you had wanted, you could have changed all of the decimals to fractions and worked from there; the steps would be mostly the same. Finally, if nothing else seems to be working for you, plug answer choices in and chug them through. Only the correct answer works.

4. The correct answer is (A). By subtracting the second equation from the first, you cause all of the 3s after the decimal point to become 0s, so you are left with $9n = 3$. Dividing both sides by 9 and then simplifying the fraction leaves you with $\frac{1}{3}$, answer (A).

5. The correct answer is (E). After 12 peaches have been eaten, 108 remain. In fractional notation, this is $\frac{108}{120}$ of the total. To convert this to a decimal, multiply by 100:
$$\frac{108}{120} \times 100 = 90.$$

6. The correct answer is (A). $P = \frac{75}{100} \times 12$ is the distance the boy has walked. By dividing the numerator and the denominator first by 25 and then by 4, you can reduce the equation to $P = 9$. But this is the distance the boy has *already* walked. Subtracting 9 from 12 leaves 3, the number of miles the boy has left to go.

7. The correct answer is (C) The first statement, "60-gallon tank is 40% full of water," can be written as $P = \frac{40}{100} \times 60$. The part of the tank that is full, P, solves to be 24. *Don't stop* here and mark answer (A). Ask what percent 24 is of 40. Algebraically, it reads $24 = \frac{c}{100} \times 40$. Solving for c gives 60, answer (C).

8. The correct answer is (B). Problems involving boys and girls usually leave out one important unstated fact: the number of boys plus the number of girls equals the total number of people. Call the number of people in the class x. This means the number of boys is 30% of x, or $\frac{30}{100} \times x$. Since the number of boys added to the number of girls equals the total number of people in the class, you can set up the equation $\frac{30}{100}x + 21 = x$. Solving for x, you get $x = 30$; that is, there are 30 people *in the class*. Subtracting 21, the number of girls in the class, leaves 9, the number of boys in the class, which is answer (B).

9. The correct answer is (D). Since both calls are made at the same rate, the ratio between the cost and the time of both calls is equal. That is, $\dfrac{\$0.24}{4 \text{ min.}} = \dfrac{\$x}{15 \text{ min.}}$. Cross multiplying and canceling units leaves $(.24)15 = 4x$. Solving for x gives $x = \$0.90$.

10. The correct answer is (B). The word *represents* implies that a ratio is being used. Call x the number of inches that represents 1 foot 6 inches in the drawing. The algebraic equation becomes $\dfrac{x \text{ in.}}{1 \text{ ft. 6 in.}} = \dfrac{3 \text{ in.}}{9 \text{ ft.}}$. Convert the feet to inches to get $\dfrac{x \text{ in.}}{18 \text{ in.}} = \dfrac{3 \text{ in.}}{9 \times 12 \text{ in.}}$.

Cross multiplying and canceling units leaves

$x \times 9 \times 12 = 3 \times 18$.   Divide both sides by 9.

$x \times 12 = 3 \times 2$.   Divide both sides by 6.

$x \times 2 = 1$.   Divide both sides by 2.

$x = \dfrac{1}{2} = .5$.

So .5 inch represents 1 foot 6 inches in the scale drawing. Notice that you did not need to do the multiplication. *Simplify before* you do the multiplication.

11. The correct answer is (B). The ratios are equal, so $\dfrac{3}{4} = \dfrac{a}{12}$. Cross multiplying and doing the simplification leaves $a = 9$.

12. The correct answer is (C). The total number of parts is $6 + 2 + 1 = 9$. Ned receives 2 of them, so Ned's share is $\dfrac{2}{9}$ of \$72, or \$16.

13. The correct answer is (C). Forty-four percent of 25 students is 11, so there are 11 boys. The 14 other students must be girls. The ratio of boys to girls is therefore $11:14$.

14. The correct answer is (B). An equilateral triangle is defined as having three equal sides; so if the length of one side is called s, then the perimeter (the sum of the lengths of the sides) must be $3s$. The ratio of the length of one side to the perimeter is therefore s to $3s$ or $\dfrac{s}{3s}$, which equals $\dfrac{1}{3}$.

15. The correct answer is (C).
$$4,836 = 4,000 + 800 + 30 + 6$$
$$= 4 \times 1,000 + 8 \times 100 + 3 \times 10 + 6 \times 1$$
$$= 4 \times 10^3 + 8 \times 10^2 + 3 \times 10 + 6.$$

16. The correct answer is 100. Set the equation up phrase by phrase: "30% of" "80" "is" "what percent" "of" "24." The algebraic expression for this is $\dfrac{30}{100} \times 80 = \dfrac{x}{100} \times 24$. Canceling a 10 twice from the first fraction leaves $3 \times 8 = \dfrac{x}{100} \times 24$. Divide both sides of the equation by 24 to get $1 = \dfrac{x}{100}$, or $x = 100$.

17. The correct answer is 15. Call my age now M and my father's age now F. The two equations take the form $\dfrac{M + 15}{F + 15} = \dfrac{1}{2}$ and $\dfrac{M - 5}{F - 5} = \dfrac{1}{4}$. Cross multiply to get $2M + 30 = F + 15$ and $4M - 20 = F - 5$. Solve the two equations in two unknowns to get $M = 15$ and $F = 45$. M represents my age, so I am 15.

Practice Problems in Exponents and Square Roots
(pp. 147–148)

1. The correct answer is (D). First change .25 to a fraction, $\frac{1}{4}$.

$$\frac{1}{y} = \sqrt{\frac{1}{4}};$$

$$\frac{1}{y} = \frac{\sqrt{1}}{\sqrt{4}};$$

$$\frac{1}{y} = \frac{1}{2};$$

$$y = 2.$$

2. The correct answer is (E).

$$4\sqrt{48} - 3\sqrt{12}$$

$$= 4\sqrt{16 \times 3} - 3\sqrt{4 \times 3}$$

$$= 4\sqrt{16}\sqrt{3} - 3\sqrt{4}\sqrt{3}$$

$$= 16\sqrt{3} - 6\sqrt{3} = 10\sqrt{3}.$$

3. The correct answer is (D).

$$\left(\frac{1}{2}x^6\right)^2 = \left(\frac{1}{2}\right)^2 x^{6 \times 2} = \frac{1}{4}x^{12}.$$

Do not forget to square the coefficient, $\frac{1}{2}$.

4. The correct answer is (E).

$$\sqrt{\frac{x^2}{4} + \frac{4x^2}{9}}$$

$$= \sqrt{\frac{9x^2}{36} + \frac{16x^2}{36}}$$

$$= \sqrt{\frac{25x^2}{36}}$$

$$= \frac{\sqrt{25x^2}}{\sqrt{36}}$$

$$= \frac{5x}{6}.$$

Do not take the square root of each addend.

5. The correct answer is (A). $7x - 7y$

$$= 7(x - y) = 20; (x - y) = \frac{20}{7}.$$

6. The correct answer is (D). The first pipe can fill 1 pool in 8 hours. You write this $\frac{1 \text{ pool}}{8 \text{ hours}}$. Likewise, the second pipe works at a rate of 1 pool in 12 hours, or $\frac{1 \text{ pool}}{12 \text{ hours}}$. Let b be the number of hours both pipes work together. The number of pools they fill in b hours is $\frac{1}{8}b + \frac{1}{12}b$. You want to fill only 1 pool, so set this expression equal to 1 and solve: $\frac{1}{8}b + \frac{1}{12}b = 1$. Multiply both sides of the equation by 24 to get $3b + 2b = 24$; $b = \frac{24}{5} = 4\frac{4}{5}$ hours.

7. The correct answer is 3. $2^{x + 2} = 32 = 2^5$; therefore $x + 2 = 5$ and $x = 3$.

8. The correct answer is 20.

$$3x - .3x = 2.7x = 54;$$

$$x = \frac{54}{2.7} = \frac{540}{27}; x = 20.$$

9. The correct answer is .11.

$$\sqrt{.0121} = \sqrt{\frac{121}{10,000}}$$

$$= \frac{\sqrt{121}}{\sqrt{10,000}} = \frac{11}{\sqrt{10^4}}$$

$$= \frac{11}{10^2} = \frac{11}{100} = .11.$$

10. The correct answer is 8. The twins are traveling away from each other at 80 miles per hour. At this rate it will take $\frac{640}{80} = 8$ hours to be 64 miles apart.

Practice Problems in Basic Geometry
(pp. 155–158)

1. The correct answer is (B).
$2x + (x + 30°) = 90°$.
$3x + 30° = 90°; 3x = 60°; x = 20°$.

2. The correct answer is (D).
$\angle ROQ + TOS = 271°$
$\angle ROQ + \angle TOS$ also equals $\angle ROS$, a straight angle, with $\angle TOQ$ counted twice; written algebraically,
$$\angle ROQ + \angle TOS = 180° + \angle TOQ$$
$$271 = 180 + \angle TOQ$$
$$\angle TOQ = 91°$$
$\angle TOQ$ and $\angle POV$ are vertical angles so they are equal.

3. The correct answer is (A). Draw a circle around the five angles like the one below. The central angles of a circle add up to 360°, so $x + 2x + 3x + 4x + 5x = 360$. Adding all of the x's on the left side, you get $15x$

= 360. From this equation, you can solve for x and find that $x = 24$.

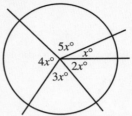

4. The correct answer is (E). *AB*, the width of the rectangle, is given as 2. *AD*, the length of the rectangle, is made up of two radii of the circles; so it must equal 4. The area equals the length times the width.
$A = l \times w = 4 \times 2 = 8$.

5. The correct answer is (D). *OA* and *OB* are both radii of the same circle; so they must have equal lengths. Mark this on the diagram along with the fact that $\angle OAB$ has a measure of 20°, which was given. Using the rule "Opposite angles of equal sides of a triangle are equal," you may fill in 20° for $\angle OBA$. Now you have a triangle, *AOB*, with an unknown angle and two 20° angles. The unknown angle, call it x, is the one you are asked to solve for. The angles of a triangle must add to 180: $x + 20 + 20 = 180$. Solving for x, you find $x = 140$.

6. The correct answer is (C). Notice that the shaded area is half the result of subtracting the areas of the smaller circles from the larger circle. The radius of the larger circle is 4, so the area of the larger circle is $A = \pi(4)^2 = 16\pi$. The diameters of the smaller circles are equal to the radius of the larger circle, so their radii are 2 and areas are 4π. The area of the larger circle minus the areas of the smaller circles is $16\pi - 2(4\pi) = 8\pi$. The area of the shaded section is half of this, 4π.

7. The correct answer is (A). The length of the line drawn by the roller after *one complete revolution* is 4, so 4 must be the circumference of the roller. The circumference equation says that $C = \pi D = 2\pi r$, where C is the circumference, D the diameter, and r the radius. Plugging 4 in for C, you have $4 = 2\pi r$, which reduces to $r = \dfrac{2}{\pi}$.

8. The correct answer is (E). The circumscribed (outside) circle has a diameter equal to the diagonal of the square. The inscribed (inner) circle has a diameter equal to the length of a side of the square. The length of a side of the square is 2, so the diagonal has a length $2\sqrt{2}$. Consequently the diameter of the outer circle is $2\sqrt{2}$ and the diameter of the inner circle is 2. Dividing the diameters by 2 to find the radii, you get $\sqrt{2}$ and 1. The areas of the circles are given by the equation $A = \pi r^2$. Plugging $\sqrt{2}$ and 1 into this equation, you find the areas to be 2π and π. The ratio of the larger area to the smaller area is $2:1$.

9. The correct answer is 72.
Let x = the measure of $\angle a$;
$2x$ = the measure of $\angle b$;
$2x$ = the measure of $\angle c$.

$\angle a + \angle b + \angle c = 180°$
$x + 2x + 2x = 180°$;
$5x = 180°$;
$x = 36°$.
$\angle b = \angle d$. Opposite angles.
$\angle b = \angle d = 2x = 72°$.

10. The correct answer is 20.
$(3x + 10°) + (x - 6°) = 84°$.
Corresponding angles are equal.
$4x + 4° = 84°$
$4x = 80°; x = 20°$.

11. The correct answer is 56. Extend one of the lines.

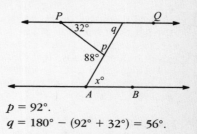

$p = 92°$.
$q = 180° - (92° + 32°) = 56°$.

Using the rule for transversals of parallel lines, $\angle x = \angle q = 56°$.

Practice Problems in Polygons and Polyhedrons
(pp. 165–168)

1. The correct answer is (C). *ABCD*'s area is 100, so the length of each side is 10. Recall, $A = s^2$ for a square. By the same reasoning, *RB* is 6. $AR = AB - RB = 10 - 6 = 4$. The length of a side of *TSRA* is 4, so its area is 16.

2. The correct answer is (C). There are several ways to proceed with this problem after you have drawn in all of the given information. One way is to say *BC* is half of one of the diagonals of *BFED* and *CF* is half of the other. The two diagonals are equal, so *BC* must equal *CF*. *BC* is a side of square *ABCD*, so it has length 4. It follows then that *CF* = 4.

3. The correct answer is (D). The side of the original sheet of metal is $x + 2 + 2 = x + 4$. Since the original sheet is a square, its area is the length of one of its sides squared $= (x + 4)^2$. However, the given information says that the area also equals $x^2 + 24x$. To solve for x, set the two expressions equal to each other. $(x + 4)^2 = x^2 + 24x$, or $x^2 + 8x + 16 = x^2 + 24x$; $16x = 16$; $x = 1$. Don't stop here. $x = 1$, so the side of the sheet is $1 + 2 + 2 = 5$, and the area is 25. Don't stop here either. Each corner has area $2^2 = 4$, so the area of the sheet without the four corners is $25 - 4(4) = 9$.

4. The correct answer is (D). By adding two line segments (as below), you can greatly simplify this problem.

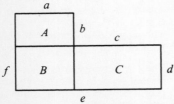

Now it is a lot easier to see that ab is the area of rectangle A and de is the area of rectangles $B + C$. All three of the smaller rectangles are accounted for, so answer (A) gives the correct area. Breaking up each of the other answers this way shows that they too give correct areas except for answer (D). In answer (D) you have af, which is the sum of rectangles A and B, and ed, which is the sum of the areas of rectangles B and C. Rectangle B is accounted for twice, so $af + ed$ is *larger* than the area of the figure.

5. The correct answer is (B). The bottom of the box is the shaded region. It has a width of two sides of the square tabs, or more simply $2s$. The length of the bottom is $3s$.

When the tabs are folded up, the height of the box formed will be the height of one tab, s. The volume of the box is length times width times height, $3s \times 2s \times 1s = 6s^3$. One hint to the answer is the exponent. Length will always be given to the first power, area to the second power, and volume to the third. Only answers (B) and (D) fit this description.

6. The correct answer is (C). The average equation says that the average equals the sum over the number. The sum of the angles in a triangle is always 180, and there are always three angles in a triangle. The average must be $\frac{180}{3} = 60$.

7. The correct answer is (A). This is a case where you must draw in an extra line. Drawing in BE, where BE is perpendicular to AC and E is on AC, forms a 45-90-45 triangle and a 30-60-90 triangle. (Numbers like 45, 30, and 60 are hints that something like this is afoot.)

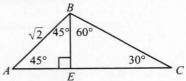

Using the rule for 45-90-45 triangles, you can solve for BE and AE to find that each equals 1. But now, since you know the length of one side of the 30-60-90 triangle (BE), you can solve for EC and get $\sqrt{3}$. The area of $\triangle ABC$ is half of its base (AC) times its height (BE).

$BE = 1$, and $AC = 1 + \sqrt{3}$.

Area $= \frac{1}{2}(BE)(AC)$

$= \frac{1}{2}(1)(1 + \sqrt{3})$

$= \frac{1}{2} + \frac{\sqrt{3}}{2}$.

8. The correct answer is 20. The figure has already been drawn in this problem, so your next step is to fill in any information that you can. Two sides of the upper right triangle are equal (they are both 2), so the angles opposite those two sides must also be equal. Call these angles x.

Now notice that $x°$, $x°$, and $40°$ make up a triangle, so their sum must be $180°$. Algebraically, you have $x + x + 40 = 180$. Solving for x gives you $x = 70$. Now fill in the new information. One of the $70°$ angles shares a vertical angle with an angle in the lower left-hand triangle; these two angles must be equal. (Some more information to fill in.)

In the lower left triangle you now have a $90°$ angle, a $70°$ angle, and a $p°$ angle. Their sum must be $180°$. Algebraically, this is $90 + 70 + p = 180$. Solving for p from this equation gives $p = 20$.

9. The correct answer is 130. This figure looks nice, but it has much more information than you need. Find the triangle with angles $20°$, $30°$, and $r°$. As with any other triangle, their sum must be 180. $20 + 30 + r = 180$. Solve the equation for r to get $r = 130$. Notice that the $100°$ and extra two line segments have absolutely no bearing on the problem.

10. The correct answer is 75. Call the length of a side of square $ABCD$ s. Since E is the midpoint of CD, ED must have length $\frac{1}{2}s$. The area of $\triangle BED$ is half of its base times its height. Use ED as its base. The corresponding height is BC; it touches vertex B and is perpendicular to ED. The length of BC is s, and the length of ED is $\frac{1}{2}s$, so the area of $\triangle BED$ is $\frac{1}{2}\left(\frac{1}{2}s\right)(s) = \frac{1}{4}s^2$. The area of the square as a whole is s^2, which means that the triangle takes up 25% of the area. The shaded area, which is everything but the triangle, takes up $100\% - 25\%$ of the area, or 75%.

Practice Problems in Coordinate Geometry
(pp. 172–173)

1. The correct answer is (B). The midpoint of AC occurs at $\dfrac{\frac{1}{4} + \frac{1}{2}}{2} = \frac{3}{8}$. You know that $\frac{3}{8}$ is greater than $\frac{1}{3}$ (point B) because $\frac{1}{3}$ can be rewritten as $\frac{3}{9}$; given two fractions with the same numerator, the one with the greater denominator is smaller.

2. The correct answer is (D). Imagine grabbing the point B and pushing it to the right. To satisfy the length constraints stated in the problem, D, E, and A must also move to the right. However, C does not have to move. You can change the length of BC without violating any of the stated constraints. Therefore, it is impossible to determine the length of BC.

3. The correct answer is (B). Drawing a set of axes and marking down where each point lies would help you decide which point to test first. If you notice that (3,1) looks a lot closer to (3,4) and test it, you'll find that the distance between (3,4) and (3,1) is $4 - 1 = 3$, not 5, so (B) is the correct answer. Notice how when the points lie on a line parallel to an axis the distance equation becomes a lot simpler.

4. The correct answer is (B). The only quadrant in which x can *not* be greater than y is the quadrant in which x is negative and y is positive. This is the case in Quadrant II.

5. The correct answer is (A). Using the formula for the midpoint would give you $(-x, -y)$ algebraically. To solve the problem graphically, put $A(x, y)$ in the first quadrant. If $(0,0)$ is the midpoint, B must be in the third quadrant. In the third quadrant x and y must *both* be negative. Hence the answer is $(-x, -y)$.

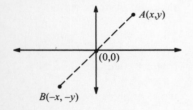

6. The correct answer is (C). Plug the two points $(a,3)$ and $(b,9)$ and the distance 10 into the distance formula. What you get is

$$\sqrt{(b - a)^2 + (9 - 3)^2} = 10.$$

Squaring both sides of the equation and simplifying $(9 - 3)^2$, you are left with $(b - a)^2 + 36 = 100$. Subtract 36 from both sides and then take the square root of both sides to get $(b - a) = 8$. The absolute value bars are included in the problem statement because $|a - b| = |b - a|$.

7. The correct answer is (B). The area of a triangle is given by the equation $A = \frac{1}{2}bh$. Call AB the base of the triangle. The altitude is then the distance from C to the x-axis, which is simply the y-coordinate of point C. Plug in 12 for A, y for the height, and 6 for the base (remember that length is always positive). What you have is $12 = \frac{1}{2}(6)(y)$. Solving for y, you get $y = 4$. Since C is in Quadrant II, y is positive; so 4 is the correct answer.

8. The correct answer is $\left(\frac{7}{3} \text{ or } 2.33\right)$. Because the line passes through the origin and (3,7) we know its slope is $\frac{7 - 0}{3 - 0} = \frac{7}{3}$. Because the line passes through (x,y) and the origin, the slope may also be written $\frac{y - 0}{x - 0} = \frac{y}{x}$. Hence $\frac{y}{x} = \frac{7}{3}$.

Practice Problems in Basic Algebra 1
(pp. 180–182)

1. The correct answer is (C). Multiply each term by 6 to eliminate the fraction. $4x + 5 = x$. Then solve for x.

2. The correct answer is (C). Remove the parentheses, collect like terms, and solve for y.

3. The correct answer is (A). If you got answer (C), you probably solved for $2y$ and not y. Other answers could mean you mixed up the + and − signs.

4. The correct answer is (E). Remember to keep your operations straight.

5. The correct answer is (C). Answer (A) comes up if you solved for $2r$ and not r. Getting (B) is a result of multiplying when you were to divide, and (E) and (D) were put in for people who jump at tempting answers. Don't be one of them; *they* usually trip.

6. The correct answer is (A). Keep your signs straight.

7. The correct answer is (E). If $b = 4$ and $c = -4$, then $a = 4 - (-4) = 8$, and $d = -4 - 4 = -8$. So, $d - a = -8 - 8 = -16$.

8. The correct answer is (A). Answer (B) comes from inverting each fraction separately, and you can't do this.

9. The correct answer is (C). Answer (A) is the answer for $y = \ldots$. (Remember *what* you are solving for.) Answers (D) and (E) both have the wrong sign.

10. The correct answer is (D). First, multiply both sides of the equation by 5 to reach $\frac{5}{x} > 1$. Since $\frac{1}{x} > \frac{1}{5}, \frac{1}{x}$ must be positive; therefore x is positive. Multiplying by x will not affect the inequality sign. After multiplying by x, we get $5 > x$. To incorporate the fact that x is positive into the inequality, add $x > 0$, yielding $5 > x > 0$.

11. The correct answer is (A). This is the perfect place for picking a number and plugging it in. Let y be 4. The first fraction is $\frac{4}{5}$, the second is $\frac{4}{3}$, the third and fourth are 1, and the fifth is $\frac{5}{4}$. Because its numerator is less than its denominator, only the first expression is less than 1; hence, it is the least.

12. The correct answer is (E). Either you can do this by picking values for a and b that make every possible answer except the correct one false, or you can apply the rules for manipulating inequalities. $a = 2$ and $b = 1$ will cull out all of the bad answers using the pick-and-plug method. To manipulate the inequalities, notice that because $a > b, \frac{a}{b} > 1 > \frac{b}{a} > 0$. Consider solution (A), $\frac{b}{a} < 1$, so $\left(\frac{b}{a}\right)^2$ is smaller than $\frac{b}{a}$.

For solution (B), $\frac{a}{b} > 1$,

so $\left(\frac{a}{b}\right)^2 > \frac{a}{b}$. Solutions (C) and (D) are disproved using the same reasoning. Solution (E) is the correct

one because $\frac{a}{b} > 1$ and therefore

$\left(\frac{a}{b}\right)^2 > \frac{a}{b}$.

13. The correct answer is (D). Again, this is a good place for pick and plug. Substitute -1 for x, and you get $3 > 3$, which is false. So solution (D) contains the value that could not be x. To perform the calculations explicitly, convert $|2x - 1| > 3$ into its two cases, $2x - 1 > 3$ or $2x - 1 < -3$. Solve each of these to get $x > 2$ or $x < -1$. The only value outside of these bounds is solution (D), $x = -1$. Incidentally, you should not have to calculate the value of 2^4, answer (E); without knowing its exact value, you should recognize that it is greater than 2.

14. The correct answer is (C). Again, this problem can be solved by plugging in values for p and q (e.g., $q = 1$ and $p = 2$) or by applying the inequality manipulations. Try to go from the given inequality to solution (C). First multiply both sides of $q < p$ by -1 and remember to flip the inequality sign to get $-q > -p$. Then, add 5 to both sides of the inequality; $5 - q > 5 - p$. This is exactly the opposite of solution (C), so solution (C) must contain the false statement.

15. The correct answer is 4. Remember to change the signs of everything inside the parentheses when you remove them since they are preceded by a $-$ sign.

Practice Problems in Basic Algebra 2
(pp. 191–194)

1. The correct answer is (B). The equation becomes $19 - (-12) = ?$

2. The correct answer is (D). The equation becomes $8(c) + (13 - 8)(2c) = ?$ Answers (A) and (B) occur if you forget that she is paid double after 8 hours. Notice that $13 - 8$ is the number of hours that the woman is paid double.

3. The correct answer is (A). Let the first number be x and the second number y.

xy	A number is multiplied by another number.
$\dfrac{xy}{(...)}$	The product is divided by . . .
$\dfrac{xy}{x-y}$	. . . the difference between the two numbers.

4. The correct answer is (B). *Volume = length* $\times$ *width* $\times$ *depth*. Replacing the length and width by their given values leaves $24 = 8 \times 3 \times depth$. Dividing both sides by 24 leaves $1 = d$. Make sure not to divide 24 by 24 and get 0. It may look silly now, but the mistake is somewhat common.

5. The correct answer is (E). x dollars equals $100x$ cents.

   y apples at 16 cents each equals $16y$ cents.

   z pears at 12 cents each equals $12z$ cents.

   The expression is then $100x - (16y + 12z)$ or $100x - 16y - 12z$.

6. The correct answer is (B). The equation is $x - 3 = 2x + 6$.

7. The correct answer is (D). The equation is $\frac{1}{3}(x + 13) = 2x + 1$. Multiply both sides by 3 to get $x + 13 = 6x + 3$; then solve for x.

8. The correct answer is (A). Let x = Tom's age. The equation is $\frac{1}{3}x$ (Tom's brother's age) + $3x$ (Tom's sister's age) + x (Tom's age) = $2(3x) - 5$.
Combine like terms.
$4\frac{1}{3}x = 6x - 5$;
$\frac{13}{3}x = 6x - 5$;
$13x = 18x - 15$;
$-5x = -15$;
$x = 3$.

9. The correct answer is (D). d dollars equals $100d$ cents. The number of stamps that can be bought is the total amount, divided by the cost of each stamp: $\frac{100d}{32}$.

10. The correct answer is (C). Let e be the size of the woman's estate, and set up the equation
$\frac{1}{4}e + \frac{1}{3}e + 10,000 = e$. Solve for e
to get $\frac{5}{12}e = 10,000$; $e = 24,000$.

11. The correct answer is (D). If the meat loses $\frac{1}{4}$ of its weight, then she really bought $\frac{3}{4}$ of a pound for $3.00. The equation is $\frac{3}{4} \times x = 3.00$. Multiply both sides by 4 and get $3x = 12.00$. Divide by 3 to get the cost, $4.00 per pound, where x represents 1 pound of meat.

12. The correct answer is (C). When the tank was $\frac{1}{3}$ full $\left(\frac{1}{3}f\right)$ and 6 gallons were added, it became $\frac{5}{6}$ full $\left(\frac{5}{6}f\right)$. Written as an equation, this is $\frac{1}{3}f + 6 = \frac{5}{6}f$. Multiply through by 6 to get $2f + 36 = 5f$ and solve to get $f = 12$.

13. The correct answer is 16. The equation becomes $(x - 4) = \frac{1}{2}(x + 8)$.

14. The correct answer is 200. The equation becomes $\frac{1}{4}x + \frac{1}{5}x + 110 = x$.

15. The correct answer is 10. The equation becomes $5x + 10x + 25x = 400$. Think that x represents the number of each type of coin and 400 is the total number of cents.

16. The correct answer is 9. The two equations are $a^2 - b^2 = 9$, and $a - b = 1$. Recall that $a^2 - b^2$ factors to $(a - b)(a + b)$. Substituting 1 for $a - b$ and 9 for $a^2 - b^2$ leaves: $9 = 1(a + b)$.

17. The correct answer is 134. If x equals the average width of each house, then the equation will be $10x + 9(x + 60) + 2(60) = 3,206$. Solve for x to get $x = 134$. Note that 10 houses are separated by 9 spaces and there is 60 feet at each end of the block.

Practice Problems in Algebraic Applications 1 (pp. 199–202)

1. The correct answer is (C).
$$\frac{(2x + 1) + (x + 5) + (1 - 4x) + (3x + 1)}{4}$$
$$= \frac{2x + 8}{4} = \frac{1}{2}x + 2$$

2. The correct answer is (E). The least average weight is when two players weigh 150 and one weighs 175. Their average is $\dfrac{150 + 150 + 175}{3} = 158\frac{1}{3}$. The greatest average weight occurs when two players weigh 175 and one weighs 150. Their average weight is $\dfrac{175 + 175 + 150}{3} = \dfrac{500}{3} = 166\frac{2}{3}$. Their average weight cannot be 167.

3. The correct answer is (D). Let x equal the other number. The average of P and x would be $\dfrac{P + x}{2} = A$. Solve for x. $P + x = 2A$; $x = 2A - P$.

4. The correct answer is (D). If the average grade of 10 students is x, then the total score is $10x$. The total of the 5 new students' scores is $5 \times 84 = 420$. The entire average is $\dfrac{10x + 420}{15}$.

5. The correct answer is (A). $(4,6 \uparrow 8,2) = (4 \times 2) - (6 \times 8) = 8 - 48 = -40$

6. The correct answer is (B). $\downarrow\dfrac{3}{4} = \left(\dfrac{3}{4} - 1\right)^2 = \left(-\dfrac{1}{4}\right)^2 = \dfrac{1}{16}$

7. The correct answer is (C). $2\ O\ (-3) = (-3)^2 - 2(2)^2 = 9 - 8 = 1$

8. The correct answer is (C). $\dfrac{3}{2} \square \dfrac{2}{3}$

$$= \left(\dfrac{\frac{3}{2} - 1}{\frac{2}{3} + 1}\right)^2 = \left(\dfrac{\frac{1}{2}}{\frac{5}{3}}\right)^2$$

$$= \left(\dfrac{1}{2} \times \dfrac{3}{5}\right)^2$$

$$= \left(\dfrac{3}{10}\right)^2$$

$$= \dfrac{9}{100}$$

9. The correct answer is (E).

$$(3x)\left(\dfrac{x}{3}\right) = x^2$$

10. The correct answer is (B). $\lfloor -2.3 \rfloor = -3$; $\lfloor 2.3 \rfloor = 2$. So, $-3 + 2 = -1$.

11. The correct answer is (E). $3 \bigstar (-2) = 3^2 \times (-2)^3 = 9(-8) = -72$

12. The correct answer is $\left(\dfrac{17}{8}\right)$.

$$\dfrac{2\frac{1}{2} + 1\frac{3}{4}}{2} = \text{average length of time}$$

$$\dfrac{\frac{5}{2} + \frac{7}{4}}{2} = \text{average}$$

$$\dfrac{\frac{10}{4} + \frac{7}{4}}{2} = \text{average}$$

$$\dfrac{\frac{17}{4}}{2} = \dfrac{17}{8} \text{ hours.}$$

13. The correct answer is $\left(\dfrac{9}{2} \text{ or } 4.5\right)$.

$$\dfrac{\frac{3}{4}}{6} = 3 \times \dfrac{6}{4} = \dfrac{18}{4} = \dfrac{9}{2}$$

14. The correct answer is 13.
$(3 + 1)^2 - (3 - 1)^2 + 1$
$= 16 - 4 + 1 = 13$

15. The correct answer is 12. $\dfrac{p}{4} = 3$;
$p = 12$.

Practice Problems in Algebraic Applications 2
(pp. 207–209)

1. The correct answer is (D). Josephine spends 45 out of every 50 minutes working. Written in fractional form, this is $\dfrac{45}{50}$, which simplifies to $\dfrac{9}{10}$. Don't forget to add the 5-minute break to the 45-minute working time when you figure the total amount of time she spends during each cycle.

2. The correct answer is (B). Start at 7:45. Add 20 minutes for the sandwich to get to 7:65, which becomes 8:05. Add 15 minutes of TV to get to 8:20. The time Donald actually spent studying is $9:45 - 8:20 = 1:25$.

3. The correct answer is (E). Remember that odd integers differ by 2. If the first odd integer is x, then the sum of the first five is $x + (x + 2) + (x + 4) + (x + 6) + (x + 8)$, which in the problem is stated to be equal to 6 more than 3 times the largest, $3(x + 8) + 6$. Combine like terms and solve to reach $x = 5$. Don't stop here. Go back and find the sum of the consecutive odd integers; $5 + 7 + 9 + 11 + 13 = 45$.

4. The correct answer is (A). There are 4 teams, so every person in a position divisible by 4 will be on the fourth team. Since 52 is divisible by 4 thirteen times, the fifty-second person will be on Team D. Counting ahead one, the fifty-third will be on Team A.

5. The correct answer is (C). You can compute all of the percentages of 60 and then sum them, or you can add the percentages to get $(90 + 75 + 95 + 90 + 85)\%$ of $60 = 435\%$ of $60 = 4.35 \times 60 = 261$.

6. The correct answer is (C). It's a little before noon because the short hand is near the 12, between the 12 and 9. The only listed time a little before 12 is 11:40.

7. The correct answer is (B). There are 4 types of coins and an equal number of each type, so there is a 1-in-4 chance of picking the quarter type. $\dfrac{25}{41}$ is greater than $\dfrac{1}{4}$ so the answer is B.

8. The correct answer is (A). The percent increase is defined as the increase over the starting value times 100.

From 1970 to 1975 the percent increase is $\dfrac{10 - 5}{5} \times 100 = 100\%$. From 1990 to 1995 the percent increase is $\dfrac{45 - 25}{25} \times 100 = 80\%$. The greatest percent increase occurred from 1970 to 1975, 100%. Do not make the mistake of marking answer (B) because Column B has the greatest increase in value; percent increase and value increase *are different*.

9. The correct answer is (10). The equation can be written as $5x = 3(x + 4)$, where x represents the middle integer. Remember to solve for the largest of the numbers, $x + 4$.

10. The correct answer is 150. 15% of $5,000 is $750; 20% savings of $750 is $150.

Practice with the Final Few
(pp. 210–212)

1. The correct answer is (B). When the set of integers is divided by a number, the *remainders form a repeating series.* Five divided into 1 has a remainder of 1, into 2 has a remainder 2, into 3 remainder 3, into 4 remainder 4, into 5 remainder 0. Dividing 5 into 6, however, brings the remainder back to 1 again. The repetition means that the remainders from five consecutive numbers must include the numbers 0 through 4 independent of which number you begin dividing with. The sum of the remainders is 10; the quantity of remainders is 5; so the average equals 10 divided by 5, or 2.

2. The correct answer is (A). There are two methods by which you could approach this problem. Randomly, call a 1, b 2, and c 3. Plugging in shows that I is the only correct statement.

   To do the problem algebraically, you plug the values of a, b, and c into the function, making sure to do what is in the parentheses first.

   (1) $a * b = \dfrac{a + b}{ab}$; $b * a = \dfrac{b + a}{ba}$.

   The two final expressions are equal, so statement I must be true.

   (2) $(a * b) * c = \dfrac{a + b + abc}{ac + bc}$

   $a * (b * c) = \dfrac{abc + b + c}{ab + ac}$

   The two final expressions are *not* equal, so statement II must be false.

   (3) $a * (b + c) = \dfrac{a + b + c}{ab + ac}$

   $a * b + a * c$

   $= \dfrac{ac + bc + ab + cb}{abc}$

   The two final expressions are *not* equal, so statement III must be false.

3. The correct answer is (C). The diagonal of the square passes through the center of the circle and has endpoints on the circle, so it must be a diameter of the circle. The diagonal of the square is $\sqrt{2}$ times the length of a side. Since the length of the side is $a\sqrt{2}$, the length of the diagonal and consequently the length of the diameter of the circle is $a\sqrt{2} \times \sqrt{2} = 2a$. Half of the diameter is the radius, a. The area of the circle is π times the radius squared, πa^2.

4. The correct answer is (D). Call the number of adults who attended the movie A, and the number of students S. $A + S =$ the total number of people who attended the movie—500. The number of students times the cost per student plus the number of adults times the cost per adult is the total amount spent for the day. Algebraically, $1.5A + .75S = 450$. Now you have two equations in two unknowns. Using either of the methods to solve for A and S, you will find that $A = 100$ and $S = 400$. The number of students is, therefore, 400.

5. The correct answer is (A). Remember that you can never come up with a fraction of a dog while working this problem. (People are the same way.) Two fifths of the number of unlicensed dogs must be an integer. Similarly, $\frac{3}{8}$ of $\frac{2}{5}$ of the number of unlicensed dogs must also be an integer. $\frac{3}{8} \times \frac{2}{5} = \frac{3}{20}$. The only number less than 30 that gives an integer answer when multiplied by $\frac{3}{20}$ is 20. Hence, there are 20 unlicensed dogs in the town.

6. The correct answer is (B). Even with the extra twist, the average equation is still used here. After two quarters, Buffy's average is 87, so her total score must be $2(87) = 174$. You are trying to find the lowest score Buffy can get in the third quarter and still have a chance of receiving 90% overall, so assume that she has a 100% average in the fourth quarter. Call X Buffy's average in the third quarter. Now the equation takes the form:

$$\frac{87 + 87 + X + 100}{4} = 90$$

Solving the equation for X gives $X = 86\%$ as the lowest possible score Buffy can receive during the third quarter and still have a chance of receiving a 90% for the year.

7. The correct answer is (A). Randomly plugging in 3 for the number of girls, 4 for the number of boys, 2 for the number of pizzas, and $1 for the cost per pizza is one way of doing the problem. Doing the problem algebraically, however, is the most direct way.

The total cost of the pizzas is the number of pizzas times the cost per pizza, which is $P \times D$ or simply PD. If only the girls pay for the pizza,

the cost per girl is the cost divided by the number of girls, $\frac{PD}{G}$. When the boys come, the cost is shared among the number of boys plus the number of girls, $\frac{PD}{B + G}$. Don't stop here! The questions asks for the *difference*, which is $\frac{PD}{G} - \frac{PD}{B + G}$. Using the rules for subtracting fractions, you first make the denominators the same and then subtract to get $\frac{PD(B + G) - PD(G)}{G(B + G)}$. Getting rid of the parentheses in the numerator leaves $\frac{PDB + PDG - PDG}{G(B+G)}$, which simplifies further to $\frac{PDB}{G(B + G)}$.

8. The correct answer is (B). "The cycle is repeated . . ." The clue is right there—you are looking for a repeating series. After the first person is done, the booth has made a profit of 15¢ − 1¢, or 14¢. The second person loses a total of 10¢, the third 5¢; and the fourth *wins* 10¢. The pattern is then repeated. The net profit for every 4 people going to the booth is therefore 14¢ + 10¢ + 5¢ − 10¢ = 19¢. After 43 people have been to the booth, the net profit is 10 × 19¢ plus the amount the booth wins from the next 3 people: 14¢, 10¢, and 5¢. The total profit is (10 × 19¢) + 14¢ + 10¢ + 5¢ = $2.19.

9. The correct answer is (E). Using polynomial multiplication, you can rewrite $(x - y)^2$ as $x^2 - 2xy + y^2$. Rearranging this expression, you have $x^2 + y^2 - 2xy$. Substitute 25 for $x^2 + y^2$, and −5 for xy, to get $25 - 2(-5) = 25 + 10 = 35$.

10. The correct answer is (E). When dealing with boy-girl problems, the unstated fact is that if one is not a boy, one must be a girl. In this problem the unstated fact is a bit less obvious: if the water comes to a fork and doesn't take one path, it must take the other. Since $\frac{5}{8}$ of the water flowing from path A takes path B, then the *other* $\frac{3}{8}$ *of the water must take path C.* The $\frac{5}{8}$ of the water that takes path B comes to another fork. From here $\frac{3}{5}$ of the water from path B, which is $\frac{5}{8}$ of the water from path A, takes path D. By multiplying $\frac{3}{5}$ by $\frac{5}{8}$ you can deduce that $\frac{3}{8}$ of the water from path A follows path D. Path F is the sum of the water from path C, which is $\frac{3}{8}$ of the water from path A, plus the water from path D, which is also $\frac{3}{8}$ of the water from path A. Adding these two quantities together, we find that $\frac{3}{4}$ of the water coming in from path A leaves by path F.

Three fourths converted to a percent is 75%. Note that during the problem the water coming in from A is used to represent all of the water, which is true since it is the only path coming in. Quite a mouthful, wasn't it?

ANSWERS TO ACTUAL SAT QUESTIONS

Math Questions				Verbal Questions			
1. B	6. A	11. A	16. 65	1. D	6. B	11. D	16. B
2. D	7. B	12. D	17. 9	2. D	7. C	12. A	17. D
3. A	8. E	13. C	18. 5 or 7	3. C	8. E	13. E	18. E
4. E	9. D	14. D	19. 7	4. B	9. A	14. A	19. D
5. C	10. D	15. A	20. 2/15 or .133	5. D	10. D	15. C	20. C

ANSWERS TO PRACTICE SAT

Section 1	Section 2		Section 3	Section 4	Section 5	Section 6
1. C	1. A	19. B	1. B	1. B	1. C	1. E
2. D	2. B	20. D	2. C	2. D	2. D	2. C
3. D	3. D	21. D	3. B	3. C	3. A	3. D
4. E	4. A	22. A	4. C	4. B	4. E	4. B
5. A	5. E	23. E	5. D	5. A	5. A	5. C
6. E	6. E	24. B	6. B	6. D	6. C	6. A
7. A	7. A	25. A	7. B	7. A	7. B	7. C
8. D	8. C	26. D	8. B	8. C	8. B	8. E
9. E	9. E	27. A	9. C	9. C	9. E	9. C
10. E	10. C	28. E	10. B	10. D	10. A	10. C
11. D	11. A	29. B	11. C	11. A	11. D	
12. A	12. D	30. C	12. C	12. C	12. E	
13. B	13. E	31. A	13. C	13. B	13. C	
14. E	14. E	32. E	14. A	14. A		
15. D	15. B	33. C	15. D	15. B		
16. E	16. E	34. B	16. 2	16. D		
17. E	17. C	35. A	17. $\frac{10}{3}$ or 3.33	17. E		
18. C	18. A		18. Any x such that $60 < x < 66$	18. D		
19. C			19. 45	19. C		
20. E			20. 9	20. C		
21. D			21. 1.25 or $\frac{5}{4}$	21. B		
22. B			22. .8 or $\frac{4}{5}$	22. D		
23. A			23. .001	23. A		
24. C			24. 36	24. C		
25. D			25. 1.33 or $\frac{4}{3}$	25. C		
				26. B		
				27. E		
				28. A		
				29. D		
				30. E		

Computing Your Score

Math Sections 1, 3, and 6

1. Count the number of right answers for all questions in Sections 1 and 6 only. All of these questions had 5 answer choices. Do not count questions with blank answer spaces—the ones you left unanswered. Record the number of right answers where indicated on the score sheet that follows.

2. Also for Sections 1 and 6, count the wrong answers and enter the number where shown. Divide the wrong answer total by 4 and subtract the resulting number from the right answer total.

3. For Section 3, count the total number of right answers. Do not count questions you left blank. Record the number of right answers where indicated.

4. For questions 1–15 in Section 3, count the wrong answers and enter the number where shown. Divide the wrong answer total by 3 and subtract the resulting number from the right answer total. Note that you are not subtracting anything for grid-in questions that you answered incorrectly.

5. Add the two totals together to get a total raw score.

6. Round the total to the nearest whole number.

7. Check the conversion table on page 306 for an approximate idea of how you would score on an SAT I.

Math Score Sheet

Total correct for Sections 1 and 6 =

_____ $- \dfrac{1}{4} \times$ _____ (no. wrong) = _____

Total correct for Section 3 =

_____ $- \dfrac{1}{3} \times$ _____ (no. wrong in questions 1–15) = _____

Add the two totals together. = _____

Round to the nearest whole number. = _____

Convert to approximate SAT score. = _____
(see page 306)

Verbal Sections 2, 4, and 5

1. Count the number of right answers in each section, and record where shown on the score sheet that follows. Do *not* count any answers left blank.

2. Count the number of wrong answers per section, and divide that number by 4, obtaining a separate total for each section. Enter totals as shown, and subtract from the number of correct answers for each section.

3. Add the total obtained from all three verbal sections to get a total raw score.

4. Round the total to the nearest whole number.

5. Check the conversion table on page 306 for an approximate idea of how you would score on an SAT I.

Verbal Score Sheet

Total correct for Section 2 =

$$\underline{\hspace{2cm}} - \frac{1}{4} \times \underline{\hspace{2cm}} \text{ (no. wrong)} = \underline{\hspace{2cm}}$$

Total correct for Section 4 =

$$\underline{\hspace{2cm}} - \frac{1}{4} \times \underline{\hspace{2cm}} \text{ (no. wrong)} = \underline{\hspace{2cm}}$$

Total correct for Section 5 =

$$\underline{\hspace{2cm}} - \frac{1}{4} \times \underline{\hspace{2cm}} \text{ (no. wrong)} = \underline{\hspace{2cm}}$$

Add the three totals together. = \underline{\hspace{2cm}}

Round to the nearest whole number. = \underline{\hspace{2cm}}

Convert to approximate SAT score. = \underline{\hspace{2cm}}
(see page 306)

Self-Evaluation on SAT Practice Test

Verbal Results

_____ correct out of 19 questions on analogies

_____ correct out of 19 sentence completions

_____ correct out of 40 based on reading passages

_____ = TOTAL CORRECT

I do the _____ questions best.

I do the _____ questions less well.

(How can you review to increase your score here?)

How was your timing? Is any particular kind of question taking you longer than it deserves? If so, watch your watch and be sure to answer your best kinds of questions first so that all possible correct answers are recorded.

Math Results

_____ correct out of 60

Problems missed were in the areas of _____

_____

_____

Problems worked correctly were of the following types:

_____

_____

How about timing? If you are short of time on a real test, circle the more difficult problems and return to them only if time permits.

Areas needing review: _____

_____

_____

_____

Converting to Approximate SAT Score

Verbal Conversion		Math Conversion	
If your score was between:	*Rough SAT I score:*	*If your score was between:*	*Rough SAT I score:*
75 and 78	800	59 and 60	800
70 and 75	740 +	55 and 59	720 +
65 and 70	690 +	50 and 55	670 +
60 and 65	650 +	45 and 50	620 +
55 and 60	620 +	40 and 45	580 +
50 and 55	590 +	35 and 40	550 +
45 and 50	560 +	30 and 35	510 +
40 and 45	530 +	25 and 30	480 +
35 and 40	500 +	20 and 25	450 +
30 and 35	470 +	15 and 20	410 +
25 and 30	440 +	10 and 15	370 +
20 and 25	410 +	5 and 10	320 +
15 and 20	380 +	0 and 5	240 +
10 and 15	340 +		
5 and 10	290 +		
0 and 5	220 +		

If you scored somewhat lower than you expected, fret not. These practice tests are usually harder for students than real SATs, and most people score a bit lower. A *real* test will be a treat, then, won't it? Also, now you can analyze what caused you to lose points and do something about the problem before the actual test day. Perhaps you can't "fix" as much as you'd like in the limited time left, but remember that *each correct answer is worth 8–10 points.* They all count and are worth working for.

Take a look at the evaluation sheet on page 305. It will help to guide your study during further test preparation. And don't look at the columns that show what you did *wrong* as your sole evaluation. What did you do *right?* If you do certain things well, you know you can learn to do *other* things well, too.

Pull out your copy of *Real SATs* and practice until you feel more comfortable with all the areas of the test.

ANSWER SHEET FOR PRACTICE TEST

Completely darken bubbles with a No. 2 pencil.
If you make a mistake, be sure to erase mark completely. Erase all stray marks.

Start with number 1 for each new section.
If a section has fewer questions than answer spaces, leave the extra answer spaces blank.

SECTION 1

1	A B C D E	8	A B C D E	15	A B C D E	22	A B C D E
2	A B C D E	9	A B C D E	16	A B C D E	23	A B C D E
3	A B C D E	10	A B C D E	17	A B C D E	24	A B C D E
4	A B C D E	11	A B C D E	18	A B C D E	25	A B C D E
5	A B C D E	12	A B C D E	19	A B C D E	26	A B C D E
6	A B C D E	13	A B C D E	20	A B C D E	27	A B C D E
7	A B C D E	14	A B C D E	21	A B C D E	28	A B C D E

SECTION 2

1	A B C D E	10	A B C D E	19	A B C D E	28	A B C D E
2	A B C D E	11	A B C D E	20	A B C D E	29	A B C D E
3	A B C D E	12	A B C D E	21	A B C D E	30	A B C D E
4	A B C D E	13	A B C D E	22	A B C D E	31	A B C D E
5	A B C D E	14	A B C D E	23	A B C D E	32	A B C D E
6	A B C D E	15	A B C D E	24	A B C D E	33	A B C D E
7	A B C D E	16	A B C D E	25	A B C D E	34	A B C D E
8	A B C D E	17	A B C D E	26	A B C D E	35	A B C D E
9	A B C D E	18	A B C D E	27	A B C D E	36	A B C D E

SECTION 3

1	A B C D E	5	A B C D E	9	A B C D E	13	A B C D E
2	A B C D E	6	A B C D E	10	A B C D E	14	A B C D E
3	A B C D E	7	A B C D E	11	A B C D E	15	A B C D E
4	A B C D E	8	A B C D E	12	A B C D E		

ONLY ANSWERS ENTERED IN THE OVALS IN EACH GRID AREA WILL BE SCORED.
YOU WILL NOT RECEIVE CREDIT FOR ANYTHING WRITTEN IN THE BOXES ABOVE THE OVALS.

16   17   18   19   20

21   22   23   24   25

Start with number 1 for each new section.
If a section has fewer questions than answer spaces, leave the extra answer spaces blank.

SECTION 4

1 ⊂A⊃ ⊂B⊃ ⊂C⊃ ⊂D⊃ ⊂E⊃	9 ⊂A⊃ ⊂B⊃ ⊂C⊃ ⊂D⊃ ⊂E⊃	17 ⊂A⊃ ⊂B⊃ ⊂C⊃ ⊂D⊃ ⊂E⊃	25 ⊂A⊃ ⊂B⊃ ⊂C⊃ ⊂D⊃ ⊂E⊃
2 ⊂A⊃ ⊂B⊃ ⊂C⊃ ⊂D⊃ ⊂E⊃	10 ⊂A⊃ ⊂B⊃ ⊂C⊃ ⊂D⊃ ⊂E⊃	18 ⊂A⊃ ⊂B⊃ ⊂C⊃ ⊂D⊃ ⊂E⊃	26 ⊂A⊃ ⊂B⊃ ⊂C⊃ ⊂D⊃ ⊂E⊃
3 ⊂A⊃ ⊂B⊃ ⊂C⊃ ⊂D⊃ ⊂E⊃	11 ⊂A⊃ ⊂B⊃ ⊂C⊃ ⊂D⊃ ⊂E⊃	19 ⊂A⊃ ⊂B⊃ ⊂C⊃ ⊂D⊃ ⊂E⊃	27 ⊂A⊃ ⊂B⊃ ⊂C⊃ ⊂D⊃ ⊂E⊃
4 ⊂A⊃ ⊂B⊃ ⊂C⊃ ⊂D⊃ ⊂E⊃	12 ⊂A⊃ ⊂B⊃ ⊂C⊃ ⊂D⊃ ⊂E⊃	20 ⊂A⊃ ⊂B⊃ ⊂C⊃ ⊂D⊃ ⊂E⊃	28 ⊂A⊃ ⊂B⊃ ⊂C⊃ ⊂D⊃ ⊂E⊃
5 ⊂A⊃ ⊂B⊃ ⊂C⊃ ⊂D⊃ ⊂E⊃	13 ⊂A⊃ ⊂B⊃ ⊂C⊃ ⊂D⊃ ⊂E⊃	21 ⊂A⊃ ⊂B⊃ ⊂C⊃ ⊂D⊃ ⊂E⊃	29 ⊂A⊃ ⊂B⊃ ⊂C⊃ ⊂D⊃ ⊂E⊃
6 ⊂A⊃ ⊂B⊃ ⊂C⊃ ⊂D⊃ ⊂E⊃	14 ⊂A⊃ ⊂B⊃ ⊂C⊃ ⊂D⊃ ⊂E⊃	22 ⊂A⊃ ⊂B⊃ ⊂C⊃ ⊂D⊃ ⊂E⊃	30 ⊂A⊃ ⊂B⊃ ⊂C⊃ ⊂D⊃ ⊂E⊃
7 ⊂A⊃ ⊂B⊃ ⊂C⊃ ⊂D⊃ ⊂E⊃	15 ⊂A⊃ ⊂B⊃ ⊂C⊃ ⊂D⊃ ⊂E⊃	23 ⊂A⊃ ⊂B⊃ ⊂C⊃ ⊂D⊃ ⊂E⊃	31 ⊂A⊃ ⊂B⊃ ⊂C⊃ ⊂D⊃ ⊂E⊃
8 ⊂A⊃ ⊂B⊃ ⊂C⊃ ⊂D⊃ ⊂E⊃	16 ⊂A⊃ ⊂B⊃ ⊂C⊃ ⊂D⊃ ⊂E⊃	24 ⊂A⊃ ⊂B⊃ ⊂C⊃ ⊂D⊃ ⊂E⊃	32 ⊂A⊃ ⊂B⊃ ⊂C⊃ ⊂D⊃ ⊂E⊃

SECTION 5

1 ⊂A⊃ ⊂B⊃ ⊂C⊃ ⊂D⊃ ⊂E⊃	5 ⊂A⊃ ⊂B⊃ ⊂C⊃ ⊂D⊃ ⊂E⊃	9 ⊂A⊃ ⊂B⊃ ⊂C⊃ ⊂D⊃ ⊂E⊃	13 ⊂A⊃ ⊂B⊃ ⊂C⊃ ⊂D⊃ ⊂E⊃
2 ⊂A⊃ ⊂B⊃ ⊂C⊃ ⊂D⊃ ⊂E⊃	6 ⊂A⊃ ⊂B⊃ ⊂C⊃ ⊂D⊃ ⊂E⊃	10 ⊂A⊃ ⊂B⊃ ⊂C⊃ ⊂D⊃ ⊂E⊃	14 ⊂A⊃ ⊂B⊃ ⊂C⊃ ⊂D⊃ ⊂E⊃
3 ⊂A⊃ ⊂B⊃ ⊂C⊃ ⊂D⊃ ⊂E⊃	7 ⊂A⊃ ⊂B⊃ ⊂C⊃ ⊂D⊃ ⊂E⊃	11 ⊂A⊃ ⊂B⊃ ⊂C⊃ ⊂D⊃ ⊂E⊃	15 ⊂A⊃ ⊂B⊃ ⊂C⊃ ⊂D⊃ ⊂E⊃
4 ⊂A⊃ ⊂B⊃ ⊂C⊃ ⊂D⊃ ⊂E⊃	8 ⊂A⊃ ⊂B⊃ ⊂C⊃ ⊂D⊃ ⊂E⊃	12 ⊂A⊃ ⊂B⊃ ⊂C⊃ ⊂D⊃ ⊂E⊃	16 ⊂A⊃ ⊂B⊃ ⊂C⊃ ⊂D⊃ ⊂E⊃

SECTION 6

1 ⊂A⊃ ⊂B⊃ ⊂C⊃ ⊂D⊃ ⊂E⊃	4 ⊂A⊃ ⊂B⊃ ⊂C⊃ ⊂D⊃ ⊂E⊃	7 ⊂A⊃ ⊂B⊃ ⊂C⊃ ⊂D⊃ ⊂E⊃	10 ⊂A⊃ ⊂B⊃ ⊂C⊃ ⊂D⊃ ⊂E⊃
2 ⊂A⊃ ⊂B⊃ ⊂C⊃ ⊂D⊃ ⊂E⊃	5 ⊂A⊃ ⊂B⊃ ⊂C⊃ ⊂D⊃ ⊂E⊃	8 ⊂A⊃ ⊂B⊃ ⊂C⊃ ⊂D⊃ ⊂E⊃	11 ⊂A⊃ ⊂B⊃ ⊂C⊃ ⊂D⊃ ⊂E⊃
3 ⊂A⊃ ⊂B⊃ ⊂C⊃ ⊂D⊃ ⊂E⊃	6 ⊂A⊃ ⊂B⊃ ⊂C⊃ ⊂D⊃ ⊂E⊃	9 ⊂A⊃ ⊂B⊃ ⊂C⊃ ⊂D⊃ ⊂E⊃	12 ⊂A⊃ ⊂B⊃ ⊂C⊃ ⊂D⊃ ⊂E⊃

NOTES

NOTES